AF326646

Dr. Vinson Synan was without equal in the Spirit-empowered movement. He had a brilliant mind, an exceptional personality, and an anointing to bridge the worlds of academia and ministry. He was respected everywhere, with Pentecostals and non-Pentecostals alike. He was an excellent teacher, preacher, writer, and historian—as well as a faithful husband, father, colleague, and friend. This tribute to him aims to honor the last two decades of his life, which were abundantly fruitful for the global Spirit-empowered movement. May his voice continue to be heard. May God bless the memory of Vinson Synan and his leadership and legacy, which live on through us.

Dr. Billy Wilson,
President, Oral Roberts University
Global Chair, Empowered21
Chairman, Pentecostal World Fellowship

A Spirit-Empowered Legacy offers a rich, authoritative witness to H. Vinson Synan's enduring impact on Pentecostal and Charismatic studies. Honoring Synan's lifetime of faithful theological and ecumenical work, this volume is both a vital academic resource and reverent tribute to one of the Spirit-empowered movement's most formative voices.

Adrian Hinkle,
Executive Director, Society for Pentecostal Studies
Dean, College of Theology and Ministry, Oral Roberts University

The death of Vinson Synan leaves a void for those who shared his commitment to Christian unity. However, the memory of his teaching, his service, and his vision remain alive here: a testimony of dialogue, faith, and communion that continues to bear fruit.

Matteo Calisi,
Founder and President, United in Christ International
Former President, Catholic Fraternity of Charismatic Covenant Communities

H. VINSON SYNAN:

A Spirit-Empowered Legacy

H. VINSON SYNAN:
A Spirit-Empowered Legacy

Authored by
H. Vinson Synan

Edited by
Younghoon Lee

ORU
PRESS

Tulsa, Oklahoma, USA

H. Vinson Synan: A Spirit-Empowered Legacy
Copyright ©2026 Oral Roberts University and Contributors

Published by ORU Press
ORU Press is the publishing division of Oral Roberts University.
7777 S. Lewis Ave., Tulsa, OK 74171 USA
https://orupress.org/

ISBN: 978-1-950971-43-5 (hardback)
ISBN: 978-1-950971-38-1 (paperback)
ISBN: 978-1-950971-39-8 (e-book)

Cover design: Jiwon Kim
Composition and Editorial Assistant: Jaime L. Riddle

Printed in the United States of America

P. H. Church Historian
Recognized
Throughout the World

Figure 1: *The Advocate* announces the success of Vinson Synan's published dissertation and its election to represent Pentecostalism in the 1973 Religious Freedom Exhibit. Copyright IPHC Archives. Courtesy of Consortium of Pentecostal Archives. Used with permission.

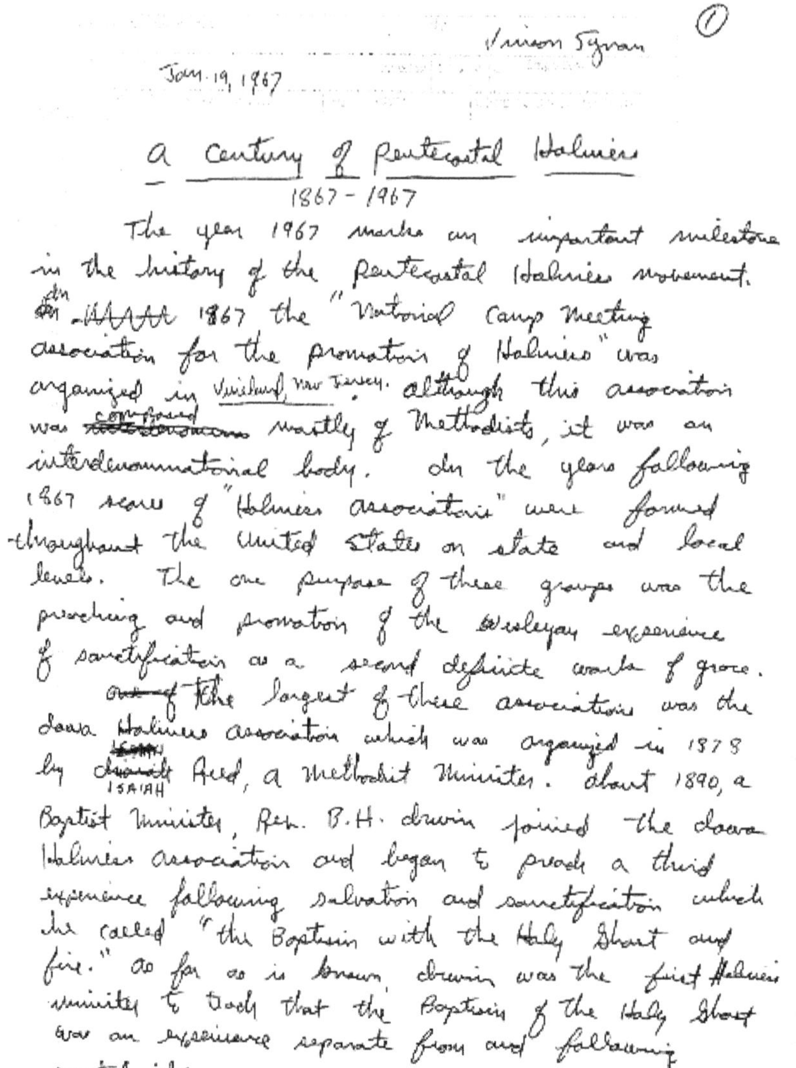

Simon Synan

① (1)

Jan. 19, 1967

A Century of Pentecostal Holiness
1867 - 1967

The year 1967 marks an important milestone in the history of the Pentecostal Holiness movement. In 1867 the "National Camp Meeting Association for the promotion of Holiness" was organized in Vineland, New Jersey. Although this association was composed mostly of Methodists, it was an interdenominational body. In the years following 1867 scores of "Holiness associations" were formed throughout the United States on state and local levels. The one purpose of these groups was the preaching and promotion of the Wesleyan experience of sanctification as a second definite work of grace.

The largest of these associations was the Iowa Holiness association which was organized in 1878 by Isaiah Reed, a Methodist minister. About 1890, a Baptist minister, Rev. B.H. Irwin joined the Iowa Holiness association and began to preach a third experience following salvation and sanctification which he called "the Baptism with the Holy Ghost and fire." As far as is known, Irwin was the first Holiness minister to teach that the Baptism of the Holy Ghost was an experience separate from and following sanctification.

Figure 2: Handwritten draft of Dr. Synan's doctoral dissertation, 1967. Copyright Holy Spirit Resource Center, Oral Roberts University. Used with permission.

PREFACE

This posthumous book celebrates the life, contributions, and influence of Vinson and Carol Lee Synan. They shaped a unique Spirit-empowered legacy. Marking the fifth anniversary of Dr. Synan's passing into glory, which was during the pandemic, this publication brings together three sections of material.

The first consists of full-length academic writings published by Dr. Synan between 2004–2020. This time was especially fruitful and included his serving Oral Roberts University as Scholar-in-Residence and helping launch its Ph.D. program in theology. Dr. Synan also served Empowered21, representing Spirit-empowered scholars and leading its annual Scholars Consultations, now part of his legacy. The second section of materials presents other scholars' reports on Dr. Synan's global and ecumenical influence, which was remarkable but less widely known. Following these, a third section gathers reflections and eulogies from close friends and colleagues shared in two memorial services—one at Oral Roberts University, in May 2020, and another at Rock Church, Virginia, in June 2020. The book also includes a eulogy from Carol Lee's memorial service in Oklahoma City, in March 2021. Vinson and Carol were lifelong partners to each other. She was the typist and editor for most of Vinson's writings. Carol Lee passed away about a year after Vinson's passing, as if she could not live without him. She is honored on the cover and in photos throughout, as is he. Finally, this publication offers a complete bibliography for further study of Dr. Synan and appreciation of this couple's life work.

This book is intended to express our gratitude to God for Vinson Synan and inspire younger generations to learn from his dedicated life as a scholar, Pentecostal ambassador, and leader in breaking new ground. I want to thank the original publishers for their kind permissions (indicated in each chapter) and the co-authors for their ready consent to be included in this book. The first section contains reprints of Dr. Synan's recent publications. Any changes made to them have been editorial, simply to maintain consistency. Likewise, I would like to express my sincere appreciation to the contributors to the second and third sections of the book, which give us a glimpse of how Dr. Synan's academic leadership looked as it played out in different contexts.

This publication project has been made possible by dedicated individuals and communities. I would like to highlight several of them. Yoido Full Gospel Church, Seoul, Korea, where I serve as Senior Pastor, provided generous financial support for the project. Vinson maintained special relationships with Dr. Yonggi Cho, the church's founder, and with me. I reflect on my relationship with him in part two of the book. Dr. Billy Wilson, President of Oral Roberts University, acted like an Asian by demonstrating deep respect for the Synan couple and providing their academic and spiritual "home" for their final years. ORU's Center for Spirit-Empowered Research, led by Dr. Wonsuk Ma, managed the project. My special thanks go to Ms. Jaime Riddle, of the Center, who oversaw the editorial process. I also want to thank Dr. Charles Scott of ORU Press. We appreciate Dr. Daniel Isgrigg, who interviewed Vinson in great depth before his passing, and meticulously archived his published and unpublished materials in the Holy Spirit Research Center.

Several other institutions also contributed to this book project. Regent University, home to Vinson's pioneering academic leadership, graciously shared Dr. Synan's material with us. The project team especially expresses our appreciation to Regent for permitting the use of the Synan couple's photo that appears on the cover. Another community we want to thank is the International Pentecostal Holiness Church, where the Synans were lifelong members. Dr. Doug Beacham, the General Superintendent, extended his support by sharing his experience with the couple in multiple denominational and ecumenical settings. I also want to mention the Flower Pentecostal Heritage Center of the US Assemblies of God for its willingness in sharing Vinson's publications and photos from *The Advocate*. We also thank Rock Church in Virginia for providing their memorial service material to be included in the book.

Finally, sincere thanks go to the Synan-Taylor family, especially Virginia Synan Taylor and her sister, Mary Synan Clark, who corresponded with us for more than a year over details associated with this book. Mary and Virginia made numerous trips to Regent University, dug through old electronic files, mailed us items, and transcribed video recordings. Because of their efforts and generosity, we now have significant contributions that we would otherwise have never had. It is our hope that this work will reflect the honor and labor of Vinson and Carol, and the grace they had to shape and steward a movement up until their precious final days.

May the Lord encourage a cycle of Spirit-empowerment in future generations out of this powerful Synan legacy!

Younghoon Lee, Editor
Senior Pastor, Yoido Full Gospel Church

Contents

Part I:
His Voice Endures

Part II:
His Legacy Endures

Part I:

His Voice Endures

1

THE CHARISMATIC RENEWAL AFTER FIFTY YEARS

Vinson Synan

> Charismatics are Christians who emphasize the baptism in the Holy Spirit
> and the gifts of the Spirit toward the proclamation that Jesus Christ is "Lord
> to the glory of God the Father." -Fr. Kilian McDonnell

It seemed to creep up on us, the realization that 2010 marked the fifty-year jubilee of the Charismatic Renewal movement that began on April 3, 1960.[1] This was when Dennis Bennett, an Episcopal priest, told his upscale St. Mark's Episcopal congregation in Van Nuys, California, about the morning in 1959 when he was baptized in the Holy Spirit and spoke in tongues in a prayer meeting led by Spirit-filled Episcopalians. This event in Van Nuys marked the beginning of what is now known as the Charismatic Renewal, which has since spread to practically every denomination and congregation in the Christian world.

For some of us, it seems only yesterday when news came in the press about this well-educated Episcopal priest who broke all the stereotypes by doing what Pentecostals had been doing for the previous sixty years: speaking in tongues, healing the sick, and casting out demons. This was the beginning of a new movement, which has gone through several names and phases and has grown enormously around the world. In his book, *Nine O'Clock in the Morning*, Bennett described the event that sparked this spiritual revolution:

> I suppose I must have prayed out loud for about twenty minutes—at least
> it seemed like a long time—and was about to give up when a very strange
> thing happened. My tongue tripped just as it might when you are trying to
> say a tongue twister, and I began to speak in a new language! Right away I
> recognized several things: first, it wasn't some kind of psychological trick
> or compulsion. There was nothing compulsive about it…It was a new
> language, not some kind of "baby talk." It had grammar and syntax, it had
> inflection and expression—and it was rather beautiful.[2]

---

1. Reprinted with permission. Originally published in Synan, *Spirit-Empowered Christianity in the Twenty-First Century* (Lake Mary, FL: Charisma House, 2011), 7–24.

2. Dennis Bennett, *Nine O'Clock in the Morning* (Plainfield, NJ: Logos Press, 1970), 20.

Although Bennett was not the first mainline pastor to speak in tongues—hundreds of others such as Richard Winckler, Harald Bredesen, Tommy Tyson, and Gerald Derstine, had preceded him—but because of widespread publicity, Bennett was the one who created the movement. Soon thousands of pastors and laymen in the mainline American churches began to seek the Pentecostal experience. When they received the baptism, many expected to be excommunicated from their churches, as the Pentecostals had experienced decades before, but Bennett and the vast majority of these new Pentecostals were allowed to remain in their churches. Some of these pioneers were: Brick Bradford, J. Rodman Williams, and James Brown (Presbyterian); Ross Whetstone and Gary Moore (Methodist); Howard Conatser and Gary Clark (Baptist); Larry Christenson and Morris Vaagenes (Lutheran); and Nelson Litwiller (Mennonite). In addition to these were thousands of others who joined the ranks and were able to remain in their churches, although, sad to say, some of them suffered severe rejection and persecution.[3]

Roots of the Charismatic Renewal

Of course, the Charismatic Renewal did not occur in a vacuum. The Pentecostal movement, with roots in the earlier Holiness movement, had rapidly spread news of the Pentecostal experience since 1901, when Charles Parham began to teach that speaking in tongues was the "Bible evidence" of the baptism in the Holy Spirit. The movement became worldwide in 1906 with the beginning of the Azusa Street revival in Los Angeles, led by the black Holiness preacher William J. Seymour. For decades the Pentecostals were pilloried from the pulpits of the mainline churches and mocked in the American press. Indeed, those who spoke in tongues were accused of being mentally and socially deprived or simply "holy rollers."[4]

The person who, more than any other one, brought Pentecostalism to the attention of the larger church world and American society at large was Oral Roberts, an Oklahoma Pentecostal Holiness preacher who started a new healing ministry in Enid, Oklahoma, in 1947. In time Roberts packed out his huge tent and the largest auditoriums in America before taking his message to television in 1955. Suddenly Americans of all church backgrounds were seeing healings and Pentecostal worship in their living rooms. Millions of people were attracted not only to the man but also to his message. Many

---

3. Peter Hocken, "The Charismatic Movement," in Stanley Burgess and Eduard M. van der Maas, *New International Dictionary of Pentecostal and Charismatic Movements* (Grand Rapids, MI: Zondervan, 2002), 477–519 [henceforth, *NIDPCM*]; Kilian McDonnell, *Charismatic Renewal and the Churches* (New York, NY: Seabury Press, 1976); Synan, *The Holiness-Pentecostal Tradition* (Grand Rapids, MI: Eerdmans, 1997), 228–30.

4. Synan, *The Holiness-Pentecostal Tradition*, 84–107; Synan, *Century of the Holy Spirit* (Nashville, TN: Thomas Nelson, 1991).

observers and historians believe that Roberts was the major person behind the beginning of the Charismatic movement in the 1960s.[5]

Another important force in spreading the movement was the Full Gospel Business Men's Fellowship International (FGBMFI), which was founded by California dairyman Demos Shakarian in 1951. With the help of Roberts, the Full Gospel laymen became the major platform for hundreds and thousands of pastors and laymen from the mainline churches, many of whom would never enter the Pentecostal church.

The "Neo-Pentecostals"

Because of the Pentecostal roots of the movement, the mainline tongues speakers were at first called "neo-Pentecostals" for want of a better name. Pentecostals often called them "neos" and "collars" while planning conferences in which they were invited to participate. At first, there was little difference between the neo-Pentecostals and the older Pentecostals in both theology and worship styles. Dennis Bennett consistently proclaimed that tongues were "part of the package" and were to be expected by everyone who claimed a full Pentecostal experience. Other leaders, such as Howard Ervin of Oral Roberts University, and J. Rodman Williams of Regent University, were very close to their Pentecostal brothers and sisters in describing the Pentecostal experience.

While the Pentecostals insisted that speaking in tongues was the "initial evidence" of the baptism in the Holy Spirit, Williams and others spoke of tongues as the "primary evidence."[6] At any rate, almost all of these neo-Pentecostals sought for and received the tongues experience. To distinguish themselves from the classical Pentecostals, they graciously called themselves "neo-Pentecostals."

Around 1965 these "new" Pentecostals adopted the term "Charismatic" to distinguish themselves from their less respected but admired Pentecostal brothers and sisters. At first these were mainline Protestants in many churches, some of whom suffered persecution for their new experience and identity. The word "Charismatic" also meant that these people emphasized all the gifts of the Spirit and not just tongues.

The term "neo-Pentecostal" was soon abandoned. In time most Charismatics dropped the idea that everyone who received the baptism in the Holy Spirit would speak in tongues. Tongues were highly valued but were seen as one of many gifts that could come with the experience.

---

5. David Edwin Harrell, *Oral Roberts: An American Life* (Bloomington, IN: University of Indiana Press, 1985).

6. J. Rodman Williams, *Renewal Theology* (Grand Rapids, MI: Zondervan, 1996). Also see his "A Theological Pilgrimage," unpublished manuscript, 68–72.

The Catholic Charismatics

For seven years, from 1960 to 1967, the movement was limited to the Protestant church world with no apparent breakthroughs into the Roman Catholic and Orthodox Churches. But in 1967, to the utter astonishment of most of the Pentecostals and Charismatics, the movement entered the Roman Catholic Church. This happened in a prayer retreat at Duquesne University led by two professors and about thirty graduate students of theology. On a night in February, the first Catholic Charismatic prayer meeting began with the students who went upstairs to tarry for a Pentecostal outpouring. Patty Gallagher Mansfield described the scene in the upper room of the Chi Rho retreat center:

> That night the Lord brought the whole group into the chapel. I found my prayers pouring forth that the others might come to know Him too. My former shyness about praying aloud was completely gone as the Holy Spirit spoke through us. The professors then laid hands on some of the students, but some of us received the "baptism in the Holy Spirit" while kneeling before the Blessed Sacrament in prayer. Some of us started speaking in tongues. Others received gifts of discernment, prophecy, and wisdom. But the most important gift was the fruit of love which bound the whole community together.[7]

From Duquesne, the movement spread rapidly to Catholic graduate students at the University of Michigan and then to Notre Dame University, the intellectual and football capital of American Catholicism. Then, like a prairie fire, the movement spread from campus to campus and parish to parish until the whole church was alive with thousands of lively prayer groups. From American the movement spread to Catholic communities all over the world. After Pope Paul VI gave his papal blessing to the movement in St. Peter's Cathedral in Rome in 1975, the Charismatic Renewal became the fastest-growing grassroots movement in the Roman Catholic Church.

Catholic bishops and scholars soon saw the value of the movement since the fires of Pentecost attracted multitudes of former Catholics back to the church. Others left the church to join Pentecostal churches that seemed to have more life and fire. In a short time, Catholic scholars such as Kevin Ranaghan and Kilian McDonnell began the task of domesticating the fire of the movement with a new Catholic theology of the baptism in the Holy Spirit that would allow the movement to gain the approval of priest, bishops, and even the Pope himself. The new view was that the Holy Spirit was given at baptism to every Catholic, but the later experience that was called "baptism in the Holy Spirit" was in reality an "actualization" or "release" of what had been received int eh sacrament of initiation. In the end, most of the

---

7. Patty Gallagher Mansfield, *As by a New Pentecost* (Steubenville, OH: Steubenville University Press, 1992), 33–66. Synan, *Century of the Holy Spirit*, 209–10.

Protestant liturgical churches, like the Episcopal and Lutheran churches, adopted this view.[8]

The High Point of the Renewal

By the late 1970s, the movement was exploding all over the nation and the world. Following the lead of Oral Roberts, new televangelists appeared on TV screens and drew millions of followers. Among them were Pat Robertson and his *The 700 Club*, Paul Crouch and his Trinity Broadcasting Network (TBN), Jim Bakker and his Praise the Lord (PTL) network, and Jimmy Swaggart, with his fiery and popular evangelist television ministry.

In a short time the movement continued to burgeon in all the denominations with large conferences and thousands of prayer groups. The Catholics held huge conferences at Notre Dame that reached thirty thousand participants in 1973. The Lutherans conducted an annual Charismatic conference in St. Paul, Minnesota, that at times reached twenty-five thousand, the largest annual gathering of Lutherans in the United States. At the same time, Baptists, Methodists, Presbyterians, and Mennonites held large conferences. This was a period of great growth and success and even "giantism" in huge rallies that burst upon the scene in the late 1970s.

It all reached a climax in 1977 with the Kansas City Conference where some fifty thousand people from all over American gathered to bear a common witness to the work of the Holy Spirit in the church. Pentecostals and Charismatics from all denominations gathered in the evenings to hear such luminaries as Léon-Joseph Cardinal Suenens of Belgium, Bob Mumford, Bishop J. O. Patterson, and Francis MacNutt. The miracle was that one-half of the people there were Roman Catholic. The other half represented all the Pentecostal churches and the mainline Protestant churches.[9]

In these years, most of the mainline renewal movements set up offices to handle the large annual conferences and the magazines that served their growing constituencies. The Catholic headquarters included Ann Arbor, Michigan, and Notre Dame, Indiana. The Lutheran headquarters was in St. Paul, Minnesota, while the Methodists worked out of Nashville, Tennessee. The Presbyterians also had a very busy renewal center in Oklahoma City. Many other renewal organizations cropped up all over the nation.

---

8. Kevin Ranaghan, *The Catholic Pentecostal Movement* (New York: Paulist Press, 1969); Kilian McDonnell, *The Baptism in the Holy Spirit as an Ecumenical Problem* (South Bend, IN: Charismatic Renewal Services Press, 1972); Larry Christenson, *The Charismatic Renewal Among Lutherans* (Minneapolis, MN: n.p., 1976).

9. David Manuel, *Like a Mighty River* (Orleans, MA: Rock Harbor Press, 1977).

Charismatic Controversies

The fast-growing movement was not without its problems and controversies during these years. The most divisive problem concerned the discipleship, or shepherding, movement led at that time by the Fort Lauderdale leaders Charles Simpson, Bob Mumford, Derek Prince, Ern Baxter, and Don Basham. In order to promote healing and provide more leadership for the huge and unwieldy movement, a group was begun in 1975. Called the Charismatic Concerns Committee, this group met annually in Glencoe, Missouri, and wrestled with the shepherding controversy. They ultimately kept a sense of unity in the movement at large. Leaders of this group included Kevin Ranaghan, Larry Christenson, Vinson Synan, Vernon Stoop, and in later years, Francis MacNutt and Scott Kelso.[10]

Because of the unity in the Glencoe group, a series of massive congresses were planned and carried out by these leaders. The first, for leaders only, was in New Orleans in 1986. Seventy-five hundred leaders registered for the event. The 1987 congress was the first open to the general public, and there were forty thousand attendees. The second was in Indianapolis in 1990, the third was in Orlando in 1995, and the fourth was in St. Louis in 2000. These were led by Vinson Synan and were supported by all the major renewal groups. After the St. Louis meeting in 2000, there were no more large ecumenical rallies held to bring all sectors of the renewal together in one great meeting. Afterward the renewal groups continued to meet separately, sometimes on a regional basis.

At the height of the renewal, Cardinal Suenens stated that the Charismatic movement should disappear into the life stream of the church" with the goal of renewing the entire church through the gifts of the Holy Spirit. At any rate, after the turn of the twenty-first century, the Charismatic Renewal began to diffuse itself into the regular life of the churches with a diminishing emphasis on separate conferences. Some of the smaller Charismatic organizations withered away as the movement lost its freshness and news value.

Also, many independent Pentecostals began to adopt the word *Charismatic* to describe their own ministries. In time, the word was used not only to describe renewal in the mainline churches but was used synonymously with "Pentecostal." By the 1990s, scholars began to speak of the "Pentecostal/ Charismatic movement" to describe the whole phenomenon.

---

10. S. David Moore, *The Shepherding Movement* (New York: Continuum International Publishing, 2004).

Worldwide Growth

While the Charismatic movement began to plateau in Europe and North America, it continued to experience enormous growth throughout the developing world. In India, Africa, and Latin America, almost all churches—Catholic, Protestant, and even Orthodox—adopted the Charismatic experience and worship styles. Historian David Harrell, an expert on Indian Christianity, stated that all the churches in India are now Charismatic.[11] The same could be said of many other nations in the world.

In Africa, the Anglican and Catholic churches experienced phenomenal growth, largely due to the energy sustained from the Charismatic Renewal. However, huge indigenous Pentecostal movements also sprang up in African and many other developing nations that were not connected to Western missions such as the Assemblies of God or Church of God. In Africa, great movements with thousands of churches developed under the leadership of such figures as William Kumuyi, Enoch Adeboye, and David Oyedepo.

Although these were clearly in the Pentecostal traditions, David Barrett and other researchers began to use a catchword name for all that did not fall clearly under the names "Pentecostal" or "Charismatic." The new term was "neo-Charismatic." Major movements under the name "neo-Charismatic" were those connected with John Wimber's Association of Vineyard Churches, which spread around the world under his dynamic ministry. In these movements there was an emphasis on signs and wonders, power encounters, healing, and exorcisms that placed them very close to their Pentecostal brothers. Like other Charismatics, many neo-Charismatics did not insist on speaking in tongues as the single initial evidence of baptism in the Holy Spirit. The ranks of the neo-Charismatic movements expanded greatly during the 1990s with the advent of the Toronto Blessing movement in 1993 and the Brownsville revival in Florida in 1995.

The Shape of the Renewal Today

As of 2006, the Pentecostal-Charismatic Renewal had appeared in three major phases, according to researcher David Barrett. These were the Pentecostal wave beginning in 1901, the Charismatic wave starting in the mainline churches in 1960, and the neo-Charismatic wave beginning in about 1980. Those individuals participating in the latter category were first called Post-denominational Charismatics and later the neo-Charismatics.[12] The

---

11. Interview with David Harrell, April 9, 2007, Virginia Beach, VA.

12. David Barrett et al., *World Christian Encyclopedia* (London: Oxford University Press, 2000).

following is the latest view of the situation as the world celebrated the fiftieth anniversary of the Charismatic Renewal in 2010:[13]

Three Waves	Demographic	Population
The First Wave	Classical Pentecostals	94,383,000
The Second Wave	Mainline Charismatics	206,579,000
The Third Wave	Neo-Charismatics	313,048,000
Total		614,010,000

Looking at these figures, it becomes obvious that the greatest growth has been and continues to be in Africa, Asia, and Latin America. The African crusades of the German Pentecostal evangelist Reinhard Bonnke are now eclipsing those of any other preacher in history with as many as one million conversions in a single-service. Although the statistics are impressive indeed, the growth has been much smaller in North America and Europe. It seems that signs and wonders are more prevalent in less-developed parts of the world. Perhaps the scientific and secular worldview of the West may act as a hindrance to the dynamics of revival that are being experienced elsewhere.

According to a Pew Forum survey in 2006, large percentages of ten nations studied had very large populations of Pentecostals and Charismatics. Together they were called "Renewalists." The nations were the United States, Brazil, Chile, Guatemala, Kenya, Nigeria, South Africa, India, the Philippines, and South Korea. Of these countries, two nations, Guatemala and Kenya, reported an absolute majority of the population that identified themselves as Renewalists.[14] The following list gives the results for all ten nations:

	Pentecostal	Charismatic	Total Pop	SE %
USA	15,0002,760	54,000,000	300,055,192	23%- 69,012,694
Brazil	27,916,919	63,278,349	186,112,794	49%- 91,195,269
Chile	1,452,079	3,388,185	16,134,219	30%- 4,840,265
Guatemala	2,458,709	4,917,418	12,293,545	60%- 7,376,127
Kenya	11,453,580	7,982,798	34,707,815	56%- 19,436,378
Nigeria	23,734,752	10,548,779	131,859,731	27%- 34,284,530
South Africa	4,187,637	10,605,034	44,187,537	34%- 15,023,797
India	10,953,520	43,814,080	1,095,351,995	5%- 54,767,600
Philippines	3,578,747	35,787,470	89,468,677	44%- 39,366,218
South Korea	976,939	4,392,140	48,846,823	11%-5,373,150)[15]

---

13. Todd Johnson and Kenneth R. Ross, *The Atlas of Global Christianity*, 2010 ed. (Edinburgh: Edinburgh University Press, 2010).

14. Pew Research Center, "Spirit and Power: A Ten-Country Survey of Pentecostals," *The Pew Forum on Religion and Public Life*, October 2006.

15. All international statistics are from the United States Central Intelligence Agency, "CIA World Factbook," (Washington, DC: CIA 2006), accessed October 29, 2010, https://www.cia.gov/library/publications/the-world-factbooks/index.html. Editor's note:

For the continents of the world, Barrett gives the following figures as of 2006, the centennial year of the Azusa Street revival:

Africa: 150 million
Asia: 165 million
Europe: 34 million

South Africa: 158 million
North America: 83 million
Oceania: 4.6 million[16]

Some Prophetic Words for the Future

Although I'm a historian with a perspective typically geared towards the past, I've often been asked to predict what might happen in the future of the Pentecostal and Charismatic Renewal. This has meant abandoning the task of surveying the past and becoming a prophet as I look toward the future. Although I've never claimed the gift of predicting the future, I do believe scholarship demands that researchers share their insights in order to warn future generations not to make the same mistakes of the past.

As I look back over a lifetime of working in my church, in the broader ecumenical world, and in academia, I try to take a long view toward the future as I share what I think lies over the horizon. With that in mind, here are ten predictions that I'll be brave enough to make:

1. The Pentecostal and Charismatic movements—in all their different forms—will grow to make up more than half of all the Christians in the world in the twenty-first century. These movements already claimed more than 25 percent of all Christians in 2000. And with present growth rates, along with the shrinking of mainline churches, this seems to be a certainty.

2. The Assemblies of God will become the largest single Protestant church family in the world. With more than 60 million members in the world in 2010, and with very rapid growth rates, this church should surpass the Anglicans, Baptists, Methodists, and Lutherans in their worldwide members, followers, and/or adherents.

3. Pentecostals will eventually claim half the population of Africa and, in the long run, will outgrow Muslims in the battle for control of the continent.

4. Classical Pentecostals and Roman Catholic Charismatics will become the majority of all Latin American national populations before the end of the twenty-first century.

5. Africa will be the salvation of the Anglican Communion as their fast-growing national churches eventually take control of the Anglican world.

---

this link is no longer available at CIA.gov, but 2020 statistics for Pentecostal-Charismatic adherents in each nation and globally are available in Todd M. Johnson and Gina A. Zurlo, *Introducing Spirit-Empowered Christianity* (Tulsa, OK: ORU Press, 2023). All U.S. statistics are taken from the United States Census Bureau Report 2006.

16. Barrett et al., *World Christian Encyclopedia.*

The North American and British branches of the Anglican world will diminish in size to become negligible and less influential parts of the church. The American Episcopal Church might actually be expelled from the Lambeth Conference of Bishops by the end of the century. This might serve as the salvation of this historical communion. The same world could well happen in other Protestant denominations.

6. Through the mass healing crusades of Pentecostal evangelists such as Reinhard Bonnke and Benny Hinn, Pentecostal and Charismatic Christianity will become more than 10 percent of the population of India.

7. China will have the largest Christian population in the world by the end of the twenty-first century. Pentecostal and Charismatic churches will make up the vast majority of these new Christians. Along with this revival will come the end of communist rule in China and the institution of true democracy.

8. Because of very high birth rates, the number of Muslims will increase in most Western nations including Britian, Germany, France, and the United States. The world population of Muslims will climb during the century because many Christians practicing birth control will have smaller families and because most Western nations have massive abortion rates. The only possibility for change in this trend would be a mighty revival of signs and wonders that will convert hundreds of millions of Muslims to Christianity.

9. In time, as the Pentecostal and Charismatic movements continue to grow, more than half of the heads of state in the world will be Pentecostals or Charismatics. Demographic growth has always been followed by political influence and power.

10. The future of Christian affairs will be more and more in the hands of the massively growing Pentecostal churches and a Roman Catholic Church that has been renewed and energized by the Charismatic Renewal.[17]

Perhaps one of the most prophetic words about the future of Pentecostalism was written by a most unlikely person, Harvey Cox of Harvard University School of Divinity. In 1994, he mildly shocked the Christian world with the publication of his book *Fire From Heaven*, with the meaningful subtitle: *The Rise of Pentecostal Spirituality and the Reshaping of Religion in the Twenty-first Century*. Already famous for his 1965 book *The Secular City*, in which he proclaimed the end of religion as a priority in the life of modern man, he was toasted by such "God is dead" theologians as Thomas Altizer, Paul Van Buren, and William Hamilton. Yet, three decades later, Cox reversed his field by celebrating the return of religion for modern man through the exploding Pentecostal and Charismatic movements of the world. He seemed to come full circle from the "God is dead" era to the "Spirit is

---

17. This is in the last chapter of my memoirs, *Eyewitness to the Century of the Holy Spirit* (Grand Rapids, MI: Chosen Books, 2010), 202–204.

alive and well" era, inspired by the rise of Pentecostalism as a major worldwide spiritual force.[18]

The initiative is now in the hands of the Pentecostals and Charismatics of the world to do as Cox suggested, i.e. to "reshape religion" in this century. This is indeed a tall order but one that I believe is possible as a new generation of brilliant Pentecostal scholars set themselves to bringing Christianity back to its earliest roots, as seen in the full Charismatic New Testament church.

---

18. Harvey Cox, *Fire from Heaven: The Rise of Pentecostal Spirituality and the Reshaping of Christianity in the Twenty-first Century* (New York: Addison-Wesley, 1994).

2

FROM GRACELESS LAW TO LAWLESS GRACE

Vinson Synan

"I have recently discovered the wonderful freedom of grace, and I have changed my views on holiness as the church has taught it," a fellow minister told me a few years ago.[1] "I have grown to see the dangers of Pharisaism and legalism that has plagued us for so long." He then exulted, "Now that I am free from the demands of the law, I am free to serve the Lord, not because I have to, but because I want to."[2]

Although this sounded interesting to me at the time, I felt a twinge of concern for this friend who had long been a stalwart champion of holy living. Years before, I had known this young man to be a devout ministerial student with extraordinary gifts. His subsequent pastorates were successful, and he was marked for future leadership in his denomination.

A few months after hearing him exult about "discovering grace," I heard the shocking news that he had left the ministry in disgrace after being caught in an affair with a woman in the community. The resulting divorce wrecked his family and forced him to resign his pastorate. For him, the discovery of grace had become a license to sin, which led to the ruin of his ministry.

Over the years, I have seen the same pattern repeated several times and usually with the same tragic results. For some people, the discovery of grace becomes a convenient way to cover sin and attempt to avoid the guilt that inevitably follows. When someone tells me he has suddenly "discovered grace," I often shudder. This "grace-discovery syndrome" is all too often the first step toward moral and ethical decline.

Graceless Law

This is not to indict sincere people who learn about the marvelous depths of truth concerning God's loving grace toward us. Many Christians are formed

---

1. Reprinted with permission. Originally published in Synan, ed. *The Truth About Grace* (Lake Mary, FL: Charisma House/Empowered21, 2017), 1–7.

2. This article was written in the early 1980s, long before the advent of the modern grace movement. (Author's note, in original).

13

in systems that can best be described as hotbeds of "graceless law." In these places, righteousness rests in obeying a set of general rules and regulations earmarked as standards for church membership. At times, zealots administer these rules in ways that destroy rather than save the sheep. Often these holiness codes become occasions for spiritual pride and the remorseless pursuit of those who fail to keep every jot and tittle of the law.

My dear friend Pauline Parham told of one of the most extreme cases of graceless law I have ever heard. In a little Kansas town, a local holiness church split over whether its male members should wear buttons or hooks and eyes on their shirts. A few members had come to believe buttons were symbols of pride, while the simpler hooks and eyes fell more in line with a holiness lifestyle. When the church split over the controversy, people in town called one group "the buttons church" and the other "the hooks-and-eyes church." Needless to say, the church became the laughingstock of the community.

To be sure, Jesus contended with the spiritual pride and arrogance of the scribes and Pharisees, who could "strain out a gnat and swallow a camel" (Matt 23:24) in their pursuit of the law.[3] This type of graceless law would stone a woman caught in adultery and then leave her equally guilty accusers to go free. Jesus, who had no patience for this hypocritical legalism, denounced it every time it reared its ugly head.

The apostle Paul, who based his entire theology on the grace of God through Christ, had no patience for this theology of graceless law either. He said, "By grace you have been saved through faith, and this not of yourselves. It is the gift of God, not of works, so that no one should boast" (Eph 2:8–9). Certainly, no Christian living in the age of grace would base his eternal salvation on the dubious grounds of performing good works rather than accepting the sacrifice of Jesus Christ, who is the only Savior.

Truly, it is the amazing grace of God through Jesus Christ that will save us in the end. No one who reads the New Testament can deny this basic truth. Jesus saves. We do not save ourselves.

Lawless Grace

At the other extreme are those who believe in a form of "lawless grace" that allows Christians to throw away the Ten Commandments and all the clear moral teachings of Christ and the apostles under the law. Those who hold to this teaching can be in as grave an error as those who live under forms of graceless law.

I often hear people in this camp deride those who live by the "thou shalt not's" of the Bible and those who posit their salvation on the sins they avoid.

---

3. Unless otherwise indicated, all scripture verses in this chapter are from the *Modern English Version* (MEV), Lake Mary, FL: Charisma House, 2014.

They often label this as "works righteousness," a favorite phrase used by these proponents to dismiss those who attempt to maintain biblical standards of holiness and righteousness.

Certainly, avoiding sin will not save anyone. Nonbelievers who live moral lives above reproach are still lost, despite their good works and moral lives, because they do not believe in Jesus Christ as their personal Savior.

Often, those who "discover grace" fall into the trap of rejecting all of the moral law given to us in the Scriptures and become laws unto themselves. This is called antinomianism, which means "against the law," and is an error as old as the gnostic heresy of the first century. These "knowing ones" taught that the spirit could remain pure even as the body sinned—a form of dualism the church has always condemned. Those who find themselves freed from the chains of graceless law should remember the advice of Paul: "Stand fast therefore in the liberty by which Christ has made us free.…Only do not use liberty as an opportunity for the flesh, but through love serve one another" (Gal 5:1, 13, NKJV).

Another grave error is to believe that a person's anointing justifies any lifestyle. I was once told by a fallen televangelist that the anointing just seemed to be present in his ministry despite the lewd sins he seemed unable to avoid in his secret private life. People were saved and healed after he preached. My answer to him was that the Lord anoints His Word and that any results are due to the faithfulness of God, not the anointing of the minister. Paul made this clear when he said, "I bring and keep my body under subjection, lest when preaching to others I myself should be disqualified" (1 Cor 9:27).

After all, "God has not called us to uncleanness, but to holiness" (1 Thess 4:7). The Scriptures are clear on this too. Paul teaches, "Do you not know that the unrighteous will not inherit the kingdom of God? Do not be deceived. Neither the sexually immoral, nor idolaters, nor adulterers, nor male prostitutes, nor homosexuals, nor thieves, nor covetous, nor drunkards, nor revilers, nor extortioners will inherit the kingdom of God" (1 Cor 6:9–10). He then says, "Such were some of you. But you were washed, you were sanctified, and you were justified in the name of the Lord Jesus by the Spirit of our God" (v. 11). The only way God's grace can reach people who commit these sins is for them to confess, repent, and abandon the lifestyles of sin that place them outside the kingdom.

The crucial point is this: your works of righteousness cannot save you, but your sinful works of unrighteousness can destroy you. The Scriptures are crystal clear on this point. Works of righteousness cannot save, but willful works of unrighteousness can damn a person in eternity, despite the grace of God, who stands ready to forgive, heal, and restore. In the end, those who practice lives of unrepented, unconfessed, and unforgiven sin will be lost, regardless of their theology of grace.

The Time is Now

Over the centuries, the pendulum has swung back and forth between graceless law and lawless grace. The nineteenth century saw a mighty revival of holiness preaching and teaching, which greatly blessed the church and the world. As historians know, the Pentecostal movement was born in a holiness cradle. Part of the success of the early Pentecostal movement was due to the godly lives of its leaders and members. In recent years, however, the pendulum seems to have swung in the other direction, toward an acceptance of lawless grace that excuses sin not only in the lives of the laity but also in the lives of its leaders. This is surely the great tragedy of this hour.

The world has seen enough of pastors, priests, teachers, evangelists, televangelists, bishops, and other church leaders who have "discovered grace," only to fall into grievous and scandalous sin. Churches are suffering untold internal harm and a drastic loss of public credibility due to the spectacle of so-called Christian leaders caught in adultery, homosexuality, child abuse, pornography, alcoholism, financial dishonesty, and many other outrageous sins. Many times, these ministers started out sincerely following the Lord, leading lives of holiness and righteousness, but later "discovered grace."

Perhaps what is needed most is a rejection of both extremes, the graceless law of the Pharisees and legalists and the lawless grace of those who think God has repealed His own basic rules of Christian living. Perhaps the church should look again at Hebrews 12:14, as did John Wesley, and contemplate the Lord's command to "pursue peace with all men, and the holiness without which no one will see the Lord."

3

HEALING IN THE EARLY PENTECOSTAL/CHARISMATIC TRADITION: A HISTORICAL PERSPECTIVE

Vinson Synan

Jesus is my Healer in my room.
Jesus is my Healer in my room.
He writes out my prescriptions;
He gives me all my medicine;
He heals me of my sickness;
Jesus is my Healer in my room.
~*Black Pentecostal Spiritual*

Introduction

During the twentieth century the Pentecostal movement grew from a small and persecuted handful of believers to become, along with their Charismatic cousins, a major Christian tradition.[1] Although mostly known for their distinctive practice of speaking in tongues, perhaps in the public eye they may be better known for their teaching and practice of divine healing. In fact, the popularity of their massive public healing crusades may account more for their worldwide growth than speaking in tongues.[2]

---

1. Reprinted with permission. Originally published as Vinson Synan, "Healing in the Early Pentecostal/Charismatic Tradition: A Historical Perspective," in *A Light to the Nations: Explorations in Ecumenism, Missions, and Pentecostalism*, ed. Stanley M. Burgess and Paul W. Lewis (Eugene, OR: Wipf & Stock, 2017), 286–300.

2. Recent broad surveys on Pentecostalism include Synan, *The Holiness-Pentecostal Tradition: The Charismatic Movement in the Churches* (Grand Rapids, MI: Eerdmans, 1997); and Synan, *The Century of the Holy Spirit* (Nashville, TN: Thomas Nelson, 2001); also Walter J. Hollenweger, *Pentecostalism: Origins and Developments Worldwide* (Peabody, MA: Hendrickson, 1997). An indispensable general source is Stanley Burgess, Gary McGee, and Patrick Alexander, *Dictionary of Pentecostal and Charismatic Movements* (Grand Rapids, MI: Zondervan, 1988) and the more recent version, Stanley Burgess and Eduard M. van der Maas, eds., *New International Dictionary of Pentecostal and Charismatic Movements* (Grand Rapids, MI: Zondervan,

17

Just who are these "Pentecostal/Charismatics" anyway? Following the great Roman Catholic Charismatic scholar, Kilian McDonnell, the broadest theological definition might be "Those Christians who stress the baptism in the Holy Spirit and the gifts of the Spirit toward the proclamation that Jesus Christ is Lord, to the Glory of God the Father."[3]

This category would include all Christians who have been called "Classical Pentecostals," (Assemblies of God, Church of God in Christ, Pentecostal Holiness Church, the Churches of God, International Church of the Foursquare Gospel, etc.) and both Protestant and Catholic Charismatics. Altogether they accounted for over 600,000,000 members in the world in 2013 and are by far the second largest family of Christians in the world after the Roman Catholic Church. Even though speaking in tongues as evidence of the baptism in the Holy Spirit is the most original contribution of the Pentecostal movement, actually the emphasis on divine healing has a much longer history than tongues in the Holiness/Pentecostal tradition and has caused not only spectacular growth, but at times resulted in confusion and turmoil within the churches. While tongues came to the fore in 1901 and 1906 with the ministries of Charles Parham in Topeka, Kansas, and William J. Seymour in the Azusa Street revival in Los Angeles in 1906, the emphasis on healing goes back to the mid-nineteenth century when efforts were made to restore New Testament signs and wonders to the church.[4]

Before this time, most Christians had seen no contradiction between faith and medicine. Most would have agreed with Sirach in the intertestamental book Ecclesiasticus when he advised:

> Cultivate the physician in accordance with the need for him, for him also hath God ordained. It is from God that the physician getteth wisdom and from the king receiveth gifts. The skill of the physician lifteth up his head, and he may stand before nobles. God hath created medicines out of the earth, and let not a discerning man reject them. Was not the water made sweet by the wood that He might make known to all men His power? And He gave men discernment that they might glory in His mighty works. By means of them the physician assuages pain. And likewise the apothecary prepareth a confection that his work may not cease nor health from the face

---

2002). Statistics are taken from David Barrett, George T. Kurian, and Todd M. Johnson, eds., *World Christian Encyclopedia: A Comparative Survey of Churches and Religions AD 30–2200* (New York: Oxford University Press, 2000).

3. Kilian McDonnell and Arnold Bittlinger, *The Baptism in the Holy Spirit as an Ecumenical Problem* (South Bend, IN: Charismatic Renewal Services, 1972), 47–48.

4. For the development of the healing movement within the Holiness movement, see Paul Chappell's, "Healing Movements," in Burgess and McGee, *DPCM*, 353–74. Also see Donald Dayton's, *Theological Roots of Pentecostalism* (Grand Rapids, MI: Francis Asbury Press, 1987), 115–41; and Faupel, *Everlasting Gospel*, 115–186. A more recent book on Pentecostals and divine healing is Kimberley Ervin Alexander, *Pentecostal Healing: Models in Theology and Practice*, Blandford Forum (Dorset, UK: Deo, 2006).

of the earth. My son, in sickness, be not negligent. Pray unto God for He can heal. Turn from iniquity and purify thy hands and from all transgressions cleanse thy heart. Give a meal offering with a memorial. Offer a fat sacrifice to the utmost of thy means. And to the physician also give a place; nor should he be far away, for of him also there is a need. For there is a time when successful help is in his power; for he maketh supplication to God to make his diagnosis successful and treatment that it may promote recovery (Sirach 38:1–9).[5]

This was written in a time when many devout Jews refused to see a doctor or take medicine because medical treatment might imply a lack of faith in God. So what I will say today is not so new in religious history.

The roots of all modern healing movements lie in Europe where healing in answer to prayer was first taught by Presbyterian Edward Irving in London (1830), by Lutheran Johann Christoph Blumhardt in Germany (1843), by Dorothea Trudel in Switzerland (1851), and by Otto Stockmayer in Switzerland (1867). These teachers developed not only the idea of the "healing home" (a hospital-like retreat where prayer was administered instead of medicines) but a theology of healing which was to affect many in America and lead to the Pentecostal doctrine of divine healing "as in the atonement." The most influential book coming out of Europe in this period was Stockmayer's *Sickness and the Gospel,* which pioneered the idea that physical healing for the body was included in the over-all atonement.[6]

Building on the pioneering work of Blumhardt, Trudel, and Stockmayer in Europe, a long list of American leaders in both the Holiness and Pentecostal movements added a flood of books on healing. They also pioneered more and more radical views of healing that eventually excluded the use of medicines or doctors in favor of prayer alone.

Charles Cullis

Although divine healing had been practiced in America by George Fox, founder of the Quakers; Joseph Smith, founder of the Mormons; and Elizabeth Mix, a black Holiness evangelist, the first person to bring healing to the attention of Americans was Charles Cullis of Boston, Massachusetts. Cullis, already a medical doctor, began his ministry in 1864 when he opened his first free faith home for consumptives where the sick could receive "the comforts of a warm home and complete medical care." His first efforts were

---

5. See R. H. Charles, *The Apocrypha and Pseudepigrapha of the Old Testament* (London: Oxford Press, 1973), 448–50.

6. For early European developments, see Chappell, "Healing Movements," *DPCM,* 355–66; on Stockmayer (no date) specifically, see Chappell, "Healing Movements," 356.

quite similar to the ministry of Mother Teresa's "home of the destitute and dying" in Calcutta.[7]

By 1870, however, Cullis added prayer to his ministry of caregiving and traditional medicine after seeing a patient, Lucy Drake, instantly healed of a debilitating brain tumor after the laying on of hands. This led Cullis to turn his homes into "healing homes" where the patients would be treated with loving care and prayer, minus medicine.[8] By the 1880s, Cullis was conducting annual healing conventions in Old Orchard, Maine, as well as holding healing conventions around the nation. By 1885, the message of healing had become international when William Boardman convened the first International Conference on Divine Healing and True Holiness in the Great Agricultural Hall in London where 2000 persons gathered to advance the cause of divine healing around the world.[9]

After this event a stream of books on healing flowed from Holiness and Evangelical presses extolling the power of healing in answer to prayer. These included Boardman's 1881 book, *The Lord that Healeth Thee*, and Kelso Carter's 1884 book entitled *The Atonement for Sin and Sickness: or a Full Salvation for Soul and Body*. These books brought healing beyond the level of anecdotal testimonies and into the arena of theological discourse and debate.[10]

Adoniram J. Gordon

The man who elevated divine healing to the level of the atonement was A. J. Gordon, the popular Boston pastor who eventually founded the seminary that bears his name today. Through his association with Cullis, Gordon became a staunch believer in divine healing, so much so that in 1882 he published his famous book, *The Ministry of Healing*, in which he asserted that healing for the body was part of the atonement. Using Psalm 103:3 [on the Lord] "…who forgiveth all thine iniquities, who healeth all thy diseases" and Matthew 8:17 [where] "He himself took our infirmities and carried away our diseases," Gordon concluded that divine healing for the body was included in the atonement side by side with the forgiveness of sins.

After many other teachers added their agreement to Gordon's formulation, including A. B. Simpson, founder of the Christian and Missionary Alliance, a host of teachers and churches asserted their belief in divine healing "as in the atonement." Decades later, when the Pentecostal

---

7. Chappell, "Healing Movements," *DPCM*, 358. See also Dayton, *Theological Roots of Pentecostalism*, 122–25.

8. Chappell, "Healing Movements," *DPCM*, 359–60.

9. Chappell, "Healing Movements," *DPCM*, 360–61.

10. Chappell, "Healing Movements," *DPCM*, 360–61.

denominations were formed, they added this phrase to their statements of faith.[11]

John Alexander Dowie

By the turn of the century, the idea of healing homes, where the sick could be cared for without cost and where the treatment would be prayer instead of traditional medical treatment, had spread far and wide. It was Alexander Dowie, the fire-breathing healing evangelist from Scotland and Australia, who made a complete break from medical treatment. Denouncing doctors as "agents of Satan," he called on his followers to trust God completely for their healing. His distrust for the medical profession may have come from his years as a surgical assistant in Scotland, where at the same time he studied theology at Edinburgh University. Later, after serving as a Congregationalist Pastor in Sydney, Australia, Dowie left his denomination to found an independent holiness church in Melbourne before emigrating to the United States in 1888.[12]

After two years of itinerant healing ministries on the West Coast where he organized local chapters of his International Divine Healing Association, Dowie settled in Chicago where in 1893 he set up a wooden tabernacle outside the entrance to the Chicago World's Fair. Soon the inside walls of the building were covered with the crutches and braces of those who claimed healing at the hands of the balding evangelist. Shortly afterward, Dowie bought the Imperial Hotel in Chicago and converted it into a healing home. In these "golden years," Dowie was lionized by the public, spoke to the largest audiences in the history of Chicago, and was received by Presidents McKinley and Roosevelt.

It was not long, however, that the ecclesiastical and medical establishments in Chicago began a concerted attack on Dowie and his healing claims with many vicious anti-Dowie articles appearing in the Chicago newspapers. By 1895 Dowie had been arrested for practicing medicine without a license and had spent 120 days in court answering over 100 arrest warrants, partly for his vociferous attacks on the corrupt politics of the city government. In response, Dowie, in April 1895, published his first but not last volley against the medical establishment. His vitriolic article entitled "Doctors, Drugs, and Devils, or the Foes of Christ the Healer" appeared in *Physical Culture* magazine. In it he made the following statements:

---

11. Dayton, *Theological Roots of Pentecostalism*, 127–30.

12. Two biographies of Dowie are R. Harlan, *John Alexander Dowie and the Christian Apostolic Church in Zion* (Evansville, WI: R. M. Antes, 1906); and Gordon Lindsay, *The Life of John Alexander Dowie* (Shreveport, LA: Voice of Healing Publishing Company, 1851). The major recent source for Dowie is Faupel, *Everlasting Gospel*, 116–35.

> I want to say today that doctors as a profession, are directly inspired by the devil. There is not an atom of foundation for science in medicine. All doctors are "poisoners-general and surgical butchers" and "professional destroyers." They are monsters who hold in their hands deadly poisons and deadly surgical knives, and in the name of the law demand that you lie down upon the altar of their operating tables, that they may deprive you of your consciousness and make you a living sacrifice."[13]

With the immense popularity gained at the Chicago World's Fair and in response to such articles, Dowie in 1896 proclaimed the founding of a new last days church for all true believers, the "Christian Catholic Church," and called on all his followers to join with him in a holy war against the religious establishment. By 1900, he began construction of Zion City on 6,500 acres 20 miles north of Chicago. Planned for 200,000 residents, Zion was to be a center of commerce and government as well as religion. In short order Dowie constructed homes, banks, schools, a hotel, and a wooden tabernacle that would seat no less than 8,000 persons. Those who took the commuter train from Chicago for Sunday services were greeted with large signs stating that Zion was "the only place where it is easy to do right and difficult to do wrong." They were also told that in Zion there would be:

> No Profanity, No vulgarity, No sorcerers, No medical poisoners, No cut throat competition, No saloons or beer gardens, No intoxicating liquors, No surgical butchers, No cigarette or tobacco stores, No vaccination: the foulest of all the foul inventions of the Devil and some dirty doctors, No drugs, No theaters, No dance halls, No opium joint, No gambling establishment, No house of ill fame assignation, No pharmacy, No apothecary's shop, or drugstore, No place for the manufacture or sale of drugs or medicines of any kind, No place or office of residence of a practicing physician or surgeon. As well as no unclean food or oysters, that scavenger of the sea, or swine, that scavenger of the earth. No place for holding secret meetings or assemblies of any oath-bound society.[14]

Indeed, Zion would be a place where holiness and healing would be in and everything else would be out! A sad footnote on Dowie's ministry was that in 1901, he suddenly proclaimed himself to be "Elijah the Restorer" in fulfillment of Scripture and announced plans to set up new Zion communities all over the world. On top of this, in 1905, he suffered a stroke that made him a living vegetable leading to power struggles over control of his vast religious empire. He died in disgrace in 1907, ignored by those who formerly adored him.[15]

---

13. J. Alexander Dowie, "Doctors, Drugs and Devils, or, the Foes of Christ the Healer," *Physical Culture* (April 1895): 81–86.

14. This passage was supplied to me by Terryl Todd of Libertyville, IL, who copied them from a contemporary photograph.

15. See Lindsay, *John Alexander Dowie*, 193–275; and Faupel, *Everlasting Gospel*, 118–33.

Dowie's stern position against all medicine and doctors, however, took root in many sectors of the Holiness movement and became the majority view of Pentecostals when the movement began in 1901 in Topeka, Kansas.

Charles Fox Parham and William J. Seymour

Although Parham is known as the man who formulated the doctrine that speaking in tongues was the "Bible evidence" of the baptism in the Holy Spirit, he was first widely known as a healing evangelist. As a Methodist pastor and later as a Holiness teacher, Parham adopted Wesleyan language to describe divine healing. He once said that sickness is instantly "cleansed away, root and branch" in answer to prayer.[16]

In 1898, after a visit to Dowie's Zion City, Parham established his Bethel Healing Home in Topeka, Kansas, where the sick could come and rest in a "spiritual hospital" where prayer and Bible reading took the place of doctors and medicine. It was only after he opened his Bethel Bible School that he and his students discovered the connection between tongues and the baptism in the Holy Spirit on January 1, 1901, the very first day of the twentieth century. After this event, Parham preached a "five-fold gospel" emphasizing the new birth, second blessing sanctification, the baptism in the Holy Spirit evidenced by tongues, divine healing "as in the atonement," and the instant rapture of the church. In this schema everything happened in an instant, including divine healing.[17]

When Pentecostalism exploded on the world scene at Azusa Street in 1906, under the African-American pastor William J. Seymour, his teaching on healing was essentially the same as his teacher Charles Parham. This included divine healing as in the atonement. In one article on healing, Seymour lamented that many Christians "will take a doctor before Jesus. They put a doctor between them and the atonement…the doctor gives you poison and you die because you dishonor the atonement."[18]

> When someone wrote a letter to Seymour's Apostolic Faith, asking "Do you teach that it is wrong to take medicine?" the answer was as follows: "Yes…medicine is for unbelievers, but the remedy for the saints of God we find in Jas. 5:14…." In another note on healing, Seymour stated that "a

---

16. The definitive biography of Parham is James Goff, *Fields White unto Harvest: Charles Fox Parham and the Missionary Origins of Pentecostalism* (Fayetteville, AR: University of Arkansas Press, 1988), 32–70.

17. Goff, *Fields White Unto Harvest*, 90.

18. William J. Seymour, "Salvation and Healing," *Apostolic Faith (Azusa Street)*, (December 1906), 2.

sanctified body is one that is cleansed from all sickness and disease. The Lord gives you power over sickness and disease."[19]

For the next decade Pentecostals generally held to Parham's and Seymour's "atonement" view that taking medicine or going to a doctor showed a lack of faith in God. Under the fiery preaching of the Pentecostals, healing was now taken out of the residential "healing homes" and preached from the rooftops. Healing evangelists laid hands on the sick in gospel tents, in schoolhouses, and in whatever church would allow them a hearing. In this period, many Pentecostal saints vowed that they would never touch another pill for the rest of their lives while "trusting God for their bodies." The standard testimony was: "I praise God that I am saved, sanctified, filled with the Holy Ghost, looking for Jesus to come, and I have trusted God for my body for 40 years," (or however many years since they had taken their last medicine).

In 1920, for example, Sam Page, one-time head of the Pentecostal Holiness Church, reported that he had been "saved and healed for 27 years." In the first church I myself pastored in Virginia, there was an elderly lady of 94 years, Sister Gayle, who testified that she had "trusted God for her body for 50 years." One preacher, W. J. Noble said, after promising not to take any medicine or see a doctor "until death," testified: "He has healed me of many diseases such as broken bones, tonsillitis, la grippe, influenza, indigestion, diphtheria, ingrown toenails, cancer, and tuberculosis in the last stage." Theirs was indeed a heroic faith.[20]

If there were any sick people among them, many Pentecostals felt that either there was sin in the body, or the person lacked the faith to be healed. If anyone suffered from depression or any other mental or emotional disorder, they were generally thought to be demon-possessed. Instead of psychiatry or psychoanalysis, exorcisms were the order of the day for those who were "oppressed of the devil." In any case, the sick often lay in their beds in a darkened sickroom for weeks, praying for a healing touch while often enduring agonies of pain and refusing any kind of medicine or visit from physicians. In this case, Jesus and Jesus alone was the caregiver and healer.

Confusion and Schism over "Remedies"

For several decades, Pentecostals made news in many communities over their views and practices on divine healing. In the period from Azusa Street to

---

19. William J. Seymour, "Questions and Answers," *Apostolic Faith (Azusa Street),* (January 1908), 2, 4.

20. Synan, *The Old Time Power: A History of the Pentecostal Holiness Church* (Franklin Springs: Advocate Press, 1973), 166–71.

World War II, some Pentecostal preachers were not only arrested for "practicing medicine without a license," but were accused of "murder" for allowing family members to die without medical aid. Some even looked on this as a mark of distinction and suffering for the faith. Francis Marion Britton of the Pentecostal Holiness Church, for instance, allowed his first wife to die "unaided" although fifty neighbors threatened to have him tried for "murder" because of a lack of medical attention. Not only did his wife die "without drugs" but so did two of their children.[21]

In the Church of God, Walter Barney, a pastor in Wytheville, Virginia, was tried and convicted of manslaughter in 1915 for refusing medical care for a daughter who later died. His conviction was later overturned with a pardon by the Governor of Virginia. To many Pentecostals, people like Britton and Barney were heroes of healing who were gladly persecuted for their faith. But to other Pentecostals they seemed to be fanatics who gave Pentecostalism a bad name.[22]

The only schism among Pentecostals over the use of medicine divided the Pentecostal Holiness church when, in 1919, a furor erupted in the church when a Georgia preacher, Hugh Bowling, wrote in the church paper *The Advocate* that it was no sin at all to take "remedies" and that going to a doctor implied no lack of faith in the patient. To some leaders this position seemed to be a compromise on the heroic stand for divine healing that many had taken over the years. One letter to the editor exhorted, "Beloved, let us never lower the standard, for if we fail to preach this wonderful truth, we are a fallen church, and if our ministers advocate drugs and doctors, something is wrong…you are not preaching the full gospel."[23]

After this, a great struggle ensued with charges and counter-charges on each side. In a later article in *The Advocate*, Bowling explained his position:

> I do not believe that those who get sick and use no remedies and drag around for weeks and after so long a time get well, are divinely healed, but that nature alone restored them.…I do not believe in lying about divine healing. I do not believe that sickness is evidence of unbelief. I do not believe that healing is paralleled with salvation in the atonement.[24]

This was the last straw! Leaders of the denomination made charges against Bowling and his friend Watson Sorrow. In the end, Bowling was given his day in an ecclesiastical court but was expelled from the church when he failed to appear for the hearing. He and some friends thereafter organized the Congregational Holiness Church in 1921. In time the controversy was largely forgotten, but in later years, the very men who criticized Bowling for

---

21. Synan, *Old Time Power*, 166.

22. Church of God, *Evangel* (December 1, 1910): 1–2; (January 23, 1915): 2.

23. Synan, *Old Time Power*, 167.

24. Synan, *Old Time Power*, 167.

advocating medicine themselves died in hospitals using the best doctors and medicines available.[25]

Oral Roberts and the City of Faith

The famous healing evangelist, Oral Roberts, was only three years old in Oklahoma when his denomination was torn with controversy over divine healing. In fact, in some places divine healing almost faded from the life of the churches. In his book, *Expect a Miracle,* Roberts says that faith for healing was at a low ebb in the Pentecostal Churches where his father and mother served as pastors. His miraculous healing from tuberculosis as a sixteen-year-old boy, however, was destined to change his life and the life of the American church in the decades to come. After his healing, young Oral answered the call to preach. The first few years of his ministry saw Roberts struggling as a traveling evangelist and pastor of small Pentecostal Holiness churches.[26] In 1947, while pastoring a small church in Toccoa, Georgia, Oral saw a man instantly healed after a motor had fallen on his foot crushing it to the bone. Impressed with this unexpected miracle, Roberts began to fast and pray for the gift of healing to be released in his ministry. After returning to Oklahoma, he pastored other churches while studying in Phillips University and helping to found Southwestern College in Oklahoma City.[27]

During a time of fasting and prayer in his Enid, Oklahoma church, Roberts heard the Lord commission him to bring God's healing power to his generation. His first healing crusade in his hometown of Ada, Oklahoma in 1948 was so successful that he immediately launched a tent-healing crusade ministry that eventually made him a household name throughout the world. A major breakthrough came in 1953 when he began televising his healing lines on national television. This brought divine healing into the very living rooms of the nation. In doing this, Roberts created a new media genre—that of the "televangelist." The income generated by his television ministry ultimately led Roberts to found his own university in 1965 in Tulsa. Here, he planned to train young people to take divine healing to the furthermost nations and peoples of the world.[28]

On top of his sensational and wildly successful healing ministry, in 1980 Roberts dedicated his 77-story hospital in Tulsa that he dubbed the "City of Faith." Here, he said, would be celebrated a "marriage between prayer and

---

25. Synan, *Old Time Power,* 169–71.

26. Of the many autobiographies of Oral Roberts, the best and most recent one is Oral Roberts, *Expect a Miracle: My Life and Ministry: Oral Roberts, an Autobiography* (Nashville, TN: Thomas Nelson, 1995). The most important biography of Roberts is David Harrell, *Oral Roberts: An American Life* (Bloomington, IN: Indiana University Press, 1985).

27. Roberts, *Expect a Miracle,* 54–56.

28. Roberts, *Expect a Miracle,* 64–100.

medicine, the supernatural and the natural, in the treatment of the whole person." The hospital included plans for a medical school where future doctors could minister healing through medicine and prayer. After an initial period of euphoria and success, however, the dream of a Pentecostal hospital ran aground on the rocks of financial disaster. Although his partners gave tens of millions of dollars to the project, few were willing to travel to Tulsa for treatment, even after the City of Faith hospital offered free plane tickets to anyone who would come. By 1990 it was clear that even Roberts' staunchest supporters would rather trust in Oral's prayers for healing than come to his hospital.[29]

With the closing of the City of Faith in 1989, the circle was complete. The healing movement had begun in the 1860s with Charles Cullis ministering prayer in a public hospital in Boston. Afterwards the healing home movement saw people abandoning hospitals in favor of entering healing homes for rest and prayer. Then, in the most radical phase, the Dowie era, people denounced all "doctors, drugs and devils" in favor of prayer alone. But, by the 1990s, Pentecostals and Charismatics had generally settled on a position in which a sick person would still ask for prayer first and trust God for healing, and then go to the doctors for regular medical care. If they got well, whether with medical treatment or without it, they claimed their healing to be a miracle from God.

Ultimately, most Pentecostals came to agree with the final position of Oral Roberts on the question of healing. After laying hands on over one million sick folk in his crusades, he concluded that all miraculous healing comes from God whether from natural processes, as the result of prayer with the laying on of hands, or through the ministry of doctors and medicine. Gone were the days when children were left to die in agony "without drugs or doctors." Still, as the century came to an end, there were those faith teachers like Kenneth Hagin who could say, "I took my last aspirin in 1934 when I had my last headache." He made a point that he had received no medicine or medical care in the 63 years since. That, by the way, was the year I was born.[30]

Conclusion

In summary, the story of healing in the Pentecostal/Charismatic movement came down to the question of who was in the sickroom. Before Cullis, the only healer in the house was the medical doctor. In his first healing homes,

---

29. It is interesting that Roberts did not mention the City of Faith in his last autobiography, evidently putting stress on his highly successful university. By 1994, the City of Faith was a source of endowments.

30. Synan, "The Faith of Kenneth Hagin," *Charisma* (June 1990): 62–70. Richard M. Riss, "Kenneth E. Hagin," in Burgess, et. al., *DPCM*, 345.

there were now two healers in the house, the doctor and Jesus. In his later years, there was only one healer in the house—Jesus. Under Dowie, doctors and drugs were not only totally excluded, they were demonized.

Later, under such Pentecostal evangelists as Aimee Semple McPherson and Oral Roberts, the healing homes were abandoned in favor of evangelistic healing crusades under tents and in large city auditoriums. With the creation of the City of Faith, prayer and medicine were again joined together. Now, Jesus and the doctor were in the same room ministering to the sick and giving God the glory for any healing that took place, whether from natural processes, from medicine or surgery, or from prayer. In the end, the long-term effect of Pentecostal/Charismatic caregiving was to invite Jesus back into the sickroom where He could add his healing touch to that of the doctors and nurses.

Indeed, by the 1990's, medical science was confirming the fact that religious faith and prayer made a measurable scientific difference in the healing process. In 1998, for example, the Templeton Foundation was sponsoring classes on religion, healing, and prayer in the major medical schools of the nation. Not only this, by the mid-1990s there was a veritable flood of magazine articles, TV specials, and scholarly studies announcing "discoveries" about prayer and healing that Christians in general and Pentecostals in particular had known for decades. One of the most important media breakthroughs was the June 1996 issue of *Time Magazine* with a cover story entitled, "Faith and Healing: Can Spirituality promote Health? Some Surprising Evidence." This story told of AIDS patients who were studied in a controlled experiment where one-half were treated with drugs alone and the other half with drugs and prayer. The results were significantly better for those who received prayer. It was also stated that "according to a 1995 study at Dartmouth, one of the strongest predictors of survival after open heart surgery is the degree to which patients say they draw strength and comfort from religion." The article concluded with a sidebar titled "Ambushed by Spirituality," which reported that 82% of Americans "believe in the healing power of personal prayer."[31]

The story of faith and healing was also carried prominently in the U.S. on national network television in March 1998 when Peter Jennings of the American Broadcasting Company (ABC) aired a series on faith and healing called "A Closer Look." He reported that in recent times "the relationship between faith and the physical is taken more seriously." He also reported on research that proves that "people with strong religious faith live longer than others" and that "faith is an essential ingredient for survival." In medical schools, he reported, religious faith and spirituality is now "a legitimate field of study." In fact, thirty American medical schools now teach courses on

---

31. Claudia Wallace, "Faith and Healing," *Time* 147, no. 26 (June 24, 1996): 58–62.

spirituality because "you cannot teach medicine in a spiritual vacuum." Dr. Tim Johnson, the medical reporter for ABC, who is also an ordained minister of the gospel, said of these developments, "This is a sea change in my lifetime."[32]

Looking back, a strong case could be made for giving credit to the Pentecostals for this "sea change" in public attitudes. Perhaps Oral Roberts was truly a prophet ahead of his times when he built a City of Faith where there would be a "marriage between prayer and medicine." The unexpected difference was that this marriage was celebrated not in just one hospital, but in hundreds more around the world. Now science is again admitting Jesus back into the sickroom where God can use the ministry of doctors and medicine while also answering the prayer of faith for miraculous healing.

---

32. Jennings, Wehmeyer, and McFadden, "A Closer Look," ABC News, March 1998.

4

"Back" to the West: Possibilities and Challenges for Pentecostal Histories and Theologies in the Twenty-first Century

Vinson Synan & Amos Yong

As the fourth and concluding volume of Global Renewal Christianity, this introductory chapter looks "back to the West" in two ways: in light of the preceding three volumes focused on renewal movements in the majority world, and in light of the much-discussed contemporary shift of the center of Christianity to the global South.[1] Following the overarching structure of the essays in all of the volumes that provided both historical and theological perspectives on renewal Christianity in various regions and countries of the world, we will proceed historically first and then more theologically second. In both parts of the following introductory reflection, we will ask: What are the possibilities and challenges for Pentecostal historiography and theological methodology, always in light of both senses of looking "back to the West," but also to provide the reader of this present work with orientation to the chapters to come.

One caveat before continuing: this volume, as part of the Global Renewal series, was conceived to review the status of the Spirit-empowered movements in North America and Europe in the first decade of the twentieth century and to discern theological currents and developments. As with the other volumes, the discussions are by no means exhaustive. Even though they are divided primarily by nations (within regions) and include some chapters devoted to larger-scale theological analyses, there are innumerable lacunae, even according to the organizational categories deployed. Arguably, marginal perspectives remain underdeveloped, even as we have attempted to be as attentive as possible to the growing edges of scholarship on the global movement. Precisely for this reason, then, the following at least highlights

---

1. Reprinted with permission. Originally Vinson Synan and Amos Yong, "'Back' to the West: Possibilities and Challenges for Pentecostal Histories and Theologies in the Twenty-first Century" in *Global Renewal Christianity: Spirit-Empowered Movements Past, Present, and Future: Europe and North America*, vol. 4, ed. Synan and Yong (Lake Mary, FL: Charisma House, 2016), xxi–xl.

what else needs to be done, even in light of the state-of-the-question research and assessments that are found in this volume and its companion texts.

Possibilities and Challenges for Pentecostal Histories

We utilize here in this first section the standard Pentecostal historiographical framework related to the classical, Charismatic, and "third wave" streams for two reasons.[2] First, it will orient us toward the content of this book, particularly when the chapters in part four on North America are prioritized. Second, recounting this standard historiography will provide opportunities to compare and contrast with Pentecostal historiography in a global perspective, precisely what has been accomplished in the other three volumes of this series.

Pentecostal Roots: North America and Europe

The modern classical Pentecostal movement with a clearly defined theology had its first beginnings in a small Bible school in Topeka, Kansas, led by Charles Fox Parham.[3] A former Methodist pastor turned evangelist and teacher, Parham established Bethel Bible School in Topeka in 1900. Here he taught his students that a tremendous revival would come at the turn of the century that would herald the second coming of Christ. On January 1, 1900, the first day of the new century, a student, Agnes Ozman, spoke in tongues to the astonishment of Parham and the student body. This experience led to Parham's teaching that speaking in tongues was the "Bible evidence" of the Pentecostal baptism in the Holy Spirit.[4] For four years, Parham and his students held revivals in towns and cities from Kansas to Texas, where utterances in tongues drew multitudes of curious onlookers to his meetings. After establishing another Bible school in Houston, Texas, by 1905 his movement attracted thousands of followers.

One of the students in Houston, William J. Seymour, a black minister, then took the Pentecostal message to Los Angeles in 1906, where a revival broke out in a tumbledown mission on Azusa Street. This meeting, which continued unabated for over three years, became one of the most notable and influential revivals in Christian history.[5] People came from all over the

---

2. For elaboration and complication of these streams, see Synan, *The Century of the Holy Spirit: 100 Years of Pentecostal and Charismatic Renewal* (Nashville, TN: Thomas Nelson, 2001).

3. On Parham, see James R. Goff Jr., *Fields White unto Harvest: Charles F. Parham and the Missionary Origins of Pentecostalism* (Fayetteville, AR: University of Arkansas Press, 1988).

4. See Cecil M. Robeck Jr., "William J. Seymour and 'the Bible Evidence,'" in *Initial Evidence: Historical and Biblical Perspectives on the Pentecostal Doctrine of Spirit Baptism*, ed. Gary B. McGee (Peabody, MA: Hendrickson Publishers, 1991), 72–95.

5. Cecil M. Robeck Jr., *The Azusa Street Mission and Revival: The Birth of the Global Pentecostal Movement* (Nashville, TN: Thomas Nelson, 2006).

world to attend the services that went on three times a day, seven days a week. Here it was said, "The color line was washed away in the Blood," as blacks and whites, among others, worshipped together under the leadership of the black pastor.[6]

Spurred on by articles written by Azusa Street onlooker Frank Bartleman in the Holiness press, visitors came to Azusa Street, spoke in tongues, and went out as Pentecostal pilgrims throughout America and to the far reaches of the world.[7] American pilgrims included G. B. Cashwell, Charles H. Mason, and William H. Durham. Pilgrims who took the Pentecostal message abroad included A. G. Garr (India), C. J. McIntosh (China), Mary Rumsey (Korea), Thomas Ball Barratt (Europe), Daniel Berg and Gunnar Vingren (Brazil), Willis Hoover (Chile), Ivan Voronaev (Russia), and Luigi Francescon (Italy). One argument is that the Azusa Street Mission became the mother church and prototype for Pentecostal churches throughout the world.

Under the pioneering ministries of many of these Pentecostal missionaries, Pentecostal revivals were ignited in many parts of the world. Yet it is also the case that around the beginning of the twentieth century, several Pentecostal outbreaks occurred outside of North America, in Korea, India, and other places, with the appearance of such charismatic phenomena as speaking in tongues, prophecies, healings, and exorcisms, apparently without any Western Pentecostal missionary influence. Because of these charismatic outbreaks and the worldwide growth of these movements, one could speak of the new century as "the century of the Holy Spirit."[8]

Yet there has also been another argument regarding Pentecostal origins that hence has not privileged North American revivals and suggested instead a polycentric model of the beginnings of this renewal movement.[9] From this perspective, Pentecostalism grew out of multiple revival centers, and Western missionaries hence arrived to connect these movements that, in turn, were able to exert greater influence than if they had remained isolated. The chapters in part 4 of this book attempt to adjudicate various aspects of these matters. Regardless of the final verdict, as we will note momentarily, in time Pentecostalism gained millions of converts during the twentieth century. Among the nations that saw the greatest growth were Chile, Brazil, Argentina, Korea, South Africa, and China.

---

6. See also Dale T. Irvin, "'Drawing All Together in One Bond of Love': The Ecumenical Vision of William J. Seymour and the Azusa Street Revival," *Journal of Pentecostal Theology* 6 (1995): 25–53.

7. See Allan H. Anderson, *To the Ends of the Earth: Pentecostalism and the Transformation of World Christianity* (Oxford: Oxford University Press, 2013).

8. See Synan, *An Eyewitness Remembers the Century of the Holy Spirit* (Grand Rapids, MI: Chosen Books, 2010).

9. See, for example, Walter J. Hollenweger, *The Pentecostals* (Minneapolis, MN: Augsburg Fortress, 1972).

In turning now to European Pentecostalism, the focus of the first three parts of this volume, we note the movement there took early root through the efforts of several Pentecostal pioneers.[10] Many look on Thomas Ball Barratt as the father of Pentecostalism in Northern and Western Europe. His first meetings in Christiania (now Oslo), Norway, in 1907, were followed by his efforts to spread the movement to Sweden with Lewi Pethrus, to Germany with Jonathan Paul, and to England with Alexander Boddy, an Anglican priest. Boddy made major contributions to the movement with his annual Whitsuntide conferences in Sunderland, England, and the publication of his magazine Confidence, which made Pentecostalism more acceptable in England and other European nations. In Eastern Europe, the movement began with the ministry of Ivan Voronaev in Odessa, in 1922, who planted some 350 Pentecostal churches in Russia and several other Slavic nations. He was martyred by the Communists later, after serving a long prison sentence for preaching the gospel. In Southern Europe, a dynamic movement was pioneered by Luigi Francescon, an Italian immigrant to the United States, who founded strong Pentecostal churches not only in Italy but also in Brazil and Argentina.

Europe was later the scene of pioneering Pentecostal ecumenism through the efforts of the South African David du Plessis, who organized the first Pentecostal World Conference in Zurich in 1947. He was later to be known as "Mr. Pentecost" due to his leading ecumenical role during the Charismatic movement in the mainline churches in the 1970s and 1980s.[11] In England, a pioneering Pentecostal journalist and Bible teacher, Donald Gee, spread news of the fast-growing Pentecostal movements of the world in his influential magazine, *World Pentecost.*

As three-fourths of this book demonstrates, European Pentecostals spoke in many tongues, literally. These Pentecostals also sent out missionaries to the ends of the earth.[12] Ironically, there is a sense in which these Western Pentecostal missionaries brought as much of their own culture with them as they did the gospel, to those they evangelized.[13] In fact, the did this not just in what we now call the global South, but also vis-à-vis the indigenous

---

10. The story is told vicariously; see William K. Kay and Anne E. Dyer, eds., *European Pentecostalism*, Global Pentecostal and Charismatic Studies, vol. 7 (Leiden: Brill, 2017); and Paul Schmidgall, *European Pentecostalism: Its Origins, Development, and Future* (Cleveland, TN: CPT Press, 2013).

11. See Joshua R. Ziefle, *David du Plessis and the Assemblies of God: The Struggle for the Soul of a Movement*, Global Pentecostal and Charismatic Studies, vol. 13 (Leiden: Brill, 2013).

12. See, for example, David Bundy, *Visions of Apostolic Mission: Scandinavian Pentecostal Mission to 1935*, Studia Historico-Ecclesiastica Upsaliensia, vol. 45 (Uppsala, Sweden: Uppsala University, 2009).

13. Allan H. Anderson, *Spreading Fires: The Missionary Nature of Early Pentecostalism* (London: SCM Press, 2007).

peoples of Europe and North America.[14] It has been, in part, for this reason that Pentecostalism has not taken off especially within Native American communities, although this is gradually changing, including among the Roma in the European continent.[15]

Latter Rain, Neo-Pentecostalism, and the Catholic Charismatic Renewal

In the late 1940s and early 1950s, a new wave of revival swept the Pentecostal movement from a local revival centered at Sharon Bible School in Saskatchewan, Alberta, Canada. Known as the "New Order of the Latter Rain," this movement represented a renewal of charismatic gifts such as prophecy, and the interpretation of tongues, as well as singing in the Spirit. In the end, the Pentecostal denominations largely rejected the revival because of perceived excesses that included the bestowal of specific gifts by the laying on of hands and a teaching called "manifest sons," where some claimed that they would never die.[16]

This movement also coincided with the beginnings of the healing revivals that began in 1948. In the following years, such men as Oral Roberts, William Branham, T. L. Osborn, and Tommy Hicks led large crusades that spilled over to many nations as these men and others began to conduct these same kinds of meetings overseas. These crusades led to the expansion of Pentecostal churches in many nations of the world.[17]

By the 1950s, laymen were joining in the revivalistic fervor that was engulfing the entire movement. In 1951, Demos Shakarian, a millionaire dairyman from Los Angeles, started the Full Gospel Business Men's Fellowship International (FGBMFI). Although women and preachers could attend and even speak at Shakarian's events, they could not be voting members of the organization. By the 1960s and 1970s, over four thousand chapters were operating all over the world, and at its height, about four

---

14. On the North American side, see Kirk Dombrowski, *Against Culture: Development, Politics, and Religion in Indian Alaska* (Lincoln, NE: University of Nebraska Press, 2001); and Angela Tarango, *Choosing the Jesus Way: American Indian Pentecostals and the Fight for the Indigenous Principle* (Chapel Hill, NC: University of North Carolina Press, 2014). On the European continent, see David Thurfjell, *Faith and Revivalism in a Nordic Romani Community: Pentecostalism Amongst the Kaale Roma of Sweden and Finland*, Library of Modern Religion, vol. 21 (London: I. B. Tauris, 2013); and David Thurfjell and Adrian Marsh, eds., *Romani Pentecostalism: Gypsies and Charismatic Christianity* (New York: Peter Lang, 2013).

15. Miroslav Atanasov's chapter discusses the Roma Pentecostal movement. For more on North American indigenous Pentecostalism, see Corky Alexander, *Native American Pentecost: Praxis, Contextualization, Transformation* (Cleveland, TN: CPT Press, 2012).

16. Richard Riss, *The Latter Rain Movement of 1948 and the Mid-twentieth-century Evangelical Awakening* (Peabody, MA: Hendrickson Publishers, 1987).

17. For the role of healing, see Candy Gunther Brown, ed., *Global Pentecostalism and Charismatic Healing* (Oxford: Oxford University Press, 2011).

million persons attended Full Gospel events each month. This Pentecostal laymen's revival brought people from all denominations to hotels and restaurants for salvation and healing meetings. Called by Oral Roberts, "God's Ballroom Saints," the Full Gospel Business Men's Fellowship helped fuel the international growth of Pentecostalism.[18]

Before 1960, Pentecostal revivalism in North America was confined mainly to Pentecostal churches coming out of the Azusa Street revival. Often scorned by the mainline churches with scathing attacks by fundamentalist and Holiness leaders, the movement grew rapidly and eventually entered the major American churches. The first neo-Pentecostal to make national news was Father Dennis Bennett of Van Nuys, California. An Episcopalian, he identified with the Pentecostals when he confessed to speaking in tongues in 1960. In the next few years, Pentecostalism entered most of the mainline churches. Some leaders were Gerald Derstine (Mennonite), Larry Christenson (Lutheran), Brick Bradford (Presbyterian), Howard Conatser and Pat Robertson (Baptist), and Tommy Tyson (Methodist). By 1965, these neo-Pentecostals adopted the label Charismatic and achieved at least some measure of approval of their ecclesiastical leaders and remained in their denominations.

In Europe, all the Reformation Protestant churches experienced Pentecostal renewals just as their co-religionists had experienced in the United States and Canada.[19] When we consider that from the earliest days of the twentieth century, Pentecostal leaders wrote of a threefold revival heritage that included the Lutheran Reformation, emphasizing justification by faith, and the Wesleyan evangelical revival, emphasizing entire sanctification, these developments may not be as surprising. It may have been precisely this ecumenical configuration of modern Pentecostalism that eventually not only accommodated but also perhaps precipitated Charismatic Renewal across the Christian traditions.[20]

In 1967, another wave of Pentecostal revival suddenly erupted in the Roman Catholic Church to the surprise of everyone, including the Pentecostals. Although there had always been Charismatics in the Catholic mystical tradition, no one expected that a Pentecostal spirituality would break out in the Church. In calling the Vatican II Council in Rome, which lasted from 1962–1965, Pope John XIII called on every Catholic in the world to

---

18. See Synan, *Under His Banner: The History of the Full Gospel Business Men's Fellowship International* (Costa Mesa, CA: Gift Publications, 1992); and Matthew Tallman, *Demos Shakarian: The Life, Legacy, and Vision of a Full Gospel Businessman* (Wilmore, KY: Emeth Press, 2010).

19. See Stephen Hunt, *A History of the Charismatic Movement in Britain and the United States of America: The Pentecostal Transformation of Christianity*, 2 vols. (Lewiston, NY: Edwin Mellen Press, 2009).

20. Walter J. Hollenweger, *Pentecostalism: Origins and Developments Worldwide* (Peabody, MA: Hendrickson, 1997). Part Five discusses what he calls the "ecumenical root" of Pentecostalism.

pray daily for the Lord to "renew [His] wonders in this day as by a new Pentecost." Debates in the Council recognized the presence of many "charisms" (gifts) in the Church and called for spiritual renewal that would "open the windows of the church" for fresh winds of the Spirit.[21]

Only two years after the Council ended, a Charismatic movement began in Duquesne University in Pittsburgh among theology students and professors. From Duquesne, the movement moved at first to Notre Dame University and the University of Michigan before spreading to the grassroots across America. Instead of adopting Pentecostal revival techniques, the Catholic renewal made use of prayer meetings and days of renewal in local parishes and Charismatic communities. Conferences at Notre Dame in 1972 and 1973 brought the movement to the attention of the Vatican. The movement soon spread to over one hundred nations of the world.[22]

By 1976, Pope Paul VI approved the renewal and appointed Léon-Joseph Cardinal Suenens of Belgium to serve as his liaison to the burgeoning movement.[23] Working with Suenens was the American Benedictine monk and scholar, Kilian McDonnell, whose books and articles paved the way for acceptance of the movement by the Vatican.[24] The Charismatic Renewal among Catholics grew fastest in Latin America and Asia. By the year 2015, estimates were that globally over 180 million Catholics were involved in the movement.[25]

Part of the result of the renewal movement across mainline Protestant and Roman Catholic traditions has been the Pentecostalization of world Christianity.[26] Across the majority world today, while some classical Pentecostal churches are looking and sounding less and less like Pentecostals, others are taking on that mantle. In addition, these historic churches and traditions are influencing Pentecostal theology and practice, in particular by

---

21. See Kevin and Dorothy Ranaghan, *Catholic Pentecostals* (Paramus, NJ: Paulist Press, 1969); and Edward O'Connor, *The Pentecostal Movement in the Catholic Church* (Notre Dame, IL: Ave Maria Press, 1971).

22. Susan A. Maurer, *The Spirit of Enthusiasm: A History of the Catholic Charismatic Renewal, 1967-2000* (Washington, DC: University Press of America, 2010).

23. See Léon-Joseph Cardinal Suenens, *Ecumenism and Charismatic Renewal: Theological and Pastoral Orientations* (Ann Arbor, MI: Servant Books, 1978).

24. Kilian McDonnell, *Charismatic Renewal and the Churches* (New York: Seabury Press, 1976); and Kilian McDonnell, ed., *Presence, Power, Praise*, 3 vols. (Collegevillle, MD: Liturgical Press, 1980).

25. This was especially vigorous in Latin America. See, for example, Edward L. Cleary, *The Rise of Charismatic Catholicism in Latin America* (Gainesville, FL: University of Florida Press, 2011).

26. See, for example, Cephan N. Omenyo, *Pentecost Outside Pentecostalism: A Study of the Development of Charismatic Renewal in the Mainline Church in Ghana* (Zoetermeer: Boekencentrum, 2002); and Jakob Egeris Thorsen, *Charismatic Practice and Catholic Parish Life: The Incipient Pentecostalization of the Church in Guatemala and Latin America*, Global Pentecostal and Charismatic Studies, vol. 17 (Leiden: Brill, 2015).

expanding the classical Pentecostal understanding of mission and evangelism to include attentiveness to social realities, consideration of social justice, and engagement in the social sphere.[27]

Late Twentieth- and Early Twenty-first Century Developments

As the twentieth century drew to a close, two major revivals broke out in local churches in North America that had reverberations around the world. The first one began in a Vineyard church in Toronto in 1994. The Vineyard movement had begun in California, led by John Wimber, who became famous as a teacher at Fuller Theological Seminary from 1975 to 1985. In the Airport Vineyard Church in Toronto, an extended revival broke out that drew thousands of visitors from all over the world. The pastor, John Arnott, saw his church explode in numbers as curious visitors came to the service that continued six nights a week. In addition to such Pentecostal manifestations as tongues and prophecy, many people at Toronto experienced unusual manifestations such as falling down, laughing in the Spirit, and roaring like lions. These unusual religious phenomena were soon dubbed the "Toronto Blessing." After Wimber investigated the revival, he characterized them as "exotic manifestations" and, in 1996, excommunicated the congregation from the Vineyard fellowship. After this, Arnott then formed his own denomination.[28]

Another revival began in 1995 in the city of Brownsville, Florida, near the port of Pensacola. This time, the revival broke out in a local Assemblies of God church. As in Toronto, multitudes attended the services in Brownsville. Before the revival began to ebb, over two million people had attended at least one service in the Brownsville church, and over one thousand students who were converted in the revival have trained as young ministers at its Bible college. Unlike the Toronto revival, the Assemblies of God denomination decided to oversee the meetings and keep the church and school within the denominational system. Both the Toronto and Brownsville revivals were highly publicized and caused many other revivals to begin in churches around the world.[29]

---

27. See, for instance, Donald E. Miller and Tetsunao Yamamori, *Global Pentecostalism: The New Face of Christian Social Engagement* (Berkeley, CA: University of California Press, 2007).

28. Guy Chevreau, *Catch the Fire: The Toronto Blessing—An Experience of Renewal and Revival* (Toronto: Marshall Pickering, 1994); and John Arnott, *The Father's Blessing* (Lake Mary, FL: Creation House, 1996). See also Margaret Poloma, *Main Street Mystics: The Toronto Blessing and Reviving Pentecostalism* (Walnut Creek, CA: AltaMira Press, 2003).

29. See Leo Sandon, "Pentecost in Pensacola: The Brownsville Revival," *The Christian Century* 114, no. 2 (1997): 748–49; and Steve Rabey, *Revival in Brownsville* (Nashville, TN: Thomas Nelson, 1999).

Part of the result of these revivals was the transformation of religion, particularly in North America, into what some have called a post-denominational landscape.[30] Independent, non-denominational and other congregational forms of churches are emerging, most of which are Pentecostal or Charismatic in spirituality, without seeking formal ecclesiastical affiliations. Yet, new networks are forming and developing, many connected to so-called apostolic leaders,[31] with others related to unique "brands" including music and worship elements, such as Jesus Culture and Hillsong.[32] This means that world Pentecostalism is continually being transformed, and now the "movement" is growing not only via traditional missionary efforts but also telecommunicatively, by way of mass media in a digital age.[33]

At the very end of the century, some of the largest Pentecostal revivalist crusades in history were taking place in Africa under the ministry of German Pentecostal evangelist Reinhard Bonnke. Going to Lesotho, South Africa, as a conventional missionary in 1967, Bonnke soon became dissatisfied with the meager results of his ministry. Therefore, in 1975, he rented a large stadium in Botswana, where he began one of the most noteworthy evangelistic ministries in the history of Christianity. Traveling throughout Africa with a tent seating 34,000, Bonnke saw hundreds of thousands of conversions in his crusades. By 1990, he abandoned the tent and began to preach in the open air. He soon began to draw enormous crowds, even surpassing the records set by Billy Graham.[34]

Perhaps the largest such crusade took place in Lagos, Nigeria, in the year 2000. In one service, it was reported that 1.6 million people attended, with over 1 million people converted. In addition to Bonnke, other Pentecostal evangelists such as the American Benny Hinn, regularly drew crowds of more

---

30. The beginnings of the discussion of ours as a post-denominational time go back two decades. See Creighton Lacy, "Toward a Post-Denominational World Church," in *Beyond Establishment: Protestant Identity in a Post-Protestant Age*, ed. Jackson W. Carroll and Wade Roof Clark (Louisville, KY: Westminster John Knox, 1993), 327–42.

31. See C. Peter Wagner, *Church Quake! The Explosive Power of the New Apostolic Reformation* (Ventura, CA: Regal, 1999). For a more scholarly analysis, see William K. Kay, *Apostolic Networks in Britain: New Ways of Being Church* (Eugene, OR: Wipf & Stock, 2007).

32. See, for example, Mark Evans, *Open Up the Doors: Music in the Modern Church* (London: Equinox, 2006); and Monique M. Ingalls and Amos Yong, eds., *The Spirit of Praise: Music and Worship in Global Pentecostal-Charismatic Christianity* (University Park, PA: Penn State University Press, 2015).

33. See Simon Coleman, *The Globalization of Charismatic Christianity* (Cambridge: Cambridge University Press, 2000).

34. Ron Steele, *Plundering Hell to Populate Heaven: The Reinhard Bonnke Story* (Tulsa, OK: Harrison House, 1998); and Reinhard Bonnke, *Living a Life of Fire: An Autobiography* (Orlando, FL: E-R Productions, 2009). For a scholarly analysis, see Paul Gifford, "Africa Shall Be Saved: An Appraisal of Reinhard Bonnke's Pan-African Crusade," *Journal of Religion in Africa* 17, no. 1 (1987): 63–92.

than 500,000 people in India and Africa. This helped the Pentecostals build mega-congregations around the world. One of these, the Yoido Full Gospel Church pastored by David Yonggi Cho in Seoul, South Korea, claimed over 700,000 members by 2000, making it the largest local church in Christian history.[35] Pentecostal movements thus have grown from being comprised of tiny groups of highly persecuted Christians in the beginning, to now being one of the fastest-growing renewal movements in history. At this writing, the Spirit-empowered movements, all together, are second only to the Roman Catholic Church in size and number—some 644 million people throughout the world.[36]

Those who consider themselves part of this global renewal movement no doubt are expectant of even further growth. Simultaneously, there are also signs that renewal Christianity is plateauing in various places, not least in North America and the Korean contexts. In the former, it is the immigration of Hispanics that is sustaining renewal growth, and that particularly among Roman Catholic Charismatics. Earlier forms of Pentecostal triumphalism and elitism are now being tempered.[37] Are these indicators of theological developments as we move further into the second Pentecostal century?

Possibilities and Challenges for Pentecostal Theologies

In the rest of this introduction, we focus on theological trajectories of contemporary Pentecostalism in light of the achievements in this volume particularly, but yet against the backdrop of the four-volume series as a whole. What are the theological challenges and opportunities as a whole? We will begin in Europe and move to Anglo-America, partly following the structure of this book, and conclude with overarching considerations in light of developments in Pentecostal academia as these have unfolded to the present.

Pentecostal and Post-Pentecostal Theologies: European Lenses

We included the chapter on Pentecostalism in the Middle East here in this book, although not without reservations, since such developments could easily have been accorded space within the volume on Asia and Oceania, even as the chapter on Pentecostal-Charismatic Christianity in Egypt, in the Africa book, also touches on important issues in this context. The challenge is that

---

35. Sung-Hoon Myung and Young-Gi Hong, eds., *Charis and Charisma: David Yongghi Cho and the Growth of Yoido Full Gospel Church* (Oxford: Regnum, 2011).

36. Todd Johnson et al., "Christianity 2015: Religious Diversity and Personal Contact," *International Bulletin of Missionary Research* 39, no. 1 (2015): 29.

37. See David J. Courey, *What Has Wittenberg to do with Azusa? Luther's Theology of the Cross and Pentecostal Triumphalism* (London/New York: Bloomsbury Academic, 2015).

there is insufficient research and scholarly documentation of renewal trends in these countries, even though there is significant Pentecostal presence and activity across the region. There is no doubt that the status of Israel in Pentecostal eschatology occludes many of the important theological issues that need to be discussed.[38] Pentecostal scholars like Calvin Smith are beginning to address these complex matters,[39] but there is much more work that needs to be done. It is not just a matter of comprehending better the challenges related to working for peace in the Middle East, although that ought to remain a priority on any agenda related to Pentecostal theology in the next generation.[40] The difficulties attend to theological questions of ecclesiology, specifically how to understand the church in relationship to Israel,[41] and of biblical hermeneutics and interpretation, especially how to read the Hebrew Bible (for Pentecostals, the "Old Testament") in the twenty-first century.[42]

The chapters in this book on Pentecostalism in Eastern Europe obviously press for consideration of what a post-Communist Pentecostal and Charismatic theological project might look like. Before 1989, of course, as many of these chapters unfold, Pentecostal theological thinking in the context of persecution and martyrdom focused, understandably, on themes of suffering for the witness of the gospel. Further, questions focused on survival in a socialist context. In an increasingly global but not definitively post-socialist environment, however, dispensationalist eschatologies identifying the Antichrist in relationship to Communist figures and realities are no longer plausible. Most immediately, Pentecostals are rejoicing at their newly-experienced religious freedom, particularly for the purposes of witness and evangelism. But how else might Pentecostal theological thinking develop in this context?

A large part of the unexplored set of questions here pertains to how to consider the relationship between Eastern Orthodoxy and the global Pentecostal movement. Much of Eastern Europe remains Orthodox in overall religious character. Historically, Orthodox communions have felt

---

38. See the discussion on Israel and Pentecostal eschatology in chapter 8 of Amos Yong, *In the Days of Caesar: Pentecostalism and Political Theology* (Grand Rapids, MI: Eerdmans, 2010).

39. Calvin L. Smith, ed., *The Jews, Modern Israel, and the New Supersessionism*, rev. ed. (London: Kings Divinity Press, 2013).

40. Leading the way courageously is this regard, even if controversially, is Paul N. Alexander, ed., *Christ at the Checkpoint: Theology in the Service of Justice and Peace*, Pentecostals, Peacemaking, and Social Justice Series (Eugene, OR: Wipf & Stock, 2012).

41. This question is confronted directly in chapter 7 of Amos Yong, *Renewing Christian Theology: Systematics for a Global Christianity* (Waco, TX: Baylor University Pres, 2014).

42. Help is on the way. See, for example, Rickie D. Moore, *The Spirit of the Old Testament*, *JPTSup* 35 (Dorset: Deo Publishing, 2011); also Jacqueline Grey, *Three's A Crowd: Pentecostalism, Hermeneutics, and the Old Testament* (Eugene, OR: Wipf & Stock, 2011).

threatened by Pentecostal proselytism in these regions.[43] Thus, building theological bridges between both traditions is a priority.[44] Pentecostals have to begin to understand the depth of Orthodox theological tradition, and Orthodox Christians also ought to query if the "new kids on the block" might have something important to retrieve from the biblical and patristic traditions for contemporary Christian life. Beyond becoming reacquainted with each other, there is potential for theological synthesis to occur, particularly in calling on the strong pneumatological and Trinitarian emphases in both traditions and their spiritualities. How, for instance, might a Pentecostal-Orthodox convergence inform Christian thought and practice in a post-Communist global context that is struggling to understand the contemporary neo-liberal economy in biblical and sustainable terms?[45] Might Pentecostal and Orthodox resources combine to present a substantive theological imagination that can engage and perhaps intervene in these matters? We invite readers to interact with the chapters in part one of this volume with questions such as these in mind.

In turning now to the northern and western European contexts, we are led to ask about the shape of what might be considered post-Pentecostal forms of theology. Three lines of inquiry regarding Pentecostal theology as post-Western, post-colonial, and post-Enlightenment suggest themselves when reading the middle two parts of this book. As will become clear, the *post*-designation in these three directions are indicative that Pentecostal theology might itself undergo drastic reformation. Will it even be recognizable as such?

We can take up this matter first by considering Pentecostalism in Europe (not to mention North America) as being transformed in the twenty-first century primarily by migration.[46] Yet, clearly these Pentecostal migrants, especially those from Africa, are not content to merely assimilate into European culture; rather, they desire to re-evangelize an obviously

---

43. The theological issues are discussed in Veli-Matti Kärkkäinen, "Proselytism and Church Relations: Theological Issues Facing Older and Younger Churches," *The Ecumenical Review* 52, no. 3 (2000): 379–90.

44. A strong initiative for this conversation is Edmund J. Rybarczyk, *Beyond Salvation: Eastern Orthodoxy and Classical Pentecostalism on Becoming Like Christ* (Milton Keynes, UK: Paternoster Press, 2006).

45. This is the project, for instance, of Daniela C. Augustine, *Pentecost, Hospitality, and Transfiguration: Toward a Spirit-Inspired View of Social Transformation* (Cleveland, TN: CPT Press 2012).

46. One set of case studies in Mechteld Jansen and Hijme Stoffels, eds., *A Moving God: Immigrant Churches in the Netherlands*, International Practical Theology, vol. 8 (Berlin: LIT Verlag, 2008); see also Michael Wilkinson, ed., *Global Pentecostal Movements: Migration, Mission, and Public Religion*, International Studies in Religion and Society, vol. 14 (Leiden: Brill, 2012).

secularized European continent.[47] There are certainly many missiological issues for consideration in this context. How are the increasingly intensifying Pentecostal evangelistic and mission practices on the European front going to impact and transform the continent? How will such mission energies interact with similar trends among Muslim immigrants across Europe?[48] But from the missiological to the theological: how ought Pentecostal scholars and theologians think about the racial and ethnic diversification of Europe in light of these developments?[49] What will Europe look like going forward? Will a post-Western Europe look like the Europe of old? These are big questions, but Pentecostal academics ought to be engaged in these matters from their own theological perspective.

The dynamics of such "reverse mission" from "the rest" back to the European West suggest that the next generation of Pentecostal theology will need to be attentive also to trends in post-colonial studies. Post-colonial perspectives are registering themselves increasingly across the theological landscape, insisting that subaltern and other indigenous and local voices be heard in Christian scholarship. Pentecostal studies is primed for such post-colonial interface, not only given the predominance of renewal vitality in the majority world, but also given the role played by women and youth in these contexts. The challenge, however, is for Pentecostal scholars to engage the current center of gravity for Pentecostal theological work, which lies in the Western academy, even while honing in creatively on global South sensibilities and commitments. Pentecostal scholars are beginning to pursue such postcolonial vantage points not only in reconsidering classical Pentecostal topics but also in articulating Pentecostal missiological approaches chastened of postcolonial presumptions.[50] Such research and rethinking is relevant not just for Western Europe and Anglo-American Pentecostal scholarship but also when applied to the post-1989 situation on the Eastern European front.[51]

The postcolonial horizon, however, is also interwoven with what can be identified as a post-Enlightenment theological methodology. If the Western and European Enlightenment bequeathed to modernity a discursive

---

47. See, for example, Claudia Währisch-Oblau, *The Missionary Self-Perception of Pentecostal/Charismatic Church, Leaders from the Global South in Europe: Bringing Back the Gospel*, Global Pentecostal and Charismatic Studies, vol. 2 (Leiden: Brill, 2012).

48. Philip Jenkins, *God's Continent: Christianity, Islam, and Europe's Religious Crisis* (Oxford: Oxford University Press, 2007).

49. See the special issue titled "Race and Global Renewal: Mulattic Tongues and Hybridic Imagination to the Ends of the Earth," *Pneuma* 36, no. 3 (2014).

50. See, for example, Samuel Cruz, "A Post-Colonial Re-Reading of Puerto Rican Pentecostalism in the Diaspora," *Apuntes* 25, no. 4 (2015): 245–57.

51. See, for example, J. D. Y. Peel, "Postsocialism, Postcolonialism, Pentecostalism," in *Conversion After Socialism: Disruptions, Modernisms, and Technologies of Faith in the Former Soviet Union*," ed. Mathijs Pelkmans (New York/Oxford: Berghahn Books, 2009), 183–99.

rationality that has fed the advance of modern science and technology, if not also spawned the scientism that insists on a reductionistic materialist and naturalist worldview, then the emergence of the postcolonial has brought with it the formulation of an alternative epistemological stance—one that does not minimize rational discursivity but that understands cognition not merely in intellectualist terms.[52] Pentecostals within their primarily oral cultural milieu and predominantly embodied and affective orientation to the world have never been tempted by the Enlightenment's definition of universal reason.[53] While not denigrating linear thinking, Pentecostals are comfortable with dreams and visions, with the divine manifesting in and through embodied expressions such as tongues, healings, active worship, and dance.[54] Pentecostal "reverse mission" initiatives in the global context of the twenty-first century will require the movement's theologians to be diligently at work on these epistemological and methodological fronts in ways that bring Enlightenment rationality into dialogue with indigenous perspectives from around the world.

The West to the Rest? American Resilience and Initiatives

Much that has been said so far about Pentecostal theology in European perspective applies also when considered within the North American frame of reference.[55] However, three additional post-perspectives loom large west of the Atlantic. In the following, we consider post-Christendom, post-secular, and postmodern forms of the emerging Pentecostal theological conversation.

---

52. For the beginnings of a Pentecostal epistemology, see chapter 3 in James K. A. Smith, *Thinking in Tongues: Pentecostal Contributions to Christian Philosophy* (Grand Rapids, MI: Eerdmans, 2010).

53. See Dale M. Coulter and Amos Yong, eds., *The Spirit, the Affections, and the Christian Tradition* (Notre Dame, IL: University of Notre Dame Press, 2016).

54. As delineated by Harvey G. Cox, *Fire from Heaven: The Rise of Pentecostal Spirituality and the Reshaping of Religion in the Twenty-first Century* (Reading, MA: Addison-Wesley, 1995).

55. We use "American" in the rest of this chapter with some misgivings since, historically, this term has by and large excluded First Nations and Native American populations. Amos Yong has worked hard to register indigenous American perspectives on the Pentecostal theological register; see Amos Yong, "Conclusion: The Missiology of Jamestown: 1607–2007 and Beyond—Toward a Postcolonial Theology of Mission in North America," in *Remembering Jamestown: Hard Questions About Christian Mission*, ed. Amos Yong and Barbara Brown Zikmund (Eugene, OR: Pickwick, 2010), 157–67. The following ought to be read with this in mind. See also Angela Tarango, "Jonathan Edwards, Early Pentecostals, and the Missionary Encounter with Native Americans," in *From Northampton to Azusa: Pentecostals and the Theology of Jonathan Edwards*, ed. Steven M. Studebaker and Amos Yong (Bloomington, IN: Indiana University Press, forthcoming). Editor's note: The source for Tarango's article that was forthcoming is now ch. 12 in *Pentecostals and the Theology of Jonathan Edwards*, ed. Steven M. Studebaker and Amos Yong (London/New York: T&T Clark, 2021), 197–209.

First, the peculiar separation of church and state in the history of the United States has shaped Pentecostal political theology no ess than it has Christian thinking about the political world in the last two centuries. Simultaneously, if not also ironically, many North American Pentecostals, much less Christian thinkers, have assumed that the state, so understood, is working out of a divinely intended framework and that such constitutional separation is uniquely Christian in its inspiration.

While the merits of such a political theological point of view can be argued, how this translates into political practice has been increasingly muddled since 1965, when immigration was opened, globalization ensued, and transnational relations complexified. In the current context, freedom of religion relates not only to Christianity but to the diversity and plurality of religious traditions now found not only across the Anglo-American world but also on the "old" continent. The point is that although "Christendom" was officially left behind with the founding of the American republic, in practice the "Christian" character of its form of government was thoroughly interwoven with the American way of life. In the present ferment, then, Pentecostal theology will need to be internationally post-Christian in approach, not only to disentangle itself from an uncritical Americanism,[56] but also to move forward with the recognition that nay theological program founded on the many tongues of the Day of Pentecost narrative will need to include, not ignore or overlook, the many voices and perspectives in a pluralistic world.[57]

Second, then, the emergence of many religious perspectives in the public even in the West, not to mention the United States, means that we no longer live in a merely secularized world. Rather, what is emerging is a post-secular public space, one in which secular values and perspectives are not absent but instead mixed in, however convolutedly, with religious sensitivities and commitments. Pentecostal scholars will need to factor into their analyses such post-secular realities and vantage points.[58]

From a more robustly theological angle, however, the questions are deeply challenging: how to live faithfully in a post-secular time when wherein there are a multiplicity of religious options in the public square that are yet all serving under the one deity of mammon? Put another way, in a post-1989

---

56. Detailed by Paul Alexander, *Peace to War: Shifting Allegiances in the Assemblies of God* (Telford, PA: Cascadia Press, 2009).

57. See Amos Yong, "The Church and Mission Theology in a Post-Constantinian Era: Soundings from the Anglo-American Frontier," in *A New Day: Essays on World Christianity in Honor of Lamin Sanneh*, ed. Akintunde E. Akinade (New York: Peter Lang, 2010), 49–61. Also see Steven M. Studebaker, *Citizens of the Cities: A Pentecostal Political Theology for American Renewal* (New York: Palgrave Macmillan, 2016).

58. Leading the way here is Nigerian Pentecostal social ethicist and theologian Nimi Wariboko; see Nimi Wariboko, *The Charismatic City and the Public Resurgence of Religion: A Pentecostal Social Ethics of Cosmopolitan Urban Life* (New York: Palgrave Macmillan, 2014).

world, nation-states are less important in a post-secular domain governed by the neo-liberal market economy. In this global economic context, Pentecostal theologians need to be speaking about what it means to be *homo economicus*—fundamentally economic creatures—governed by the so-called invisible hand of the market.[59] If Pentecostal theologians continue to fight among themselves and with others about religious pluralism, they will lose the war to the late modern capitalist regime. The point is that contemporary Pentecostal thinking about the public square in post-secular terms will need to proceed in an interdisciplinary mode, in conversation with political theologians, globalization theorists, and economists of religion, no less than with theologians of the religions.[60]

Post-Christendom and post-secular approaches work alongside post-modern sensibilities and efforts. Pentecostals are already beginning to engage this perspective,[61] as complex as is the discussion because the notion of *postmodern* is subject to so many different understandings. While each strand of the multifaceted postmodern conversation needs to be engaged, our interests are driven primarily by the concern that the West's encountering "the rest" and the arrival of "the rest" here in the West require that Pentecostal theologians come to grips with modern science and its challenges.

The issue here is not that Pentecostals should buy into the so-called mainstream science or the "consensus" around evolution[62] but that these matters need to be engaged. Part of the challenge is that the "enchanted" cosmologies of the majority world—which include a populated "middle level" between God and humanity filled with innumerable spirit beings and other nondivine and nonhuman creatures—blames evil spirits for poverty rather than taking on political corruption, engaging in sociopolitical and economic development initiatives, or integrating modern medicine into a more holistic frame.[63]

---

59. Nimi Wariboko is also at the forefront of thinking about these matters from a Pentecostal perspective. See Nimi Wariboko, *Economics in Spirit and in Truth: A Moral Philosophy of Finance* (New York: Palgrave Macmillan, 2014).

60. An exploratory foray into this nexus is found in Katherine Attanasi and Amos Yong, eds., *Pentecostalism and Prosperity: The Socioeconomics of the Global Charismatic Movement*, Christianities of the World, vol. 1 (New York: Palgrave Macmillan, 2012).

61. See, for example, Bradley Truman Noel, *Pentecostal and Postmodern Hermeneutics: Comparisons and Contemporary Impact* (Eugene, OR: Wipf & Stock, 2010).

62. About which topic, in any case, rapprochement may yet be possible; see Amos Yong, *The Spirit of Creation: Modern Science and Divine Action in the Pentecostal-Charismatic Movement* (Grand Rapids, MI: Eerdmans, 2011), chapters 4–5.

63. See Samuel Zalanga and Amos Yong, "What Empire? Which Multitude? Pentecostalism and Social Liberation in North America and Sub-Saharan Africa," in *Evangelicals and Empire: Christian Alternatives to the Political Status Quo*, ed. Bruce Elliss Benson and Peter Goodwin Heltzel (Grand Rapids, MI: Brazos Press, 2008), 237–51; cf. David

The point here is that the postmodern spirituality is open again to the many spirits, but we need more discipline theological reflection about his pluralistic cosmology even as this can be facilitated by a more vigorous consideration of theology in relationship to modern science.[64] Pentecostal theology needs to get beyond the natural-supernatural binary, itself bequeathed by Enlightenment thinking, in order to reconsider how the spiritual is interrelated with, not disparate from, human materiality, community, and history. Such an allegedly postmodern insight, one could argue, is closer to the spirituality of the biblical authors than is the modern dichotomy between the material and spiritual worlds.[65]

The point here is that Western and North American Pentecostals can no longer do their theological work apart from their colleagues in the southern hemisphere. Such collaboration involves mutual and reciprocal learning and interrogation. We cannot assume that any group holds a privileged perspective in this contemporary period. So if the first generation of Pentecostal and Charismatic believers founded Bible schools, colleges, and university to deepen the historical and theological understandings of the movements, the most recent generation has seen the formation of theological and academic societies that are globally interrelated. Since the founding of the Society of Pentecostal Studies in 1970, a veritable number of scholarly groups have appeared, many with their own conferences, journals, and book series, thus perpetuating the global Pentecostal theological conversation. The following highlights the West meeting "the rest" and vice-versa:

- The European Pentecostal Theological Association and its *Journal of the European Pentecostal Theological Association*
- The Pentecostal-Charismatic Theological Inquiry International and its *Cyberjournal for Pentecostal-Charismatic Research*
- The Asian Pentecostal Society and its *Asian Journal of Pentecostal Studies*
- The Canadian Pentecostal Research Network and its *Canadian Journal of Pentecostal-Charismatic Christianity*

Tonghou Ngong, *The Holy Spirit and Salvation in African Christian Theology: Imagining a More Hopeful Future for Africa* (New York: Peter Lang, 2010).

64. As developed primarily in Veli-Matti Kärkkäinen, Amos Yong, and Kirsteen Kim, eds., *Interdisciplinary and Religio-Cultural Discourses on a Spirit-Filled World: Loosing the Spirits* (New York: Palgrave Macmillan, 2013).

65. This unhelpful bifurcation is addressed in Amos Yong, *The Spirit Poured Out on All Flesh: Pentecostalism and the Possibility of Global Theology* (Grand Rapids, MI: Baker Academic, 2005), chapter 7; see also Amos Yong, ed., *The Spirit Renews the Face of the Earth: Pentecostal Forays in Science and Theology of Creation* (Eugene, OR: Pickwick Publications, 2009); and James K. A. Smith and Amos Yong, eds., *Science and the Spirit: A Pentecostal Engagement with the Sciences* (Bloomington, IN: Indiana University Press, 2010).

- The European Research Network on Global Pentecostalism (GloPent), which developed an informal relationship with *PentecoStudies: An Interdisciplinary Journal for Research on the Pentecostal and Charismatic Movements*

In addition to the above, there are regional centers for Pentecostal studies that have emerged, including the Centre for Pentecostal Theology at the Pentecostal Theological Seminary in Cleveland, Tennessee, that initiated the *Journal of Pentecostal Theology* in the early 1990s, with its Journal of Pentecostal Theology Supplement book series; the Centre for Pentecostal and Charismatic Studies at the University of Birmingham, United Kingdom, that initiated and remains connected with, among other initiatives, the Global Pentecostal and Charismatic Studies book series published by Brill; and the Center for Renewal Studies at Regent University in Virginia Beach, Virginia, with its *Renewal Dynamics* blog and, as an offshoot (since both editors began at, but are no longer affiliated with, the institution), the CHARIS: Christianity and Renewal—Interdisciplinary Studies book series published by Palgrave Macmillan. Alongside these are two other book series: the Asbury Theological Seminary Series in World Christian Revitalization Movements—Pentecostal and Charismatic Studies section, published by Emeth Press, and the Pentecostal Manifestos series published by William B. Eerdmans (which is winding down at the time of this writing). Each of these represent global Pentecostal theological discussions, reflecting where Western and non-Western perspectives meet and cross-fertilize.

Overarching Theological Matters: Going Away, or Which Way?

We conclude our introduction with comments on three important theological topics: eschatology, pneumatology, and theology proper, or the doctrine of God. Each arena is fraught with opportunities and challenges. Global conversations, both within Pentecostal scholarly communities and engaging with ecumenical voices outside the movement will be requisite for advancing the discussion into the middle of the present century.

First, as many of the following essays highlight, there is the issue of Pentecostal eschatology. How is the Pentecostal theological community going to grapple with the dispensationalist emphasis prominent at the popular and lay levels on the rapture of the church as motivating Christian and Pentecostal mission over the last century[66] but which is less plausible in the present time? This question is, of course, not unique to Pentecostalism, since the delay of the Parousia is one that Christians across the ecumenical spectrum have had to engage for the last two thousand years. Promising

---

66. See William Faupel, *The Everlasting Gospel: The Significance of Eschatology in the Development of Pentecostal Thought*, JPTSup 10 (Sheffield: Sheffield Academic Press, 1996).

trajectories are those charted by Pentecostal theologians who are not captive to the dispensational framework,[67] an incongruous alliance considering that dispensationalist schemes have often denied the ongoing validity of the charismata. The way forward is reconceiving biblical eschatology in terms of the Spirit being poured out on all flesh "in the last days" (Acts 2:17) without embracing a dispensational escapism. How Pentecostal theologians, not to mention churches, grapple with this important matter will be central for Pentecostal mission and its capacity to engage with important global issues in the twenty-first century.

Second, then, and clearly, Pentecostal pneumatology will need to be reconfigured. Up until now, much effort has been expended to shore up the Pentecostal doctrine of glossolalia as initial physical evidence of the Spirit baptism, as well as to argue for the ongoing relevance of the charismatic gifts, especially healings and exorcisms being among the more "spectacular." Yet the future for Pentecostal pneumatology, not to mention Pentecostal theology, spirituality, and practice, may lie less in these emphases than in the capacity to integrate its pneumatological commitment to Christocentric and Trinitarian theological vision.[68] The goal here is not focusing on the Spirit and the gifts for their own sake but revitalizing Christian thinking across the theological spectrum and empowering Christian living "in the Spirit." The latter means that the Spirit-filled life involves, not extinguishes, the life of the mind,[69] so that a robustly Pentecostal theology for the twenty-first century will be one that is pneumatologically Christocentric and Trinitarian in every respect.

Last but not least, a fully Trinitarian Pentecostal theology for the next century, if not the third millennium, will need to include, not dismiss, the Oneness Pentecostal point of view. As David A. Reed's chapter in this volume shows—not to mention other discussions of the Oneness perspective in the other books in this series—the unity of the Godhead is non-negotiable for a biblical monotheism in any age. The question is how to be informed by such Oneness commitments while also yet bringing this witness into the ecumenical conversation. There are deep ecumenical issues to be adjudicated on this front, but these are as missiologically and

---

67. See, for example, Peter Althouse, *Spirit of the Last Days: Pentecostal Eschatology in Conversation with Jürgen Moltmann*, *JPTSup* 25 (New York: Bloomsbury Academic, 2003); and Matthew K. Thompson, *Kingdom Come: Revisioning Pentecostal Theology*, *JPTSup* 37 (Blanford Forum: Deo Publishing, 2010).

68. See, for instance, Amos Yong, *Spirit of Love: A Trinitarian Theology of Grace* (Waco, TX: Baylor University Press, 2012); see also Veli-Matti Kärkkäinen, *Toward a Pneumatological Theology: Pentecostal and Ecumenical Perspectives on Ecclesiology, Soteriology, and Theology of Mission*, ed. Amos Yong (New York: University Press of America, 2002).

69. Amos Yong argues this in his "The Spirit, Vocation, and the Life of the Mind: A Pentecostal Testimony," in *Pentecostals in the Academy: Testimonies of Call*, ed. Steven M. Fettke and Robby Waddell (Cleveland, TN: CPT Press, 2012), 203–20.

ecclesiologically relevant as they are of theological import.[70] In many respects, how Pentecostal theologians, Oneness and Trinitarian alike—engage with one another on this matter will be indicative of how far Pentecostal theology will make its mark in the wider ecumenical arena moving forward. Any incapacity to listen to and learn from each other in this intra-Pentecostal area will inhibit contribution to the wider discussion.

As the preceding hints at, and as the next few hundred pages unfold, there is much to be optimistic about, even as there are undeniable challenges ahead. Pentecostal theology will need to mature while not losing its distinctive voice. Can this happen? The possibilities are charted in this and its companion books. Welcome to the conversation of and amidst global renewal Christianity.

---

70. For instance, Talmadge L. French delineates the ecumenical relevance of the Oneness question in his *Early Interracial Oneness Pentecostalism: G. T. Haywood and the Pentecostal Assemblies of the World (1901-1931)* (Eugene, OR: Pickwick, 2014).

5

PENTECOSTAL AND CHARISMATIC UNITY

Vinson Synan & William M. Wilson

As the many Pentecostal and Charismatic movements exploded around the world, there was little attention given to unity. Pastors, evangelists, and a myriad of witnesses were too busy planting churches and sending out missionaries to worry about unity.[1] They were just too busy. But, as time went on, it became clear that their disunity was a scandal to the mainline churches. Much criticism was levelled against these empowered movements that were seen as fragmented and lacking a common witness. Denominational rivalry between churches meant that some places had a surplus of Pentecostal churches while other places were left untouched. Also, leaders had little idea about the tremendous growth of the movement beyond their own flocks.

In North America, theological differences soon appeared and divided the movement into three major divisions: the Wesleyan Pentecostals, which included the Church of God in Christ, the Pentecostal Holiness Church, and the Church of God (Cleveland, TN); the "Finished Work" Pentecostals, which included the Assemblies of God, the International Church of the Foursquare Gospel, and the Pentecostal Church of God; and the "Oneness" Pentecostals, which included the Pentecostal Assemblies of the World and the United Pentecostal Church. For decades, these groups hardly spoke to each other. Similar divisions took place in many other areas of the global movement.[2]

Unity After World War II

It was only after World War II that the first attempts were made to bring these brethren together after decades of separation. The first of these was the World Pentecostal Conference, which convened in Zurich, Switzerland in 1947. The visionary organizer of this event was David du Plessis from South

---

1. Reprinted with permission. Originally Vinson Synan and Billy Wilson, *As the Waters Cover the Sea: Empowered 21 and the Movement it Serves* (Tulsa, OK: ORU Press, 2021), 45–52.

2. Synan, *The Holiness-Pentecostal Tradition* (Grand Rapids, MI: Eerdmans, 1997), 149–64.

Africa. This group has met once every three years in different cities of the world since that time. Thousands of Pentecostals gathered in these conferences from many parts of the world to celebrate their unity. When the Europeans met together in Zurich, many questions arose about unity among the Pentecostal churches in North America, which remained severely divided. Du Plessis encouraged the Americans to come together as the Europeans had done.[3]

The very next year after Zurich, 1948, North American Pentecostals met together for the first time in Des Moines, Iowa as the Pentecostal Fellowship of North America (PFNA). This came soon after major American Pentecostal denominations joined the newly formed National Association of Evenagelicals. Since Black Pentecostals and Oneness Pentecostals were not included, this was an all-white Trinitarian fellowship. This group met annually until 1994.[4]

One of the first forces that brought cooperation between the Pentecostal churches in America was the healing crusade movement that flourished after 1948. Many pastors who had never met each other gathered together to invite and support such evangelists as William Branham, Oral Roberts, T.L. Osborn, and Jack Coe. They were delighted to meet each other at last. Soon, many local pastor associations held regular meetings where Pentecostal pastors enjoyed fellowship and discussions of common problems. The same situation existed in Europe where many national groups knew nothing of each other.

Charismatic Unity

In the meantime, Pentecostalism suddenly appeared unexpectedly in the mainline Protestant denominations. This began in 1960 when Dennis Bennett, an Episcopal priest from Van Nuys, California, spoke in tongues. This event made national headlines, which eventually caused the movement to grow strongly in all the other Protestant denominations. At first these Spirit-filled Protestants were called "neo-Pentecostals." Other leaders of this phase of Pentecostalism included: Brick Bradford (Presbyterian), Larry Christenson (Lutheran), Ross Whetstone (Methodist), Vernon Stoop (United Church of Christ), Nelson Litwiller (Mennonite), and Pat Robertson (Baptist). Through the foreign missions programs of these churches, Pentecostalism spread around the world in these mainline churches in Africa,

---

3. Burgess and van der Maas, *NIDPCM*, 589–93.

4. David du Plessis, *The Spirit Bade Me Go: The Astounding Move of God in the Denominational Churches*, (Gainesville, FL: Bridge-Logos, 1970). David du Plessis (as told to Bob Slosser), *A Man Called Mr. Pentecost* (Plainfield, NJ: Logos International, 1997).

Asia, Latin America, and Europe. Up to this point, the movement was entirely a Protestant phenomenon.[5]

All of this changed drastically in 1967 with the unexpected appearance of Pentecostalism in the Roman Catholic Church. This happened during a weekend retreat of graduate students from Duquesne University in Pittsburgh. Professors from Duquesne heard about the Pentecostal movement and felt that it could be a blessing to the Roman Catholic Church. After studying *The Cross and the Switchblade* and the first four chapters of the Acts of the Apostles, the students were ready to receive the baptism in the Holy Spirit. Several of them gathered in the upstairs chapel and soon were praising God in other tongues and with prophecies. News spread rapidly to Notre Dame University and the University of Michigan. Soon hundreds and then thousands of Catholics were rushing to prayer meetings to receive the Pentecostal experience. Early leaders of the movement included Patti Gallagher, Kevin Ranaghan, and Francis MacNutt, who saw the movement mushroom into the thousands and then millions around the Catholic world.[6] At first the Spirit-filled Catholics called themselves "Pentecostal Catholics," but in a short time they adopted the name "Catholic Charismatics." The word "Charismatic" was also later adopted by most of the Protestant renewal movements.

The Charismatic movement also entered the Orthodox Church in North America in 1971. Among the leaders of the Orthodox Charismatics were Athanasius Emmert, Eusebius Stephanou, and Boris Zabrodsky. According to Timothy Cremeens, himself a convert to Orthodoxy from the Assemblies of God, the movement was "marginalized" when no Orthodox bishops approved of the movement. Unlike the Roman Catholics, the Orthodox renewal touched only a few thousand persons in the Church.[7]

The Charismatic Concerns Committee at Glencoe

By the beginning of the 1970s, there were three major groupings of Pentecostals and Charismatics: classical Pentecostals, Protestant Charismatics, and Catholic Charismatics. The first attempt to bring these groups together was the Glencoe gathering that met near St. Louis in the 1970s and 1980s. First called together by Dennis Bennett and David du Plessis in 1971 in Seattle to settle problems among Charismatic leaders, the

---

5. Synan, *Century of the Holy Spirit* (Nashville: Thomas Nelson, 2001), 149–208. Also see Synan, *The Twentieth Century Pentecostal Explosion* (Lake Mary, FL: Creation House, 1987).

6. Patti Gallagher Mansfield, *As by New Pentecost: The Dramatic Beginning of the Catholic Charismatic Renewal* (Nottingham: New Life Publishing, 2016). Also see Edward O'Connor, *The Pentecostal Movement in the Catholic Church* (Notre Dame: Ave Maria Press, 1971).

7. Timothy B. Cremeens, *Marginalized Voices: A History of the Charismatic Renewal in the Orthodox Church in North America, 1972-1993* (Eugene, OR: Pickwick Publication, 2018).

group faced the growing problems caused by the shepherding teachings of the "Fort Lauderdale Four," which included Bob Mumford, Derek Prince, Charles Simpson, and Don Basham. In addition to du Plessis and Bennett, some of the early attendees were Larry Christenson, Jamie Buckingham, Kevin Ranaghan, and Francis MacNutt. In 1975, the conflict exploded in the "shootout in the Curtis Hotel" in Seattle. Here, Bennett and Pat Robertson strongly objected to the shepherding teachings. Also strongly opposing the shepherding group was Demos Shakarian, head of the Full Gospel Business Men's Fellowship International (FGBMFI). Both Robertson and Shakarian refused to allow the shepherding leaders to speak on their programs.

In 1976, these leaders met in Oklahoma City to struggle with the "shepherding movement," which was now dividing the whole movement in the United States. This was called the Charismatic Leaders Conference. Little was accomplished in this meeting. From 1973 to 2001, the group met annually in the Marianist Retreat Center in Glencoe, Missouri, at the invitation of Francis MacNutt. Led by Kevin Ranaghan and Larry Christenson, in 1976 the group changed its name to the "Charismatic Concerns Committee," with the goal of attempting to settle controversies that sprang up within the movement over the years. Two of these involved questions about water baptism and the place of women in ministry. However, the shepherding movement continued to be the most absorbing controversy to face the group. About forty leaders of all segments of the renewal met annually in the Glencoe Marianist Retreat to give some guidance to the various movements represented. Attendance was by invitation only to leaders with "trans local" ministries. No records were kept, so members could speak freely. Speakers who addressed the group included John Wimber, David Barrett, C. Peter Wagner, Benny Hinn, and others.[8]

By the mid-1970s, the group decided to conduct a major Charismatic conference in Kansas City to impact the nation and the world with the message of the renewal.[9] The Kansas City General Conference on Charismatic Renewal met in Arrowhead Stadium in the summer of 1977. Some 45,000 persons registered for the gathering to make a "common witness" to the world that "Jesus is Lord." Speakers included Léon-Joseph Cardinal Suenens (Catholic Primate of Belgium), Kevin Ranaghan, Bob Mumford, and Jim Forbes. In some ways, this conference marked the highwater mark of the Charismatic Renewal in the United States and brought the movement to the attention of the nation.[10]

---

8. Bob Garrett, *The Charismatic Leaders Fellowship* (Augusta, GA: n.p., 2019).

9. For the shepherding controversy that concerned the Glencoe meetings, see David Moore, *The Shepherding Movement: Controversy and Charismatic Ecclesiology* (New York: T&T Clark, 2024).

10. The story of the conference is told in David Manual, *Like a Mighty River: A Personal Account of the Charismatic Conference of 1977* (Orleans: Rock Harbor Press, 1997).

North American Renewal Service Committee (1985–2000)

For almost a decade, the Glencoe leaders showed little interest in conducting another expensive and exhausting conference like the one in Kansas City. But in time, a vision formed for another similar conference to take place in 1987. This time, the Glencoe leader was Vinson Synan, who led the group from 1984-2001. Synan worked closely with Kevin Ranaghan in planning the conference. It was decided to form a new corporation that would own and conduct the conference. It was named the "North American Renewal Service Committee" (NARSC). The chosen city was New Orleans. It was also decided to conduct a leaders' conference in 1986 in the Superdome, followed by a general conference in 1987. After months of planning, the Leaders Conference convened with about 7,500 leaders from all sectors of the renewal in attendance. Among the speakers were Oral Roberts and Paul Yonggi Cho.[11]

In the very hot summer of 1987, the General Conference on Charismatic Renewal and World Evangelization convened in the Superdome. Upwards of 40,000 people attended this gathering, where all the workshops and plenary sessions emphasized world evangelization. Major speakers included Vinson Synan, Reinhard Bonnke, and Fr. Tom Forrest, with special videos from Billy Graham and Pope John Paul II. A unique feature of the congress was a Charismatic parade down Bourbon Street, complete with twenty-five blocks of floats, bands, and clowns. It was the second largest parade in the history of New Orleans other than Mardi Gras.[12]

After the New Orleans Congress, the NARSC conducted large congresses in Indianapolis in 1990, Orlando in 1995, and a concluding congress in St. Louis in 2000. These congresses emphasized the goal of winning half the world's population to Christ by the end of the century, a challenge given to the leadership by Fr. Tom Forrest. After the St. Louis Congress, the NARSC leaders felt that its mission was now completed and never met again.[13]

After the year 2000, the Pentecostal World Conference continued to meet every three years and the PFNA, every year. A major change came in 2004 when all the all-white PFNA was disbanded and the Pentecostal/Charismatic Churches of North America (PCCNA) was born. In what the press called "the Memphis Miracle," for the first time since Azusa Street, "the color line was washed away in the Blood." Leading in this change was Bishop Bernard E. Underwood and Vinson Synan of the Pentecostal Holiness Church, and Bishop Ithiel Clemmons of the Church of God in Christ.

---

11. Synan, *The Holiness-Pentecostal Tradition*, 267–70.

12. Synan, *The Century of the Holy Spirit*, 367–78.

13. For a detailed account of the NARSC story, see my autobiography, *Where He Leads Me: The Vinson Synan Story* (Franklin Springs, GA: Life Springs Resources, 2019), 157–68.

Although a large number of Oneness Pentecostals attended the Memphis meeting, only Trinitarians were admitted for full membership. In subsequent meetings, Oneness Pentecostals were invited to attend the sessions with Trinitarians.[14]

In all these organizations, there were huge neo-Charismatic and independent denominations in the world that were not active or represented. This situation called for a new paradigm to bring all the elements of the Pentecostal-Charismatic movements together in unity. Thus, the vision for Empowered21 was born.

---

14. See Harold Hunter, *Reconciliation Magazine* (Springfield, MO: n.p., 1998).

6

Empowered21: A Global Network

Vinson Synan & William M. Wilson

Of all the attempts to bring unity to the Pentecostal-Charismatic movements of the world, Empowered21 has created the widest global network in history.[1] This story involves three men who conceived the vision and brought it into being. The three were Dr. William (Billy) M. Wilson, a preacher from Kentucky, his friend, Mart Green, a businessman from Oklahoma, and Dr. Rob Hoskins, a missionary from Florida. Both Wilson and Green were born and raised in a vibrant Pentecostal denomination known as the Church of God of Prophecy. The two young men met while ministering at youth camps for their church. They became fast friends for life. Working closely together in future years, these two men not only founded the Empowered21 movement, but helped save Oral Roberts University from bankruptcy and led it on to become a strong and solvent institution.

Billy Wilson

Billy Wilson was born in Owensboro, Kentucky, on October 4, 1958. After graduating from Daviess County High School, he earned a Bachelor of Science degree at Western Kentucky University. Later he earned the Master of Arts and Doctor of Ministry degrees from Pentecostal Theological Seminary in Cleveland, Tennessee. Raised in the Church of God of Prophecy, he was licensed to preach in 1978 and was ordained bishop in 1984. Over the years, he pastored churches in Ohio and Tennessee. In 1983, he was appointed as the International Director of Youth and Camping Ministries for his denomination. In this position, he worked globally with over 100 national and state youth ministries, conducting youth camps and training sessions for youth. It was in this capacity that he met Mart Green, as they worked together in youth camps. Wilson also served as the International Director of

---

1. Reprinted with permission. Originally Vinson Synan and Billy Wilson, *As the Waters Cover the Sea: Empowered21 and the Movement it Serves* (Tulsa, OK: ORU Press, 2021), 55–68.

Evangelism from 1994 to 1998 and as Communications Director in his denomination from 1994 to 2003.[2]

His work caught the attention of the leaders of the Church of God (Cleveland, TN), which also had headquarters in Cleveland. The Church of God of Prophecy began as a split from the Church of God in 1923, after which the two churches went their separate ways. In a unique move, both churches accepted Wilson as an ambassador extraordinaire to work between their denominations. In 2003, Wilson was also ordained as a bishop in the Church of God. He was the only person in history to be ordained bishop and accepted by both churches. In this position, Wilson was given the title of "International Minister of Outreach" and led the "International Ministry of Outreach: A Cooperative Ministry of the Church of God and the Church of God of Prophecy," which focused on joint evangelistic efforts between the two denominations. During this time, he attempted without success to bring both churches to the point of amalgamation or merger. Later in 2011, Wilson resigned his ministry in the Church of God of Prophecy and remained with the Church of God.

During these years, Wilson branched out in into several national ministries. In 2008, he helped found the Awakening America Alliance, which consisted of over 250 Pentecostal, Charismatic, and Evangelical denominations and parachurch ministries. Another ministry he led was the World Impact with Billy Wilson television show. Throughout all his other activities, this TV ministry has continued for decades. In 2006, Wilson was named Executive Director of the Center for Spiritual Renewal in Cleveland, Tennessee, which was founded by Robert Fisher in 2002. Fisher was planning a centennial celebration for the Azusa Street Revival of 1906-1909. Tragically, Fisher passed away before the event took place. After Fisher's passing, the Board of Directors of the Center for Spiritual Renewal asked Wilson to lead the celebration. In 2006, Wilson led the Azusa Street Centennial Celebration in Los Angeles. Speakers came from all over the world to mark this important event. Meetings were held in many other Los Angeles venues. More than 50,000 people attended this celebration from 112 nations. During these days, a tent was raised on the very spot where the Azusa Mission once stood. Even Al Jazeera covered the event for the Muslim world. In this meeting, Wilson made contact with Pentecostal and Charismatic leaders from around the world who were to become the core leaders for the forming of Empowered21.

Over the next few years, Wilson led in calling international scholars together to study the Pentecostal and Charismatic movements of the world.

---

2. The information on Billy Wilson came from his personal bio entitled "William (Billy) Wilson" and the Wikipedia article entitled "Billy Wilson (academic)." Also, a personal interview with the author on January 16, 2019 at Oral Roberts University in Tulsa, Oklahoma. Editor's note: Wikipedia article currently "William Wilson (American academic)."

The first of these convened in London, with Harold Hunter leading the gathering of the scholars. After this, Vinson Synan was chosen to lead the scholars' meetings. Important scholar meetings were conducted in Germany, Chile, London, and Ecuador. Joining with Synan in Quito was the decorated scholar Amos Yong of Fuller Theological Seminary. The papers collected in these sessions became chapters in five books that were later published under the sponsorship of E21. In 2008, Wilson was contacted by his friend, Mart Green, during the time of crisis at Oral Roberts University, which was at the point of closure because of a huge debt. David Green, Mart's father, sensed a burden from the Lord to help ORU, and Mart asked Wilson to get involved. Wilson and Green were destined to work together at ORU, with Green as chairman of a newly formed Board of Trustees and Wilson as vice chairman.[3]

In August of 2019, Wilson was selected as the chair of the Pentecostal World Fellowship during the Pentecostal World Conference in Calgary, Canada. Wilson has published numerous books, articles, and circulars over the years. Most notably, he authored the books *Fasting Forward: Advancing Your Spiritual Life Through Fasting*, *Foundations of Faith*, *Father Cry*, *The Power of One*, *Generation Z: Born for the Storm*, and *Empowered to Lead*.

Mart Green

Mart Green was born in Lawton, Oklahoma, on September 2, 1961, to a middle-class business family. His father, David, was later to found the major store chain Hobby Lobby. Green was raised in a family surrounded by preachers in the Church of God of Prophecy. All five of his father's siblings were preachers or married preachers, and both grandparents were as well. As a young man, he attended Tomlinson College in Cleveland, Tennessee, and Southern Nazarene university in Bethany, Oklahoma, for only one semester in each school. Like his father, Green was not called to preach; he entered the world of business.[4]

Green began his retail career in the home of his parents as a youth. With $600, his family started Hobby Lobby in their living room. The business now has over 900 arts and crafts stores in the United States. Green serves as the ministry investment officer for Hobby Lobby and as the board chair. In 1981, Green established Mardel, a chain of Christian and education stores headquartered in Oklahoma City. Mardel now has thirty-four stores in seven states. In June 2002, Green founded and was the producer and CEO of Every Tribe Entertainment, a feature film production company. Two of his films were "The End of the Spear" and "Beyond the Gates of Splendor." From

---

3. Jennifer LeClaire, "ORU Names Billy Wilson as Fourth President," *Charisma News*, January 31, 2013.

4. The information on Mart Green is taken from his bio on Wikipedia and a personal interview with the author on January 13, 2019 in Oklahoma City, Oklahoma.

2008 to 2014, Green served as Board Chair of the Board of Trustees of Oral Roberts University. During this time and later, the Green family gave over $250 million to rescue and build the university. Also serving on the Board of Trustees was Billy Wilson, who later became president of the university.[5]

In later years, Green, through a collective alliance called Every Tribe Every Nation (ETEN), built the Digital Bible Library whose purpose was to digitize, centralize, standardize, and finalize the biblical texts of the world. One of his driving passions is illumiNations, which has a vision that all 6000+ vital languages on planet Earth will have some portions of Scripture by 2033. Green's personal motto is "This Book is Alive." The Green family's most ambitious project, spearheaded by Mart's brother, Steve Green, and Steve's wife Jackie, was the construction of the Museum of the Bible in Washington DC, which was dedicated in 2017. These projects demonstrated the Green family's great respect for the Bible as the living Word of God.

Rob Hoskins

The third man who helped envision Empowered21 was Mart Green's friend, Rob Hoskins, who worked closely with Green on these projects. Hoskins served as an ordained missionary in the Assemblies of God before becoming the president of OneHope Ministries in 2004. Along the way, he earned a Bachelor of Arts degree at Vanguard University. In recognition of his ministry of distributing millions of books and other media materials to young people all over the world, he was given the John Maxwell Leadership Award in 2005 and was named as one of the twenty-one emerging leaders of the church in *Charisma* magazine, in 2010. Hoskins completed his Doctor of Ministry degree at Gordon-Conwell Seminary in 2019 and was also granted an honorary Doctor of Divinity degree from Oral Roberts University in 2017.

Working closely with Mart Green in reviving Oral Roberts University, Hoskins joined the Board of Trustees in 2008 and went on to chair the Board of Trustees from 2014 to 2017. From 2008 to 2010, he worked diligently with Wilson and Green in planning for and founding the Empowered21 movement. Hoskins now serves on the E21 Global Council and is a liaison for E21 Next Gen, which works with next generation leaders all around the world.

Founding a Global Network

The Empowered21 movement had its origins in a vision given to Dr. Robert Fisher concerning a fitting celebration of the centennial of the Azusa Street

---

5. Bill Sherman, "ORU receives another $10 million donation," *Tulsa World*, (December 17, 2010).

Revival that began in 1906. The celebration, held in Los Angeles in April 2006, was a resounding success as more than 50,000 persons attended the various events that were celebrated in several Los Angeles venues.

After the Azusa Street celebration in 2006, the Center for Spiritual Renewal began a connection with Oral Roberts University (ORU) when Wilson's friend, Mart Green, was chosen to chair the Board of Trustees of the university. At this time, Wilson also joined the Board of Trustees. From this association came a vision for another meeting on the campus of ORU. Although the meeting was under the auspices of ORU, the International Center for Spiritual Renewal was chosen to administer the event. Called the "Global Congress on Holy Spirit Empowerment," the Tulsa meting drew 10,000 persons to the campus in April 2010. In preparing for the Tulsa meeting, Mart Green and his associates conducted a broad-ranging survey of the next generation to find out what term best described the Pentecostal-Charismatic Renewal in their minds. In the end, the word "empowered" won out over the terms "Pentecostal," "Charismatic," or "full gospel." Also, since everyone wanted to look toward the future instead of the past, the numeral 21 was added, referring to the twenty-first century. Thus the term "Empowered21" (or E21) was born, becoming formally organized in 2009.

Vision for Empowered21

The vision statement of Empowered21 is powerful and pointed: "That every person on earth would have an authentic encounter with Jesus Christ through the power and presence of the Holy Spirit…by Pentecost 2033." Its mission statement proclaims that "Empowered21 will help shape the future of the global Spirit-empowered movement throughout the world. We will do this by focusing on crucial issues facing the movement and by connecting generations for intergenerational blessing and impartation." Thus, the major focus is on what is called "next gen" (next generation) in order to continue the "spiritual grace" of the Pentecostal-Charismatic Renewal into future generations. Underling all the efforts of this vision is a prayer for a "fresh outpouring of the Holy Spirit in the twenty-first century." These themes have permeated all the events and planning sessions of E21 from the beginning.

In the two years before the formation of the E21 movement, Wilson led 17 unique conversations with some 500 church leaders and scholars from 54 nations and 15 universities with the goal of answering these questions: "What does it mean to be Spirit-empowered in the twenty-first century?" and "What steps can be taken to engage new generations in the Spirit-filled experience?" Armed with the wealth of knowledge from these conversations, E21 conducted two major events on university campuses.

A Global Movement

The first was the aforementioned Global Congress on Holy Spirit Empowerment, which drew 10,000 persons to Oral Roberts University in April 2010. Approximately 210 workshops produced a futuristic book edited by Vinson Synan entitled *Spirit-Empowered Christianity in the Twenty-first Century*. The second was a meeting at Regent University in 2012, which emphasized the convergence of Spirit-empowered generations and movements. More than 500 leaders registered for this event. During this time, the E21 movement was organized on an international scale with a global council and fourteen regional cabinets around the world. Included in these groups were leaders from almost all of the Pentecostal and Charismatic movements. Wilson and Pastor Jack Hayford served as co-chairs of the Global Council in the beginning, with Dr. George Wood as the chair of the World Assemblies of God Fellowship and then superintendent of the Assemblies of God USA, replacing Hayford in 2014.

The first global gathering after the American events at ORU and Regent University was the E21 Asia Congress held in Jakarta, Indonesia, in October 2011, which drew some 15,000 persons. Other plans for the future included worldwide celebrations on Pentecost Sunday each year to celebrate the birthday of the church and the outpouring of the Holy Spirit in the Upper Room (Acts 2). On Pentecost Sunday 2012, many thousands gathered in local celebrations around the world. Totally ecumenical, the vision is to see Pentecost Sunday rise to the level of Easter and Christmas as opportune days to make a common witness to the world.

An important part of the E21 vision has been to gather scholars from around the world to study the past, present, and future of the empowered movements on every continent and from as many nations as possible. To accomplish this goal, three meetings convened before the Global Congress in Jerusalem in 2015. One was held in Oxford, England, in 2012 under the leadership of Dr. Harold Hunter. Another took place in Sydney, Australia in 2013, where the focus was on Asia. Vinson Synan and Amos Yong directed this latter consultation and those that followed. The third meeting was in Quito, Ecuador in 2014, where the focus was on Latin America.

Meetings of Scholars

Another meeting of scholars gathered during the Empowered21 Global Congress in Jerusalem in 2015 in a culminating congress where thousands of people gathered for one of the largest Christian meetings held in the Holy Land in modern times. Here, the scholars read papers focusing on Africa, North America, and Europe. In the end, four volumes of the papers read in these gatherings were published and edited by Synan and Yong. Entitled *Global Renewal Christianity: Spirit-Empowered Movements Past, Present, and Future,* the four volumes were 1) Asia and Oceania 2); Latin America 3) Africa and 4) North America and Europe. Many of the papers published in these volumes were initially presented in the above-mentioned conferences and consultations.

Another book published by E21 came as a result of the scholars gathered in London in 2016. E21 leaders from around the world asked for a book that addressed the so-called "hyper-grace" teaching that was gaining popularity on some televangelists' programs. The papers were gathered and edited by Vinson Synan, and appeared in 2018 with the title, *"The Truth About Grace: Spirit-Empowered Perspectives."* This book featured all sides of the grace question and included chapters by Michael L. Brown and Joseph Prince, among others. It was also published by Charisma House. Other scholars' consultations have been conducted in Singapore, Johannesburg, and Bogota, with each session focusing on a different issue and with a book published by ORU Press following each consultation. Dr. Wonsuk Ma, Dean of the College of Theology and Ministry at ORU, now co-chairs the Scholars' Consultation annually.

The Importance of Empowered21

In looking back, it is evident that the Empowered21 movement is the most widespread and important global network of Pentecostal and Charismatic movements that have appeared since the glory days of Azusa Street in 1906. Wilson, with the financial help of the Green family, has tirelessly traveled around the globe, organizing events and regional cabinets of leaders. He has done all this while serving as president of Oral Roberts University, a position where he has excelled. Under his leadership, the university has operated with no indebtedness and has built new buildings, including a new dormitory to house the growing student population.

While leading a great university, Wilson has also led E21 congresses in Singapore and Kiev, Ukraine in 2017. In 2018, major congresses gathered in Sao Paulo, Brazil; Jakarta, Indonesia; Johannesburg, South Africa; Dublin, Ireland; Riga, Latvia; and again, in Brazil. In 2019, E21 meetings were convened in Dubai; Athens, Greece; and Bogota, Colombia. Other meetings will gather in the years leading up to the greatest E21 meeting of all. Preliminary plans are being drawn up to celebrate the 2000th anniversary of the Resurrection of Jesus Christ in Jerusalem 2033. By that time, it is fervently hoped that "The earth will be filled with the knowledge of the Lord as the waters cover the sea" (Isa 11:9, NIV).

7

ORAL ROBERTS: SON OF PENTECOSTALISM, FOUNDER OF THE CHARISMATIC MOVEMENT

Vinson Synan

Abstract

Oral Roberts was one of the most important religious figures of the twentieth century.[1] He was born and raised in the Pentecostal Holiness Church, hence, a "son" of the Pentecostal movement. He first became famous as a Pentecostal preacher who conducted large healing crusades under his huge tent. By the 1960s, he became the best-known Pentecostal in the world, founding Oral Roberts University in 1965. In the last part of his life, Roberts became a father of the Charismatic movement in the mainline churches through his television ministry. For nineteen years, Roberts was a member of the United Methodist Church and helped lead the Charismatic movement in the denomination. In his last years, he and his university strongly identified with the Charismatic movement. Thus, the title, "Oral Roberts: Son of Pentecostalism, Father of the Charismatic Movement."

Introduction

Oral Roberts was a Pentecostal pastor from Oklahoma who gained fame as a healing evangelist, television personality, and educator. Roberts not only founded Oral Roberts University (ORU) in Tulsa, Oklahoma, but in his lifetime served as a leader in the burgeoning world Pentecostal movement and later as a founding father of the Charismatic movement. In the late 1940s, Roberts emerged from the Pentecostal subculture in Oklahoma to become one of the most acclaimed and influential religious figures of the twentieth century. In his long life of ninety-one years, he served as a Pentecostal pastor, a healing tent evangelist, a television pioneer, and the founder of a major university named after himself. He brought Pentecostal healing evangelism to the attention of the American public through his televised healing

---

1. Reprinted with permission. Originally published as Vinson Synan, "Oral Roberts: Son of Pentecostalism, Founder of the Charismatic Movement," *Spiritus: ORU Journal of Theology* 2, nos. 1-2 (Tulsa, OK: ORU Press, 2017): 5–21.

crusades, his many books and magazines, and in his later years, through his prime-time programs on national television.[2]

Oral Roberts was born into a movement that was persecuted, denounced, and ridiculed by the public and rejected by the mainline churches. According to David Barrett, the lowly Pentecostals were "more harassed, persecuted, suffering, martyred than perhaps any other Christian tradition in recent history."[3] As a young man, Roberts felt the sting of this rejection but rose above it all during his amazing life and ministry. In school, he and his brother were often called "Holy Rollers," a term he resented. He also had a severe problem with stuttering. As a child, he was derided by his schoolmates when he could not get out the words he wanted to say. Despite all of this, it was Roberts who, above all others, turned the tide and brought Pentecostals into the accepted mainstream of American society.[4]

Roberts grew up in the Dust Bowl days of the 1930s. Many Okies, as they were called, decided to move to California to escape the poverty they faced in Oklahoma. The most famous migrants from Oklahoma to California were the Tatham family from Sallisaw, Oklahoma. Members of a Pentecostal Holiness Church, the family was immortalized as the Joad family in John Steinbeck's great American novel, *Grapes of Wrath*. In the novel, Grandma spoke in tongues. After arriving in California, the family worked in migrant camps but later went on to find prosperity in Sacramento.[5]

The Roberts family did not follow the tempting trail to California but suffered through the dark days of the Great Depression in Oklahoma. His father, Rev. Ellis Roberts, made a scant living through farming and pastoring local Pentecostal Holiness churches in the area of Ada, Oklahoma. Besides, he also held revivals in other Pentecostal Holiness Churches.[6] Offerings were

---

2. The definitive biography of Oral Roberts is David Edwin Harrell, *Oral Roberts: An American Life* (Bloomington, IN: Indiana University Press, 1985). A fine biography by Paul Chappell appeared in *NIDPCM*, 1024–25. His career in the Pentecostal Holiness Church can be found in Vinson Synan, *The Old Time Power* (Franklin Springs, GA: Advocate, 1973, 1998). A critical account of Roberts' life and ministry is Jerry Sholes, *Give Me That Prime-Time Religion: An Insider's Report on the Oral Roberts Evangelistic Association* (Hawthorn Books, 1979).

3. See David Barrett, "The Twentieth Century Pentecostal/Charismatic Renewal in the Holy Spirit with the Goal of World Evangelization," *The International Bulletin of Missionary Research* 12, no. 3 (July 1988): 1.

4. Among all Oral Roberts' books, two were autobiographies. The first was *The Call: An Autobiography* (Garden City, NY: Doubleday, 1972). The more important one was *Expect a Miracle: My Life and Ministry, an Autobiography* (Nashville, TN: Thomas Nelson, 1995). A warm book of memories was written by his daughter, Roberta Roberts Potts, *My Dad, Oral Roberts* (Noble, OK: ICON Publishing, 2011).

5. See John Steinbeck, *Grapes of Wrath* (New York: Viking, 1939); and Dan Morgan, who traced the Tatham family from Sallisaw to Sacramento in his book, *Rising in the West: The True Story of an "Okie" Family from the Great Depression Through the Reagan Years* (New York: Knopf, 1992).

6. Chappell, "Granville Oral Roberts," *NIDPCM*, 1024–25.

small, and Pastor Roberts barely eked out a living for his family of seven children. Oral Roberts never forgot the grinding poverty of his childhood.[7]

Oral Roberts: A Son of Pentecostalism

Oral Roberts (born on January 24, 1918; died on December 15, 2009) was born Oral Granville Roberts in Pontotoc County, Oklahoma, the fifth and youngest child of the Reverend Ellis Melvin Roberts and Claudius Priscilla Roberts (nee Irwin). Both parents were ministers of the Pentecostal Holiness Church and members of the East Oklahoma Conference. He was raised in a Pentecostal church typical of the time and place.

The Pentecostal Holiness Church in which Oral Roberts was born and raised was formed out of the Holiness movement that flourished in the last decades of the nineteenth century. The denomination was the result of a merger of two Holiness/Pentecostal churches in 1911 in Falcon, North Carolina. They were the Fire-Baptized Holiness Church and the Pentecostal Holiness Church. The Fire-Baptized Holiness Church was founded by Benjamin Hardin Irwin in 1896 in Iowa. Irwin was a dynamic healing evangelist who taught a "third blessing" (after salvation and sanctification) which he called the "baptism of the Holy Ghost and fire" or simply "the fire." The national church was organized in 1898 in Anderson, South Carolina, with both blacks and women serving as "Ruling Elders." The Pentecostal Holiness Church was pioneered by the Methodist evangelist Abner B. Crumpler, who emphasized the second blessing of "entire sanctification" as taught by John Wesley.[8]

Both churches accepted the Pentecostal baptism in the Holy Spirit as a third blessing and became Pentecostal after being influenced by the Azusa Street revival under the black pastor William J. Seymour. A member of the Pentecostal Holiness Church, Gaston B. Cashwell, brought Pentecost to both churches in 1907, after traveling to the Azusa Street Mission in 1906 and speaking in tongues. All the churches in Oklahoma were originally part of the Fire-Baptized Holiness section of the church.[9]

Oral was raised in abject poverty. On his mother's side, he was descended from the Cherokee Indians and was proud of his Indian heritage in Oklahoma. In high school, Roberts played basketball on his Ada, Oklahoma,

---

7. Roberts, *The Call*, 20–26; and Roberts, *Expect a Miracle*, 10–13.

8. See Synan, *The Old Time Power*, 44–92, and Synan, *The Holiness Pentecostal Tradition* (Grand Rapids, MI: Eerdmans, 1971, 1978) 44–67. Also see Vinson Synan and Dan Woods, *Fire Baptized: The Many Lives of Benjamin Hardin Irwin* (Wilmore, KY: Emeth, 2017). A major source for these two churches may be found in Joseph E. Campbell, *The Pentecostal Holiness Church: 1898–1948* (Franklin Springs, GA: Publishing House of the Pentecostal Holiness Church, 1950): 192–253.

9. Synan, *The Old Time Power*, 94–113.

high school team and for a short time joined a local Methodist church with his teammates. In 1935 at seventeen years of age, however, he contracted tuberculosis and was bedridden for five months. Some of his family feared that he might never recover. Yet in his darkest hour of despair, Roberts heard a voice telling him about his future: "Son, I am going to heal you and you are to take my healing power to your generation. You are to build me a university and build it on My authority and the Holy Spirit."[10] He was suddenly healed, however, after his parents and his older brother, Elmer, took him to a tent revival. When the evangelist, George W. Moncey, laid hands on him and prayed a healing prayer, he was instantly healed, although it took months for him to totally recover. Roberts soon preached his first sermon and returned to the Pentecostal Holiness Church, where he was ordained in 1936.[11]

In 1938, he married Evelyn Lutman Fahnstock, the daughter of a Pentecostal Holiness minister, a marriage that lasted until her death in 2005. To this marriage was born two sons and two daughters: Ronald, Richard, Rebecca, and Roberta. The Roberts' suffered great tragedy at the early death of Rebecca in an airplane crash and of Ronald, who fell into drug addiction and later committed suicide.[12]

A young man with limitless drive and ambition, from 1941–1947, Roberts pastored local Pentecostal Holiness Churches in Enid and Shawnee, Oklahoma, Toccoa, Georgia, and one independent church in Fuqua Springs, North Carolina. In Toccoa, he experienced his first striking miracle of healing when a deacon in his church, Clyde Lawson, was instantly healed after a falling motor had crushed his foot. When Roberts laid hands on his foot and prayed, the man was instantly healed.[13] At this time, he also was becoming one of the most important young ministers in the Pentecostal Holiness Church. With his rising influence, he was elected as a delegate from East Oklahoma to the General Conferences of 1941 and 1945, the highest governing body of the church. He was looked on as a very loyal son of the church with a bright future in the denomination.

After returning to Oklahoma in 1942, Roberts attended Oklahoma Baptist University and Phillips University, studying for two years in each school. He never earned a degree, however, since he soon became a traveling evangelist holding revivals in many parts of the nation. In 1947, while pastoring Enid Pentecostal Holiness Church, he felt the call to become a full-time healing evangelist after visiting the meetings of William Branham, whom he admired. His first city-wide crusade was also in 1947, a healing service held in the civic auditorium of his hometown of Enid, attended by 1,200 people. From there, he purchased a tent seating 3,000 persons and began his meteoric

---

10. Roberts, *Expect a Miracle*, 32.
11. Roberts, *Expect a Miracle*, 33–35.
12. Roberts, *Expect a Miracle*, 195–250. Also R. R. Potts, *My Dad, Oral Roberts*, 140–62.
13. Roberts, *Expect a Miracle*, 35.

rise to prominence in American religious life. The same year he published his first book on healing, *If You Need Healing Do These Things*. He then went to the radio airwaves with a national radio broadcast. He also soon started his own monthly magazine *Healing Waters*.

In one of his earliest tent meetings in Tulsa, Oklahoma, in June 1947, a sniper fired a shot at Roberts that whizzed by just above his head. When the Tulsa press found out about it, stories were written about the incident that appeared in newspapers all over the United States. Overnight, Oral Roberts became a nationally recognized figure. Because of his increasing fame, Roberts was invited by J. A. Culbreth to preach in the famous Falcon camp meeting in 1948. The other invitation was from Joseph A. Synan, who later served as the presiding bishop of the Pentecostal Holiness Church.[14] His healing crusades became so successful that he soon bought another much larger tent seating 12,500 people, which he filled to overflowing. He called it his "tent Cathedral." As the crowds continued to grow, he soon was attracting crowds that rivaled those of Billy Graham, the famous Baptist evangelist. Like Graham, Roberts refused to segregate his crowds on the basis of race. Blacks could sit anywhere in his tent, a striking exception to the Jim Crow segregation practiced in the South at the time.

Most of his followers were fellow Pentecostals who packed his tents and sent huge offerings to support his ministry. Several Pentecostal Holiness members helped Roberts in his early ministry. They were O. E. Sproull, who served as his first Master of Ceremonies for the tent crusades; Collins Steele, who oversaw the moving and setup of the huge tent; Lee Braxton, who helped him organize his radio and television ministries; and Oscar Moore, who helped run the huge Tulsa office. Other prominent Pentecostals from many churches helped in Roberts' tent ministry. Two of them were Bob DeWeese from the Open Bible Church, who assisted him in the healing lines, and Vep Ellis, from the Church of God (Cleveland, Tennessee), who led music and wrote many songs for the Roberts ministry.[15]

In 1951, Roberts helped Demos Shakarian found the Full Gospel Business Men's Fellowship International (FGBMFI), which, in time, attracted millions of men to their monthly meetings, held mostly in hotels. Roberts' ministry skyrocketed in 1955 when he went on national television, attracting a huge audience across the nation. Americans saw Roberts lay hands on thousands of the sick who stood in lines waiting for his healing touch. Many claimed to be healed. Part of Robert's attraction was his dynamic preaching and positive message which emphasized salvation, sanctification, baptism in the Holy Spirit with tongues as initial evidence, the second coming, divine healing, prosperity, and "seed faith" for finances. During his

---

14. Harrell, *Oral Roberts*, 81–82. Roberts always felt that the publicity from this sniping incident was the breakthrough that brought him to the attention of the American public.

15. Harrell, *Oral Roberts*, 80–110.

healing ministry, Roberts conducted some 300 crusades in America and around the world. He claimed to have personally laid hands on over two million people. Many historians credit Roberts with playing a major role in the beginning of the Charismatic movement in the mainline churches because of his riveting television specials. Many of his critics called Roberts a "faith healer," a term which he hotly denied. He said that Jesus did the healing and not Roberts himself.[16]

Because of his burgeoning ministry, in 1950 Roberts built a modern multistoried headquarters building in Tulsa that became his center of operations. From here, millions of books, tracts, articles, and magazines flowed out to his dedicated followers. He also inaugurated a weekly Sunday morning television program that for thirty years was the number one rated religious program in the nation. In 1956, he began publishing *Abundant Life Magazine,* which, at its height, went to some two million subscribers. In a 1980 Gallup Poll, Roberts' name was known to 84% of the America public. He became the most prominent Pentecostal in the world. In the decade of the 1980s, he published a daily devotional magazine called *Daily Blessing* that went to a quarter of a million subscribers. In addition to this, the 88 books that he wrote sold some fifteen million copies.[17]

With this notoriety, Roberts embarked on one of his most ambitious projects, the founding of a liberal arts university. Beginning in 1962, he financed and built one of the most futuristic campuses in the world, naming it Oral Roberts University. In 1960, Roberts had penned a vision for the new university: "Raise up your students to hear my voice, to go where my light is dim, where my voice is heard small, and my healing power is not known, even to the uttermost bounds of the earth. Their work will exceed yours, and in this I am well pleased."[18]

When classes began in 1965, the university was an undergraduate school with one graduate component, the School of Theology.[19] After a few years, the student body grew to over 5,000 in several undergraduate and graduate schools. These included schools of Medicine, Nursing, Dentistry, Law, Business, Education, and Theology. Although teachers and administrators came from diverse church backgrounds, many of the core leaders were from the Pentecostal Holiness Church. Some of these scholars who helped in the early years of ORU were Dr. Raymond O. Corvin, who served as the

---

16. See Synan, *Under His Banner* (Costa Mesa, CA: Gift Publications, 1992).

17. Chappell, "Granville Oral Roberts," *NIDPCM,* 1025. Harrell, *Oral Roberts,* 116–20.

18. Larry Hart, "The Seminary: A History of Graduate Theological Education at Oral Roberts University" (unpublished manuscript, Oral Roberts University, 2016) 3.

19. The first catalogue was titled *Information for Prospective Students and Other Interested People* (1965), 1–11. The second catalogue, titled *Oral Roberts University Bulletin 1966–1967,* contained a full list of the Board of Regents, the administration and faculty, and the curriculum for the new university.

Chancellor in the beginning and also the first dean of the School of Theology; Dr. Carl Hamilton, who led the university to full accreditation; Dr. Harold Paul, a history professor; and Dr. Paul Chappell, who later led the School of Theology for many years. Other important scholars came from the Assemblies of God, the Church of God, and other Pentecostal denominations.[20]

As time went on and the university began to grow, Roberts became uncomfortable with his identity as a Pentecostal. Of necessity, he was forced to hire professors for his university who came from mainline churches, because there were few Pentecostals with Ph.D. degrees and with administrative experience on the graduate level. Also, records showed that his donor base showed growing income from mainline donors. In fact, the largest donor base was from Methodists. Among the mainline administrators and professors Roberts hired were Dr. Howard Ervin, an American Baptist, along with Dr. John D. Messick, Tommy Tyson, and Bob Stamps, Methodists all. Although Messick came to ORU as a Methodist who had once headed East Carolina University, he was raised in the Pentecostal Holiness Church. In time, Roberts' vision began to broaden far beyond his humble Pentecostal origins as he became friends with many non-Pentecostal Christian leaders, including the most famous one of all, Billy Graham.[21]

During these years, the Charismatic movement broke out in the mainline denominations, beginning in 1960, under the leadership of Father Dennis Bennett, pastor of St. Luke's Episcopal Church in Van Nuys, California. Soon thousands of ministers and lay people from all the Protestant churches spoke in tongues and created Charismatic movements in their churches. In 1967, a similar but unexpected Charismatic movement broke out among Roman Catholics at Duquesne University in Pittsburg, Pennsylvania. In explaining the beginnings of this renewal, Father Kilian McDonnell explained that behind every new Charismatic stood a classical Pentecostal.[22]

The most important of these was Oral Roberts, whose televised healing crusades came into the living rooms of every American. It was reported that Roman Catholic bishops in New York City, Philadelphia, and Chicago were becoming concerned by the rising tide of Catholics who loved to watch Oral Roberts on TV, and, to their alarm, also sent him large donations, rather than putting them in church offerings. Clearly something was happening in

---

20. Harrell, *Oral Roberts*, 211–13.

21. Roberts, *Expect a Miracle*, 315–30.

22. For the beginning of the Episcopal Charismatic renewal, see Dennis Bennett, *Nine O' Clock in the Morning* (Plainfield, NJ: Logos, 1970). Patti Gallagher Mansfield tells of the start of the Catholic renewal in her *As by a New Pentecost: The Dramatic Beginning of the Catholic Charismatic Renewal* (Steubenville, OH: Franciscan University Press, 1992). For a summary of the renewals in all the churches see Kilian McDonnell, *Charismatic Renewal and the Churches* (New York: Seabury, 1971). Also see Synan, *Century of the Holy Spirit: One Hundred Years of Pentecostal and Charismatic Renewal* (Nashville, TN: Thomas Nelson, 2001).

American religious life. This has led some historians to see Roberts as a father of the Charismatic movement.[23]

Oral Roberts: A Father of the Charismatic Movement

Roberts reached an early pinnacle of acceptance when he attended Billy Graham's Berlin Congress on World Evangelism in 1966. For years, Roberts and Graham had been close personal friends, but in planning the Berlin Congress, Graham was reluctant at first to invite Roberts, fearing a backlash from his supporters. Graham later wrote about this in his book, *Just as I Am*:

> Whom should we invite as participants to the Congress? We carefully formulated general guidelines, but they did not automatically resolve every issue. For example, the growing charismatic movement, much of it associated with Pentecostal denominations, was somewhat outside of mainstream evangelicalism. We did not bar these denominations from our crusades, but we did not particularly encourage their participation either; some of their ecstatic manifestations were controversial and disruptive within the broader Christian community. I felt that my longtime friend Oral Roberts, world renowned for his preaching and healing ministry as well as for the university bearing his name in Tulsa, Oklahoma, should be included among the delegates. I was not ready to assign him a place on the program, but I was convinced that his presence would mark the beginning of a new era in evangelical cooperation.[24]

When Roberts accepted Graham's invitation, he went to Berlin with many fears and trepidations. He was a delegate with a seminar on healing as part of the program. At first, he hung out with his church friends, including R. O. Corvin and Bishop Synan. But soon other non-Pentecostals began to befriend him. In the end, Graham invited him to greet a plenary session and lead in prayer. The results were explosive. Roberts' greeting "was an electric moment. When the applause began, pandemonium broke out. They jumped up from every angle and applauded and applauded." But his prayer moved the delegates more and "moved the entire congress."[25] This broke the ice as hundreds of world leaders clamored to meet and thank him for his ministry. It was indeed "the beginning of a new era of cooperation" as Graham had said. Roberts then returned to America with a wider view of the body of Christ and a new sense of mission.[26]

The next year was a momentous one for Oral Roberts, as he planned to dedicate his new and growing university. In the afterglow of the Berlin

---

23. Personal conversation with Bishop Synan in Franklin Springs, GA, ca. 1965.

24. Billy Graham, *Just as I Am: An Autobiography of Billy Graham* (New York: Harper, 1999), 536.

25. Harrell, *Oral Roberts*, 204–5.

26. Harrell, *Oral Roberts*, 204–5.

Congress, Roberts invited Billy Graham as the main speaker at the dedication ceremony. Graham gladly accepted. It was a windy day, as some 18,000 people showed up for the service, which was held outdoors. In honor of his denomination, Roberts invited his bishop of the Pentecostal Holiness Church, J. A. Synan, to read the scriptures. But the star of the day was Billy Graham, who lauded Roberts on his accomplishments and warned the president and faculty that a curse from God might fall on the university if it ever left its biblical moorings.[27]

From that point on, Roberts began a move to remake Oral Roberts University (ORU) from a narrower Pentecostal school to a university that would reflect the entire body of Christ. In 1968, Roberts ended his healing crusades. The *New York Times* stated that Roberts' "tent was folded and replaced by a television studio."[28] A hint of things to come was a growing conflict between Oral and his childhood friend R. O. Corvin, dean of the ORU School of Theology since 1963. As the seminary grew, it soon became apparent to Roberts that Corvin's vision was for the seminary to serve as a training center for the Pentecostal churches and more particularly the Pentecostal Holiness Church, to which both Roberts and Corvin belonged. But after the Berlin Congress, Roberts' view had expanded to include all the mainline churches and not just the Pentecostal movement. In 1968, the two men collided several times over the future of the seminary. In the end, Roberts fired Corvin and closed the seminary in 1969. A drastic step indeed.[29]

In the meantime, the Oklahoma Methodist bishop, Angie Smith, a friend of Roberts, invited him to join the Methodist Church. At first, Roberts did not take him seriously, since there was a wide theological chasm between the more liberal United Methodist Church and the much more conservative Pentecostal denominations. However, eventually Roberts joined the influential Boston Avenue United Methodist Church in Tulsa, which was pastored by Finis Crutchfield. This move was made with the added influence of Tommy Tyson, the Methodist chaplain of the university, and Wayne Robinson, who had already left the Pentecostal Holiness Church for Methodism. Roberts then shocked the religious world on May 28, 1968, when he was recognized as an elder in the Oklahoma Conference of the Methodist Church. Pentecostals around the world as well as many mainline church leaders were equally mystified by Roberts' unexpected move. He was not re-ordained, however. Until the end of his life, Roberts' ordination remained with the Pentecostal Holiness Church. For a time, Roberts was a favorite preacher at Methodist events in the United States and overseas.[30]

---

27. Roberts, *The Call*, 203–5.
28. Harrell, *Oral Roberts*, 303.
29. Harrell, *Oral Roberts*, 234–35.
30. Roberts, *Expect a Miracle*, 315–20. The United Methodist "Certificate of Recognition of Orders" for Oral Roberts is in the Oral Roberts University archives in Tulsa,

At first, Roberts led a fast-growing charismatic movement among Methodists and was invited to preach in many leading churches and Annual Conferences. In time, the number of Methodist Charismatics grew to number someone million in the United States. Oral Roberts, now a professed Charismatic, became their hero. To cement his Methodist connection, Roberts re-opened his seminary in 1976, with Jimmy Buskirk as dean of the seminary. Buskirk was a Spirit-filled professor of evangelism at Emory University in Atlanta. Shortly after his coming, the new school was fully accredited, not only by the Association of Theological Schools (ATS) but also by the United Methodist Church as an approved seminary for Methodist workers. In a short time, most of the faculty were Methodists.[31] Moving in another direction, in 1969, after abandoning his healing crusades, Roberts began a series of prime-time television programs that made him a national TV celebrity.[32]

Roberts' most ambitious project was the founding of a hospital in 1981, which he called "the City of Faith." At a cost of $250 million, the hospital consisted of three buildings of 20, 30, and 60 stories that would house a hospital and a research facility that Roberts claimed would "merge prayer and medicine." In raising money for the hospital, Roberts was roundly criticized by the press for claiming to see a "nine hundred foot Jesus" and for saying that Jesus would "take him home" if he did not raise $8,000,000 to finish the project. The money came in, but Roberts' reputation suffered irreparable harm. In spite of heroic fund-raising efforts, the City of Faith was forced to close in 1989.[33]

As a result of this and other negative publicity, the leaders of the United Methodist Church became uncomfortable having Oral Roberts as a member of the church. A blow to Roberts came when Buskirk resigned to become pastor of Tulsa's First Methodist Church. Another bitter blow came in 1987 when the United Methodist Church withdrew its accreditation of ORU for the training of Methodist ministers. After this decision, nineteen Methodist faculty members resigned and left the university. A short time later, the Oklahoma Methodists unceremoniously excommunicated Roberts from the United Methodist Church. He was not even notified by the church officials but learned about his ouster in the *Tulsa World* newspaper while eating

---

Oklahoma. Roberts was not re-ordained but accepted as an "elder" not in "full connection." Roberts was a Methodist minister for 19 years. In 1987, he was excommunicated from the United Methodist Church due to rising opposition to his ministry.

31. Roberts, *Expect a Miracle*, 320–23.

32. Harrell, *Oral Roberts*, 235–99.

33. Harrell, *Oral Roberts*, 423–35.

breakfast at home. After this, Roberts returned to fellowship with his Pentecostal and Charismatic friends.[34]

Soon after, Roberts brought Larry Lea, a leading Southern Baptist charismatic pastor, to Tulsa to serve as the new dean of what he called "the Signs and Wonders Seminary." Later in 1986, Roberts organized a "new fellowship" of charismatic leaders which he called the International Charismatic Bible Ministries (ICBM). Roberts and ORU were henceforth identified with the burgeoning Charismatic movement that was sweeping the world. Clearly his Methodist days were over.[35]

As a Charismatic school, the university and its School of Theology experienced a boom in enrollment. Seminary Academic Dean Paul Chappell reported in 1987 that "with its clear identity as a Charismatic Bible believing/teaching institution and with a Charismatic faculty, we have grown to be the 34th largest seminary in North America. We are the fastest growing seminary in North America."[36]

In 1993, Roberts turned ORU over to his son Richard, who was not able to attract enough students and money to maintain the quality envisioned by the founder. Despite his best efforts, Richard Roberts was not able to raise funds to the level that his father had. More and more, the university lived on borrowed money, so much so that the debt soared to over $50,000,000. In 2007, Richard was asked to resign and a new president, Dr. Mark Rutland, was installed. Soon afterward, the David Green and Mart Green families of Oklahoma City gave the university over $100 million dollars to save the school. Under the leadership of Mart Green, the campus was renovated, and the board adopted realistic policies that are helping the university become self-supporting.[37]

In Closing

Oral Roberts died on December 15, 2009, at 91 years of age. He was one of the most prominent American religious leaders of his time, second only to Billy Graham. His emphasis on healing and prosperity still inspires millions of Pentecostals and charismatics around the world. In the end, Roberts was the most famous and influential leader ever produced by the Pentecostal Holiness Church. At the same time, he was the one man above all others who brought Pentecostalism to the attention of the world. In his lifetime, Roberts

---

34. Roberts, *Expect a Miracle*, 326–28. The *Tulsa World* stated that Roberts had been "cast out of the Methodist Church by a special committee of leaders," 328.

35. Roberts, *Expect a Miracle*, 327–30.

36. Hart, "The Seminary," 14–15.

37. See David Green, *Giving It All Away…And Getting It All Back* (Grand Rapids, MI: Zondervan, 2017). Also see NBCNews.com, "Businessman Rescues Oral Roberts University," February 5, 2006.

spent his first fifty years as a Pentecostal, nineteen years as a Methodist Charismatic, and twenty-two years as an independent Charismatic.

But in a broader sense, Roberts was not only the leading Pentecostal in the world but also one of the most important fathers of the worldwide Charismatic movement that swept into all the mainline churches after 1960. By the year 2017, the Pentecostals and Charismatics globally numbered some 669,000,000, according to Todd Johnson of Gordon-Conwell Seminary.[38] As one of the foremost historic figures in both movements, Oral Roberts must now be recognized as one of the major Christian leaders of world Christianity in the past century.

---

38. Todd Johnson et al., "Five Hundred Years of Protestant Christianity," *International Bulletin of Mission Research* 41, no. 1 (July 2017): 49.

8

AN EARLY ACCOUNT OF ORAL ROBERTS' HEALING TESTIMONY

Daniel D. Isgrigg & Vinson Synan

Abstract

The story of Oral Roberts' healing is well documented. However, recently a discovery was made of an early testimony in the *East Oklahoma Conference News* of the Pentecostal Holiness Church that provided new details about the early years of his life and ministry. This testimony, from 1939, includes details from the first few years of Roberts' evangelistic ministry and a different account of both the nature of his sickness and the circumstances of his healing. This article will also explore the possible factors that contributed to the differences in this testimony from his later accounts.

This edition of *Spiritus* is dedicated to new research on the impact Oral Roberts has made on the global Spirit-empowered movement.[1] A volume like this might warrant a biographical sketch of Roberts' life, although his story is well documented. However, while doing research for this volume, the authors discovered some previously unknown information on Roberts' early ministry in *East Oklahoma Conference News* of the Pentecostal Holiness Church, held in the Holy Spirit Research Center.[2] As a young evangelist in Oklahoma, Roberts contributed several articles to the paper and was featured as an evangelist prior to becoming the pastor of the Shawnee Pentecostal Holiness Church. To our delight, we discovered that he also served a year as the editor of the paper (September 1943 to September 1944) while he was the pastor in Shawnee.

---

1. Article reprinted with permission from *Spiritus: ORU Journal of Theology* 3, no. 2 (Fall 2018): 169–77. This issue was specially devoted to new and reflective research on Oral Roberts' life and ministry. Synan and Isgrigg were feature contributors.

2. David E. Harrell, Jr., *Oral Roberts: An American Life* (San Francisco: Harper & Row), 43, notes that Roberts wrote articles for the *Pentecostal Holiness Advocate* as early as 1937 but was not aware that he also wrote in the *East Oklahoma Conference News* (henceforth, *EOCN*).

In 1943, Roberts was asked to step in as editor for Rayford Bullard, who was called away to work at the publishing house in Franklin Springs, Georgia.[3] During his year as editor, Roberts often wrote about issues taking place in the denomination and continued the tradition of highlighting evangelistic works taking place in the conference,[4] including that of his parents.[5] Shortly after Bullard returned to resume his duties, Roberts decided to leave his pastorate in Shawnee for evangelistic meetings in North Carolina in August of 1945.[6] From there, he spent a short time as a pastor in Toccoa, Georgia, before returning to Oklahoma to pastor in Enid and enroll in Phillips Seminary in 1946.[7] A year later, Roberts made the decision to launch into full time healing ministry.

Below is a reprint of an article in the *East Oklahoma Conference News* (*EOCN*) from October 5, 1939, in which the editor, Oscar Moore, asked Roberts to give a short account of his testimony to introduce himself to the readers.[8] This account is the earliest known telling of Roberts' early life and gives several details of his early career as a rising evangelist. He reports that in the first few years of his ministry in early revivals in Texas, Arkansas, and Oklahoma, he preached a staggering 600 times and recorded over 400 salvations.

> ***Moore:*** In keeping with my announced plan, I am giving you a brief life story of another one of our young ministers. This month I introduce Rev. Oral Roberts, who I believe is the youngest Ordained Minister in the East Okla. Conf. I have asked him to write the story for me, here it is:

> ***Roberts:*** I was born Jan. 24, 1918, in a little log cabin fifteen miles from N. W. of Ada. I met a cold reception for the day was blustery. The day of rejoicing was soon over, however, and I settled down to the regular routine of life. There is nothing eventful in my life until the day of my conversion and call to the ministry—except a few things which led up to it. At the age of fifteen, I felt as if I wanted to leave home and try life alone—so against the advice of my parents I went with my old High School Coach to Atoka to play ball and go to school. All was well for the first seven months but one night while in the second game of a basketball tournament, I took the flu, my health broke, and I had to go back home—a sick boy.

> For sixty days death hovered near and had it not been for the love of a merciful Savior I could not have lived through the suffering. Fearing my hour of death was near, I called in my school mates and gave them my

---

3. Rayford Bullard, "Back Again," *EOCN* (September 1944): 4.

4. "Can Our Soldier Boys Be Saved?" *EOCN* (May 1944): 2–3; "Will God Repeat the Upper Room Revival?" *EOCN* (November 1943): 1, 7; "Suggestions for the P. H. Y. S. Rallies and Young People's Work," *EOCN* (January 1944): 2–3.

5. *EOCN* (October 1943): 1, 7; (July 1944): 3.

6. "Former Editor Goes East," *EOCN* (August 1945): 3.

7. Oral Roberts, *Expect a Miracle* (Nashville, TN: Thomas Nelson, 1995), 56–57.

8. *EOCN* (October 5, 1939): 1.

books, and at the same time told them goodbye, meanwhile my parents were praying for me—even whole churches—and at last I opened my heart, prayed with all the earnestness of my soul, and God saved me.

My strength returned and with it came the call from God to the ministry. I really intended to preach, but I began an association with a number of unsaved boys and girls and soon lost my experience. In 1934, after my parents moved to Stratford, I started school there but at the end of the 6th week I had a nervous breakdown and had to quit. I stayed in bed for five months. Those were lonely days for all of us, but on the 7th of Feb. during family prayer, I called on God in my distress and suffering, and God heard my earnest cry and saved me again. A call came the second time to enter the ministry—and immediately, I began to mend.

In the month of August 1935, I preached my first sermon in Homer School house five miles east of Ada. Three were saved that night. In 1936 I was licensed to preach by the Conference and entered full time ministry—since my father was sent to pastor the Westville church. Since then I have been preaching the glorious gospel in my humble and simple way, and have seen numbers of souls come to God. On Christmas day, 1938, I was united in holy wedlock with Evelyn Lutman Fahnestock, who had been teaching school for the past three years.

During this time I've written a thirty-two page book entitled "Salvation by the Blood" and a four- page pamphlet on "Character Building." It has been my pleasure to conduct revivals in the following places: Gainesville and Weslaco, Texas; Rogers, Ark.; Memphis, Tenn.; Ada, Westville, Wagoner, Sand Springs, Okmulgee, Muskogee, Braggs, Konawa, Seminole, Fox, Okemah, Cromwell, Sulphur, Durant, and Okla. City in 2nd church in Oklahoma. I have preached approximately 600 times, 400 have been saved, 125 sanctified, 98 received the Holy Ghost, 187 added to the church, 69 baptized in water, and I have performed 5 wedding ceremonies. In conclusion let me say that life with this glorious Pentecostal Experience is a happy one, and I can see greater things ahead, if I stay true to Christ.

What is noteworthy about this biographical sketch is the way Roberts tells the testimony of his healing. In his later autobiographies, he describes the details of his collapse during a basketball game, being diagnosed with tuberculosis, and being bedridden for months.[9] During this time of sickness, he had two significant experiences that led to his recovery. The first took place when at his weakest point his father prayed all night at his bed. Because of these prayers, Roberts received salvation, and God gave him strength to

---

9. Oral Roberts wrote five autobiographies in a forty-three year span between 1952 and 1995: *Oral Roberts' Life Story as Told by Himself* (Tulsa, OK: Oral Roberts, 1952); *Oral Roberts, My Story* (Tulsa, OK: Summit Books, 1961); *Oral Roberts, My Twenty Years of a Miracles Ministry* (Tulsa, OK: Oral Roberts, 1967); *Oral Roberts, The Call: An Autobiography* (Garden City, NJ: Doubleday, 1971); *Oral Roberts, Expect a Miracle: My Life and Ministry* (Nashville, TN: Thomas Nelson, 1995).

stand up for the first time in months.[10] A few weeks later, after his parents moved to Stratford, Oklahoma, he attended a tent revival where he was prayed for by Rev. George Moncey.[11] After Moncey rebuked the sickness, Roberts testified that power touched his lungs, and he was instantly healed of tuberculosis.[12]

In this previously unknown 1939 account, Roberts tells a somewhat different story. He curiously describes his illness as only "a flu" that "broke his health," but does not mention it was tuberculosis. The diagnosis by the doctors that it was tuberculosis is a significant part of his story considering his family history and Native American heritage.[13] There is no doubt that he was fully aware that it was tuberculosis. In later accounts, Roberts recalls, "I began to think of all the Indians I had seen with tuberculosis, of those I had seen die as I accompanied Papa on his preaching tours among the Indian people."[14] Yet, in the 1939 account, Roberts says he recovered from his "broken health" after his father prayed for him and he received his first salvation experience before moving to Stratford. He goes on to claim that after they moved to Stratford, he had a second salvation experience wherein he would "begin to mend" and was called to ministry. Furthermore, Roberts' testimony in the July 11, 1935 edition of *The Advocate* indicates he was still struggling with sickness despite having been saved, sanctified, and called to preach.[15]

---

10. Roberts, *Oral Roberts' Life Story as Told by Himself*, 46.

11. Roberts, *The Call*, 34; Roberts, *Expect a Miracle*, 32–33; E. M. and Claudius Roberts, *Our Ministry and Our Son Oral* (Tulsa, OK: Oral Roberts, 1960), 58–59.

12. Roberts, *Oral Roberts' Life Story as Told by Himself*, 50. Roberts testifies that following Moncey's prayer, his lungs began to tingle, he saw a light above him, and he ran on the stage declaring "I am healed! I am healed! I am healed!"

13. Based on his later accounts, Roberts clearly understood the nature of his illness, having testified that his doctor and his parents told him that it was tuberculosis. Roberts, *My Story*, 16–17. Roberts knew that tuberculosis was common in Native American communities and his Cherokee mother's father and sister had died of the same illness. Roberts, *Expect a Miracle*, 32, also recounts that Moncey encouraged him, "An Indian boy was healed here a few nights ago." To which he commented, "I suppose that someone had told him I had Indian blood."

14. Roberts, *Expect a Miracle*, 24.

15. "Testimonies," *The Advocate* (July 11, 1935): 14. Roberts' account of his testimony notes, "I have been bedfast for 130 days, and I praise God for it. During this time I have been saved and sanctified. I have had several doctors, medical and chiropractic, but they seem of no avail. It seems that God is the only one that knows my condition…I feel the call definitely, but before I recover and enter into the work I must have the abiding Comforter, the Holy Ghost, to comfort and help me to overcome my infirmities." It is unclear exactly when Roberts visited Rev. Moncey's tent meeting and was healed, but it would presumably be after this testimony. Nevertheless, this account further contradicts the 1939 testimony, which places this event in February.

It is also noteworthy that there is no mention of his healing experience with George Moncey in the tent revival near Ada, Oklahoma.[16] The only healing he reports is recovering from a "nervous breakdown" that kept him in bed for five months. Later accounts describe the agony of his suffering during the sickness, but do not mention such a mental episode.[17] Instead of one sickness (tuberculosis) that was healed during the process of two experiences (salvation and healing) by two individuals (his father and George Moncey), Roberts describes recovering from two separate issues (flu and nervous breakdown) by means of two salvation experiences by the same individuals (family prayer).

What should we make of these additions/omissions in this early account? Why would Roberts downplay a central piece of his story that would later establish him as America's leading healing evangelist? First, this account demonstrates that Roberts learned early in his life to tailor his testimony in a way that would lend credibility to his ministry. For decades, Roberts used his story of healing from tuberculosis as a way of validating his ministry as a healing evangelist. His healing ministry was motivated by his healing testimony. As David Harrell comments, "Roberts's view on healing depended not so much on an ideological base but on experience. Over and over he traced his passion for healing back to the enchanted moment when he himself had experienced God's touch."[18] In the same way, in order to validate his evangelistic ministry, Roberts placed the majority of his focus on how his salvation experiences were instrumental in his call as an evangelist. The way he carefully constructs his story, coupled with the impressive reports of the number of salvations in his revivals, suggests he designed his testimony in a way that would lend credibility to his ministry as an evangelist.

Another possible explanation for the differences may come from Roberts' traumatic experience of sickness within the context of a Pentecostal environment. While he was suffering with tuberculosis, Roberts testified that nearly every Sunday someone from the church or the community came to his house to pray for him, but at the same time would declare that it was God who put sickness upon him. Roberts notes that during this time, many Pentecostals not only questioned if healing was possible, they often felt it was "sacrilegious to call on God to help them individually."[19] This left Roberts

---

16. Roberts, *The Call*, 34; Roberts, *Expect a Miracle*, 32–33; E. M. and C. Roberts, *Our Ministry and Our Son Oral*, 58–59.

17. Roberts, Oral *Roberts' Life Story as Told by Himself*, 36, says nothing of his mental state except, "During those 163 days, I never had a good day." It is also possible that he refers to this episode when he describes his mental anguish from tuberculosis in his 1952 account. He says, "I lived in a state of unreality except for the suffering in my body. My mind was in a shadow and it felt as if I was away off from normal things…A stupor engulfed me and at last it was as if I didn't see or hear anyone." Roberts, *The Call*, 30–31.

18. Harrell, *Oral Roberts*, 449.

19. Roberts, *Expect a Miracle*, 29.

with feelings of bitterness and resentment towards his church. He recounts, "One Sunday afternoon, I got mad. The room was crowded with people and they were all trying to get me saved while in the same breath they were telling me God had afflicted me." Roberts finally sat up and said, "I don't believe it. I don't want to hear any more of it."[20] Roberts resented the fact that during this time his faith community saw sickness as a sign of disobedience and judgment from God and he refused to validate those assumptions. Roberts' belief that God was a good God who wanted to heal people did not fully develop until nearly a decade later.

A final explanation may have to do with the nature of the illness itself. Roberts' unwillingness to divulge his illness could be due to the stigma that came with tuberculosis, especially as a Native American. Roberts had contracted tuberculosis during a time in history when the disease was associated with social problems and class distinctions.[21] When the diagnosis came from his doctor, Roberts expressed fear that he would be confined to a sanatorium or left to die, and blamed "his mother's people" for passing that gene on to him.[22] Although he later fully embraced his Native American heritage, it is possible that at this time he was uneasy about publicly admitting this aspect of his story out of fear of how it would affect his popularity. Whatever the reasons for this differing account, this fascinating early version of Roberts' story provides a unique summary of his early life and provides an interesting addition to what we know about this giant in American religious history.

---

20. Roberts, *Oral Roberts' Life Story as Told by Himself*, 18.

21. For example, *The American Review of Tuberculosis* 2 (1918–1919), 234, notes that tuberculosis was seen as a lower-class disease. The journal describes the fate of infected workers who miss work in order to spend months in a sanatorium, only to be barred from work when they returned because of its "consumptive" nature and "danger to his fellows."

22. Roberts, *Expect a Miracle*, 26.

9

PENTECOSTAL ROOTS OF ORAL ROBERTS' HEALING MINISTRY

Vinson Synan

Abstract

This article delves into the development of the healing doctrine of the Pentecostal Holiness Church in which Oral Roberts was born, raised, and ordained to the ministry. Attention is given to the roots of healing teachings from both Europe and America, which were adopted by the Pentecostal movement. The main part of the paper describes the doctrinal statements on healing in the founding documents of the Pentecostal Holiness Church, the widespread acceptance of the Alexander Dowie position on refusing the use of doctors and medicine, the division over the use of remedies that produced the Congregational Holiness Church, and the later changes that emphasized the value of both prayer and medicine in the 1940s. This became the basic healing theology of Oral Roberts' ministry.

Introduction

It could truly be said that Oral Roberts was a son of the Pentecostal movement and a father of the Charismatic movement.[1] Born in 1918 and raised in the home of Ellis and Claudius Roberts, Pentecostal Holiness ministers, Roberts' formation was in classical Pentecostalism. The only exception was the seven years after he joined the Methodist Church in Stratford, Oklahoma, and a few months as a teenager when he also joined the Atoka, Oklahoma, Methodist Church, along with the entire basketball team. After almost dying from tuberculosis, he was healed in 1935 and returned to the Pentecostal Holiness Church where he flourished as an evangelist and pastor until 1947. In that year he began his healing ministry under huge tents that made him a national figure. By 1954, he went on television and became a household name as millions watched his dynamic

---

1. Reprinted with permission. Originally Vinson Synan, "Pentecostal Roots of Oral Roberts' Healing Ministry," *Spiritus: ORU Journal of Theology* 3, no. 2 (Fall 2018): 287–302.

sermons and his healing lines. His national television ministry planted the seeds of the Charismatic movement that broke out in all the mainline churches after 1960.[2]

Perhaps the pivotal event in his entire life was when Roberts was healed of severe tuberculosis in 1935. The first sign of his illness was when he fell on the floor playing basketball in Atoka, Oklahoma, hemorrhaging blood. He was taken from there to his home in Stratford, Oklahoma, where he lay bedridden, coughing up blood and wasting away for 163 days. During these days he was finally converted due to the passionate prayers of his father and mother. Before this, despite the prayers of his father, Oral had left home and lived a dissolute life in high school before falling ill. All of this changed when Elmer Roberts, Oral's older brother, took him to a tent meeting in nearby Ada, Oklahoma, where a Church of God of Prophecy evangelist, George W. Moncey, was holding a healing crusade. For the first time, Oral saw a healing line; Rev. Moncey's hands were laid on over 200 persons. After the prayer line ended, Moncey came to where Oral was sitting and said the unforgettable words: "'O Lord, heal this boy'"…and then he said, 'You foul tormenting disease, I command you in the name of Jesus Christ of Nazareth, come out of this boy. Loose him and let him go free.'"[3]

Immediately Oral said, "I felt the power of the Lord. It was like your hand striking me, like electricity going through me. It went into my lungs, went into my tongue, and all at once I could breathe. I could breathe all the way down. Before that when I tried to breathe all the way down I would hemorrhage."[4] This was the great turning point in Oral Roberts' life that would soon lead him into the Pentecostal Holiness ministry as pastor and evangelist and later into a worldwide healing ministry that would change the face of Christianity in the twentieth century.

Red-Letter Days

It was a red-letter day for the city of Tulsa, Oklahoma, and in the life of Oral Roberts when the dedication of the gleaming new Oral Roberts University

---

2. See Vinson Synan, "Oral Roberts: Son of Pentecostalism, Father of the Charismatic Movement," *Spiritus* 2, nos. 1–2 (2017), 5–21. The major sources for Oral Roberts' life are two of his five autobiographies, *The Call: An Autobiography* (Garden City, NJ: Doubleday, 1972) and *Expect a Miracle: My Life and Ministry, an Autobiography* (Nashville, TN: Thomas Nelson, 1995); also the biography by David Edwin Harrell, *Oral Roberts: An American Life* (Bloomington, IN, Indiana University Press, 1985). A short biography by Paul Chappell appeared in "Granville Oral Roberts," in *NIDPCM*, 1024–25. Roberts' career in the Pentecostal Holiness Church can be found in Vinson Synan, *Old Time Power* (Franklin Springs, GA: Advocate Press, 1973, 1998). For the dedication service see Harrell, *Oral Roberts*, 228–30.

3. Roberts, *Expect a Miracle*, 30–34. A striking description of this event can be found in Harrell, *Oral Roberts*, 3–7.

4. Roberts, *The Call*, 27–35.

took place on April 2, 1967. Over 18,000 friends came to hear Billy Graham dedicate the university while Roberts' bishop from the Pentecostal Holiness Church, Joseph A. Synan, read the Scriptures. The presence of these two men on the platform spoke volumes about Roberts' recent rise from the Pentecostal subculture in Oklahoma to become a world-renowned religious leader with millions of followers. After being lionized at Billy Graham's Berlin Congress for evangelists in 1966, Roberts invited the famous Graham to dedicate his university.[5]

Another red-letter day occurred on November 1, 1981, when Roberts dedicated his City of Faith hospital before a crowd of 13,000 followers who gathered in the nearby Mabee Center due to torrential rains outside. Instead of Billy Graham, Roberts' Charismatic friends filled the platform, including such luminaries as Demos Shakarian, Pat Robertson, and Oklahoma Governor George Nigh, who assisted in the dedication. Also on the platform was the Methodist educator, Jimmy Buskirk, whom Oral Roberts tapped to head the new ORU School of Theology after joining the Methodist Church in 1968.[6]

These two events highlighted the two major periods in Oral Roberts' life: his ministry as a Pentecostal Holiness evangelist and pastor, and his life as a Methodist leader in the burgeoning Charismatic Movement. Indeed, after becoming a well-known healing evangelist, Roberts claimed that his ministry began in 1947 when he held his first healing crusade in his hometown of Enid, Oklahoma. But as a matter of fact, Roberts' ministry began on the very night he was healed of tuberculosis in 1935. After the healing prayer by George Moncey, Roberts sprang to his feet, ran across the platform and exclaimed "I'm healed! I'm healed!" and preached his first sermon. He later said that the Lord spoke to him that very night saying, "Son, I am going to heal you, and you are going to take my healing power to your generation. You must build me a university and build it on my authority and the Holy Spirit."[7]

Oral Roberts and the Pentecostal Holiness Church

After he regained his strength, Roberts joined his father in preaching local revivals where his audiences were amazed at his eloquence although he had stuttered badly since childhood. After this, Oral went on to be licensed to preach in 1936 and ordained to the Pentecostal Holiness ministry in 1937.[8] In a few short years, Roberts gained attention as an effective evangelist

---

5. For the dedication see Harrell, *Oral Roberts*, 228–30.

6. Harrell, *Oral Roberts*, 295, 390–91; and Roberts, *Expect a Miracle*, 271–88. A long account of his joining the Methodist Church can be found in Roberts, *The Call*, 125–46.

7. Harrell, *Oral Roberts*, 5–7; Roberts, *Expect a Miracle*, 30–33.

8. Roberts, *Expect a Miracle*, 37. Also see "Minutes of the East Oklahoma Conference," 1937, 10.

preaching all over the nation and in faraway Canada. His meetings attracted overflow crowds with many hundreds converted.

He also published two books that helped to put him on the denominational map. They were *Salvation by the Blood* in 1938, and the *Drama of the End-Times* in 1941, both published by the Pentecostal Holiness Church. In addition to this, he was elected to represent his East Oklahoma Conference in the denomination's General Conferences in Franklin Springs, Georgia, in 1941, and in Oklahoma City in 1945. All this marked young Roberts as a young rising star in the Pentecostal Holiness Church.[9]

Figure 3: Oral Roberts, 1948, (second from left) next to IPHC Bishop J. A. Synan (second from right); Bishop Synan was the father of Vinson Synan. Used with permission. Copyright Synan Collection, Holy Spirit Resource Center, Oral Roberts University.

During these years, although Roberts regularly testified to his healing experience in 1935, he seemed to be more interested in evangelism and prophecy than in divine healing. His sermons bristled with expositions and defenses of the five "cardinal doctrines" taught by the Pentecostal Holiness Church: salvation, sanctification, baptism in the Holy Spirit with the initial evidence of speaking in tongues, divine healing as in the atonement, and the imminent second coming of Christ. He also became a master of the dynamic Pentecostal style of preaching. Two of his models were Joseph Synan, his bishop, and G. H. Montgomery, editor of the Pentecostal Holiness *Advocate*, both of whom honed their skills in camp meetings and revivals in local churches. At this point Roberts was clearly a creature of his denomination.

For six years, from 1941 to 1947, Roberts pastored Pentecostal Holiness congregations in Shawnee and Enid in Oklahoma as well as in Toccoa, Georgia, and Fuqua Springs-Varina, North Carolina. He was successful and dissatisfied at the same time as a local pastor. All the churches grew under his leadership and his pay rose to one of the highest levels in the church. It was in the parsonage of the Enid Pentecostal Holiness Church that Roberts received his definite call to the healing ministry in 1947. He said that he heard the Lord say, "Son, don't be like other men, don't be like any other

---

9. Harrell, *Oral Roberts*, 35–54.

denomination. Be like Jesus, and heal the people as he did." It was also in Enid that he held his first healing service, which eventually launched him into becoming one of the most popular evangelists in the history of the United States.[10]

In 1947 Oral Roberts published his third book, *If You Need Healing—Do These Things*, and the next year began publication of his monthly magazine *Healing Waters*. At the same time he purchased his first "Tent Cathedral," which seated some 3,000 persons. He later bought a much larger tent that seated 12,500. In May 1951, Roberts was featured along with Billy Graham in *Life* magazine as "the loudest and splashiest revivalist to appear since Billy Graham."[11] Roberts' attractions were not only his spellbinding sermons, but his healing line where hundreds of people came each night to feel the healing touch of Oral Roberts' hand. He now was the most noted healing evangelist since the death of Aimee Semple McPherson in 1943. All of this success came while Roberts was an ordained minister in the Pentecostal Holiness Church.[12]

Roots of the Healing Movement

As a son of the Pentecostal Holiness Church, Oral Roberts received his under-standing of divine healing from his parents and his church. Long before the birth of the Pentecostal Holiness Church, the doctrine of divine healing had been developed by leaders of the American Holiness movement who were influenced by such European healing teachers as Presbyterian Edward Irving in London (1830), Lutheran Johann Christoph Blumhardt in Germany (1843), Dorothea Trudel in Switzerland (1851), and Otto Stockmayer in Switzerland (1867). The most influential book coming out of Europe in this period was Stockmayer's *Sickness and the Gospel*, which pioneered the idea that physical healing for the body was included in the overall atonement.[13]

American Holiness writers were not far behind in producing a flood of books on healing. These included: William Boardman's 1881 book *The Lord that Healeth Thee*; Kelso Carter's 1884 book titled *The Atonement for Sin and Sickness: Or a Full Salvation for Soul and Body*; and Adoniram J. Gordon's *The Ministry of Healing*. Added to these writers were such healing practitioners as Dr. Charles Cullis of Boston, Massachusetts and Alexander Dowie of Chicago, Illinois. By saying that healing for the body was in the atonement, these writers were elevating divine healing into the center of the gospel mystery. In a way they were placing healing on the same level as salvation for

---

10. Roberts, *Expect a Miracle*, 75–82; Roberts, *The Call*, 37–44; Harrell, 55–69.

11. See "A New Revivalist," *Life* (May 30, 1951): 73–78.

12. Harrell, *Oral Roberts*, 80–170.

13. See Stanley Burgess and Paul Lewis, eds., *A Light to the Nations* (Eugene, OR: Pickwick, 2017), 286–300.

the soul. Dowie went much further than the others by teaching that true believers should not only pray for healing, but that they should not take any medicines or see any doctors, but "trust God for their bodies." To Dowie, doctors were "poisoners general and surgical butchers" and "Doctors, Drugs, and Devils" are "the Foes of Christ the Healer."[14]

When the Pentecostal Movement began after 1901, a large proportion of Pentecostals agreed with Dowie and promised God that they would never resort to doctors or medicines, but rely only on prayer for healing. The Dowie position was later immortalized in the Black Pentecostal spiritual "Come on in the Room":

Come on in the room,
Come on in the room;
Jesus is my doctor
and He writes out all of my prescriptions,
He gives me all of my medicine in the room.[15]

Healing Doctrine in the Pentecostal Holiness Church

The Pentecostal Holiness Church in which Oral Roberts was born and raised was a merger of two holiness churches with roots in the nineteenth-century Holiness movement. The first was the Fire-Baptized Holiness Church founded by former Primitive Baptist preacher Benjamin Hardin Irwin in 1898 in Anderson, South Carolina. It was an interracial church that offered ordination for women equal to that of men. Irwin became known as a healing evangelist who drew large crowds to his meetings in America and Canada. All the Pentecostal Holiness Churches in Oklahoma began as part of the Fire-Baptized Holiness Church.[16]

The other church was the Pentecostal Holiness Church founded in 1900 in Fayetteville, North Carolina, by Abner B. Crumpler, a Methodist evangelist. Both churches became Pentecostal in 1907–08 from direct contacts with Azusa Street and accepted tongues as the "initial evidence" of the baptism in the Holy Spirit. Both churches also were strong advocates of divine healing "as in the atonement." In 1911, the two churches merged and

---

14. J. Alexander Dowie, "Doctors, Drugs and Devils, Or, the Foes of Christ the Healer," *Physical Culture* (April 1895): 81–86.

15. Lyrics from https://www.elyrics.net. Editor's update: Covered by Georgia Mass Choir, "Come on in the Room," https://www.invubu.com/music/show/song/Georgia-Mass-Choir/Come-On-In-the-Room.html, accessed July 23, 2025. With slightly different lyrics but additional verses, see *African American Heritage Hymnal*, "Come on in my Room," https://hymnary.org/text/come_on_in_my_room, accessed July 23, 2025.

16. For the story of Benjamin Hardin and the Fire-Baptized Holiness Church, see Vinson Synan and Dan Woods, *The Many Lives of Benjamin Hardin Irwin* (Lexington, KY: Emeth Press, 2017). All Pentecostal Holiness Churches in Oklahoma were organized out of the Fire-Baptized Holiness Church in Oklahoma City, which met in the Blue Front Saloon. After the 1911 merger, they took the name "Pentecostal Holiness."

took the name of the smaller group—The Pentecostal Holiness Church.[17] Both churches included strong doctrinal statements on divine healing in their founding documents. The Constitution of the Fire-Baptized Holiness Church, first adopted in 1898, contained the following short statement on divine healing: "We believe also in divine healing as in the atonement. (Isa. 53:3–5; Matt. 8:16, 17; Mark 16:14–18; James 5:14–16; Ex. 15:26)."[18]

The Pentecostal Holiness statement was one of the most liberal ones for the times. Although it accepted divine healing as in the atonement, it also allowed its members to use doctors and medicines in addition to prayer. In Section I of the Articles of Faith, it read:

> The healing of the body of its sickness is a blessed provision of the atonement which is to be appropriated according to James 5:14–15, and other Scriptures. We do not consider it an evidence of sin or a mark or divine displeasure because a person is sick or employs a medical aid. Neither do we believe that it is an evidence in itself that a person is of God because he is healed in answer to prayer.[19]

When the two churches merged in 1911, the language of the Fire-Baptized Holiness Church was adopted, indicating that the newly-merged church rejected the more liberal view on healing and opened the door for its members to adopt Dowie's view of no doctors or medicines.

The 1921 "Remedy" Controversy

As time went on, the Dowie position became the accepted view of the church leadership, as well as a probable majority of church members. Many took vows of never taking medicines or seeing doctors for themselves or for their families. They would "trust God for their bodies" for life. The popular testimonies of the time were: "Praise God, I am saved, sanctified, filled with the Holy Ghost, and have trusted God for my body for 20 years," the last claim referring to how long they had refused to see doctors or take medicines. One leader, Samuel D. Page, reported that he had been "saved and healed" for twenty-seven years.[20]

Inevitably, some passionate believers ran afoul of the law for refusing medical treatment for dying spouses or children. One leader, F. M. Britton, was threatened with arrest in South Carolina for allowing his wife and a son to die in agony after Britton "refused medicine" for them.[21] Some top leaders

---

17. For the founding of Pentecostal Holiness Church, see Synan, *Old Time Power*, 68–92.

18. "Constitution of the Fire-Baptized Holiness Church," 1905, 3.

19. "The Discipline of the Pentecostal Holiness Church" (n.p., n.d.). [Hand-written notes on the cover say "Possibly 1909"] (A. H. Butler), "Before 1911" (W. E. Morris), 12.

20. Synan, *Old Time Power*, 162.

21. F. M. Britton, *Pentecostal Truth* (Royston: Publishing House of the Pentecostal Holiness Church, 1919), 244–46.

in the church, such as Joseph H. King and George F. Taylor, made similar vows and refused to see doctors or take medicines. But there were others who disagreed with the majority view, including Hugh Bowling, Superintendent of the Georgia Conference, and his friend Watson Sorrow, a leading evangelist. In 1919 Bowling published an article in the church paper, *The Advocate*, stating that "it was no sin at all to take 'remedies' and that going to a doctor implied no lack of faith in the patient."[22]

This led to a firestorm on the pages of *The Advocate* with hot letters and articles following pro and con on the issue. In defending his position, Bowling wrote in April 1920:

> I do not believe those who get sick and use no remedies and drag around for weeks and after so long a time get well are divinely healed, but that nature alone restored them. I do not believe in lying about divine healing. I do not believe that sickness is an evidence of unbelief. I do not believe that healing is paralleled in the atonement.[23]

This was the last straw for Taylor and King. In short order, Bowling and Sorrow were summoned to Franklin Springs to stand trial for their views on divine healing. When they failed to appear for the trial, the two men were expelled from the church, not for preaching false doctrine, but for failure to appear for the trial. But they did not go alone. On January 21, 1921, Bowling and Sorrow took fourteen churches out of the denomination and organized the Congregational Holiness Church in the town of High Shoals, Georgia.[24]

As a matter of interest, both King and Taylor changed their minds and at the end of their lives made use of doctors and medicines. In fact, the Pentecostal Holiness Church Manual added a "Doctrinal Emphasis" written by Bishop King in 1945, which, after reaffirming that divine healing was "wrought solely by the application of the atonement to the body," added the following statement:

> Natural means viewed as a product of the law of recovery are not to be despised. Neither are we to look upon their use as sinful on the part of believers in Christ. The healing of Calvary's stream is the "better way," and the way to secure complete and permanent healing of all sickness and disease.[25]

Added to this was the doctrinal "Amplification" written by Bishop J. A. Synan in 1961, which presented the same view as King. He stated:

> And while we do not condemn the use of medical means in the treatment of physical disease, we do believe in, practice, and commend to our people

---

22. Synan, *Old Time Power*, 163.
23. Hugh Bowling, *The Advocate* (April 1920): 3–5.
24. Synan, *Old Time Power*, 165–66. Also see B. L. Cox, *History and Doctrine of the Congregational Holiness Church* (Greenwood: n.p., 1958), 7–9.
25. The Pentecostal Holiness Church Manual, 1989, 35–36.

the laying on of hands by the elders or leaders of the church, the anointing with oil in the name of the Lord, and the offering of prayers for the healing of the sick.[26]

As a postscript to the "remedies controversy" that divided the church in 1921, the original cause of the division was eventually resolved and the Pentecostal Holiness Church admitted that they were on the wrong side of the question. But all attempts to heal the division that produced the Congregational Holiness Church, including apologies, failed to heal the breach between the two denominations that have since gone their separate ways.

Oral Roberts was born in 1918 so the division in his church took place when he was three years old. By the time of his healing in 1935, he felt that the teaching on divine healing had waned somewhat among Pentecostals in the parts of Oklahoma where he lived. So when he began his healing ministry in 1947, Roberts had formed his healing theology from his roots in the Pentecostal Holiness Church. In short, by that time the church still believed that divine healing was provided for in the atonement and that sick persons should first ask for healing prayer with the laying on of hands, but that medicine and doctors could also be used to hasten the healing process. Therefore, healing prayer and medical means were both acceptable to members of the church.

Oral Roberts' Innovations

Adding to the teachings of his church, Roberts began to read widely and expanded his theological and pastoral horizons. Two secular books that deeply affected his future outlook were Dale Carnegie's famous book *How to Win Friends and Influence People*, which was recommended by his friend Lee Braxton. Another influential and controversial book that influenced Roberts was Napoleon Hill's *Think and Grow Rich*, a secular handbook on how to envision your way to wealth.[27] Roberts also was influenced by some of the healing evangelists of the middle 1940s, including Thomas Wyatt from Portland, Oregon and William Branham from Jeffersonville, Indiana. There is a famous photo of Oral Roberts standing with Branham and Gordon Lindsay, in Kansas City in 1948, at the outset of Roberts' healing ministry. These evangelists challenged Roberts to launch out as a major healing evangelist.[28]

Roberts soon developed some new approaches to his healing ministry. He continued the laying on of hands as he had been taught, and indeed laid

---

26. The Pentecostal Holiness Church Manual, 1989, 47.

27. Roberts, *Expect a Miracle*, 123. Also see Harrell, *Oral Roberts*, 115.

28. For the photo see Paul Chappell, "Healing Movements," in *DPCM*, 353–74.

hands on more than one million persons in his healing lines. He also added that he had special healing power in his right hand and that this "point of contact" brought special healing power to the sick persons to whom he ministered. He also erected special prayer tents near the main tent where he could go and pray for people in wheelchairs who could not make it to the healing lines.[29]

Perhaps his most important innovation was bringing his healing services to television audiences in 1954. Now millions of people who might never enter his tent could hear his sermons and witness his healing prayers in their own living rooms. The results were electric. Multiplied millions of Roman Catholics, Methodists, Baptists, Presbyterians, Episcopalians, and others could witness dynamic Pentecostal religion in their own homes. In time, Roberts' television programs made him the most popular television evangelist of his time.[30]

Another major innovation was the founding of Oral Roberts University (ORU) in 1965. Roberts had been interested in higher education before the beginning of his healing ministry. In 1946 he had helped his friend R. O. Corvin to found the Southwestern Pentecostal Holiness College in Oklahoma City and briefly served on the faculty. He also raised money for Emmanuel College in Georgia in the late 1940s. The founding mission for Oral Roberts University was summarized in Roberts' visionary statement that was written on a napkin while dining with Pat Robertson in Norfolk, Virginia, in 1960:

> Raise up your students to hear my voice, to go where the light is dim, where my voice is heard small and my healing power is not known, even to the uttermost bounds of the earth. Their work will exceed yours and in this I am well-pleased.[31]

After the dedication of ORU in 1967 with Billy Graham as the main speaker, ORU grew to some 5,000 students at its height in the 1970s.[32] Perhaps Roberts' most original innovation was the building of the three-towered City of Faith hospital that was dedicated in 1981. Here he planned to "merge prayer and medicine" in a profound new way. This slogan was exactly the position of the Pentecostal Holiness Church on healing after the "remedies" controversy of the early 1920s. Although the City of Faith was a

---

29. Eventually Roberts issued prayer cards that admitted people to the prayer lines. All others were sent to the prayer tent. See Harrell, *Oral Roberts*, 96–97.

30. Harrell, *Oral Roberts*, 171–72. Also see Roberts, *Expect a Miracle*, 142–59. Roberts was encouraged to go into television by his friend, Rex Humbard, who had pioneered television ministry since 1952 from his church in Akron, Ohio.

31. See Roberts, *Expect a Miracle*, 161–62. There are two versions of where the dinner took place. Harrell says it was in Richmond, Virginia, while Oral Roberts says it was in Norfolk, Virginia. See Harrell, *Oral Roberts*, 207; Roberts, *Expect a Miracle*, 161.

32. ORU story in Harrell, *Oral Roberts*, 199–252.

financial disaster resulting in the closing of the hospital in 1989, the university later converted the towers into office space and maintained the property as an endowment. It was later renamed CityPlex Towers.[33]

What Roberts Retained from His Pentecostal Formation

When he joined the United Methodist Church in 1968, Roberts declared that he would still and always be a Pentecostal. To his new pastor, Finis Crutchfield, at the Boston Avenue United Methodist Church, and his new bishop, Angie Smith, Roberts said, "there will be no change in my standard of the Full Gospel message or of my life, my ministry, or of ORU." He later elaborated, "I was a classical Pentecostal and charismatic before I joined the Methodist Church. I was the same during the nineteen years I was in the Methodist Church."[34]

Becoming a Methodist was probably the most controversial action of his entire life, causing puzzlement in the press, among liberal Methodists, and among his friends in the Pentecostal Holiness Church. Indeed, his financial support dropped drastically at first as Pentecostals withdrew their support. But in time his new Methodist supporters more than made up the shortfall, especially after Roberts began his prime-time television shows in 1969. All went well with Roberts' ministry for several years after he joined the Methodist Church, but underneath the surface, opposition to Roberts being a Methodist minister began to grow among Methodist leaders who were embarrassed by Roberts' controversial public image. In 1987, *Tulsa World* stated that Roberts was "cast out of the Methodist Church by a special committee of leaders."

After this, Roberts organized the International Charismatic Bible Ministries (ICBM) organization in where he could spend his time with his Pentecostal and Charismatic friends until his death in 2009 at 91 years of age.[35] In 1995, Roberts wrote positively about his upbringing and ministry for almost fifty years in the Pentecostal Holiness Church: "I had become a spoon-fed denominational preacher. I had accept-ed about 95 percent of everything the denomination taught and did without questioning why or studying the Word of God for myself to 'see if these things were true.' I had become an echo, not a 'voice of one crying in the wilderness.'" He went on to describe what he received from the church on the matter of divine healing, which he felt was not being adequately emphasized at that time.

---

33. City of Faith story in Harrell, *Oral Roberts*, 381–96; Roberts, *Expect a Miracle*, 251–70.

34. Harrell, *Oral Roberts*, 294; Roberts, *Expect a Miracle*, 322.

35. See Synan, "Oral Roberts: Son of Pentecostalism," 5–21. For ICBM, see Paul Chappell, "Granville Oral Roberts," *NIDPCM*, 1024–25.

He said, "Whether by divine design or by my belonging to that denomination and submitting wholly to it, that calling of taking God's healing power to my generation became submerged." He added: That denomination had a little book called *The Discipline*, and in it were printed the fundamental doctrines and practices of that church. It included a strong section on the healing of the sick being in the atonement of Christ on the cross. That was a powerful doctrine and statement of purpose. There was, however, no major emphasis on healing as being a practice of the church that I could observe, other than a belief that if you got sick, you were to have faith, and if you could hold out, you were not to go to a doctor I do know one thing: I became intensely loyal to believing in the exclusivity of that denomination, although I differed with it on medical science as a viable part of what God has placed on earth for our better health, and the small-ness of its vision.[36]

Figure 4: Vinson Synan (left) with Oral Roberts (far right) at a meeting of International Charismatic Bible Ministries (Edwin Cole, center). Roberts' handwritten remarks to Dr. Synan reads, "Vinson, thank you for your word at the June 1986 CBM founding conference. Your partner, Oral." Used by permission. Copyright Synan Collection, Holy Spirit Resource Center, Oral Roberts University.

He further went on to say:

> I cannot blame the Pentecostal Holiness Church, the denomination I belonged to for the first years of my ministry. The people of that denomination were there long before I was converted and healed and given the call of the healing ministry. They had paid the price to form their own beliefs and denomination and had worked hard for it. In many ways they were a blessing to me. They helped form the patterns of my life in learning the value of being baptized in the Holy Spirit, of living a holy life, of learning loyalty and developing integrity. I made lasting friendships among the people.[37]

---

36. Roberts, *Expect a Miracle*, 376.
37. Roberts, *Expect a Miracle*, 375.

Conclusion

Looking back over his life, one can see an amazing simplicity and consistency in Roberts' life and ministry. Despite his worldwide acclaim, his amazing accomplishments, and his persuasive influence on American religious life, one must agree with his biographer David Edwin Harrell who said in his *Oral Roberts: An American Life*:

> Oral had not changed. He still believed what Ellis and Claudia had taught him in the little [Pentecostal Holiness] churches of Southeast Oklahoma. He believed in miracles, in visions and anointed prayer cloths. He was still that marveling, faith filled little Oklahoma boy who had clamped his hand on thousands of heads.[38]

---

38. Harrell, *Oral Roberts*, 436.

10

CHARLES STANLEY'S PENTECOSTAL ROOTS

Vinson Synan

Abstract

Charles Stanley, pastor of First Baptist Church in Atlanta, Georgia, is probably best known for his television program *In Touch with Dr. Charles Stanley*. Yet, few know about Stanley's early formation in Pentecostal circles. This article examines Stanley's early formation in these circles and the role these Pentecostal roots have played in his ministry as a Southern Baptist minister.

Introduction

Charles Stanley, Pastor of the First Baptist Church in Atlanta, Georgia, is probably the best-known Baptist minister in America since the death of Billy Graham.[1] His television ministry, *In Touch with Dr. Charles Stanley*, is seen in nearly every major television market and viewed by millions of people each week. By 2006, *In Touch* could be heard in 107 languages worldwide. He has also authored over forty books, many which have been religious bestsellers. His publisher, Thomas Nelson, estimates that over 3.5 million copies of his books have been sold. He also served two terms as President of the Southern Baptist Convention. Under his leadership Atlanta First Baptist Church has grown to over 15,000 members. With his strong Baptist identity, few people know about Stanley's Pentecostal roots, which have deeply influenced his life and ministry.[2]

---

1. Reprinted with permission. Originally published (post-humous) as Synan, "Charles Stanley's Pentecostal Roots," *Spiritus: ORU Journal of Theology* 5, no. 2 (Fall 2020): 275–86. The late Charles Stanley passed April 18, 2023. He was still alive at the time of this writing.

2. Charles Stanley's most autobiographical books are: Charles Stanley, *Courageous Faith: My Story from a Life of Obedience* (New York: Howard Books, 2016); Charles Stanley, *How to Handle Adversity* (Nashville, TN: Thomas Nelson, 1989); Charles Stanley, *The Wonderful Spirit Filled Life* (Nashville, TN: Thomas Nelson, 1995); and Charles Stanley, *How to Listen to God* (Nashville, TN: Oliver-Nelson, 1985). Two major histories of the Pentecostal Holiness Church are: Synan, *The Old Time Power: A Centennial History of the International Pentecostal*

Charles Frazier Stanley was born on September 25, 1932, in the rural farming community of Dry Fork, Virginia, near the city of Danville, Virginia. His parents, Charley and Rebecca Stanley, were members of the local Emmanuel Pentecostal Holiness Church, a congregation co-founded by his grandfather George Washington Stanley.[3] Since his father died when Charles was only nine months old, he never knew his father and was raised by his mother who later moved to Danville and worked in the Dan River Mills to support her family. Despite their poverty, Rebecca faithfully paid tithes to her church. Charles Stanley was deeply moved by his mother's prayers and deep faith in God. As he grew up, Stanley delivered newspapers to 125 homes in Danville, both morning and evening editions, to add to the family income. He arose at 5:00 A.M. for his first deliveries. As a result he earned poor grades in school, which he deeply regretted. During this time Stanley suffered from severe loneliness since he was by himself at home much of the time.[4]

Charles Stanley as a Young Pentecostal

In his teenage years, Charles was a member of the North Danville Pentecostal Holiness Church on Main Street, pastored by F. A. Dail, a pioneer Pentecostal Holiness minister. Here he heard sermons on the "cardinal doctrines" of the church, which included salvation, sanctification as a second blessing, the baptism in the Holy Spirit evidenced by speaking in tongues, divine healing, and the imminent second coming of Christ. He also saw the fervent altar calls where people loudly sought for the "deeper experiences." Dail was known for supporting the owners in the hard-fought Dan River Mills strike in 1930–1931 while pastoring the Schoolfield Pentecostal Holiness Church near Danville. Dan River Mills was the largest textile mill in the nation and a prime target for labor unions. The union lost the battle. Because of his outspoken sermons against the unions and the violence of the strikers, his church was dynamited. A few months later, after the 4,000 workers returned to work, the mill owners donated money for Dail to build a new church.[5]

At the age of 12, Stanley was converted to Christ in the Danville Church and began a Christian life of deep prayer and devotion. Despite his active prayer life, he later confessed, "I spent the early years of my Christian life

---

Holiness Church (Franklin Springs, GA: Lifesprings Resources, 1998); and A. D. Beacham, Jr., *A Brief History of the Pentecostal Holiness Church* (Franklin Springs, GA: Lifesprings Resources, 1983).

3. G. W. Stanley reported on the Dry Fork revivals in the church paper. See *The Pentecostal Holiness Advocate* (August 1, 1918): 7, and (January 16, 1919): 12.

4. George W. Stanley, *My Life's Experiences for God* (Franklin Springs, GA: Publishing House, n.d.), 20–25. Also see C. Stanley, *Courageous Faith*, 9–25.

5. Synan, *Old Time Power*, 188.

struggling. Call it carnal; call it fleshly; call it whatever you wish. It was anything but wonderful."[6] In spite of his struggles, young Stanley also felt a definite call to preach. It is not known if he experienced second blessing sanctification or the baptism in the Holy Spirit with speaking in tongues, as taught by his church, at this time. The three most important influences in his life in this period were his mother, Rebecca, his Sunday school teacher, Craig Stowe, and his grandfather, George Washington Stanley.

Early Influences

Stanley's mother, Rebecca, was a staunch Pentecostal woman who always led family prayer on their knees with young Charles. For the rest of his life, Stanley would always pray on his knees at bedtime. His mother worked hard to support him on her meager salary at Dan River Mills. As a child Charles and his mother lived in fourteen different rented houses in Danville. Another great influence on young Charles was his Sunday school teacher, Craig Stowe. A very kind and loving man, Stowe took an interest in Stanley and even bought newspapers from him on the streets although he already had the paper at home. Stowe was a prominent layman in the Western North Carolina Conference of the Pentecostal Holiness Church serving as Sunday School Director for the Conference. Stowe was the father figure and role model that young Charles never had at home. In later years Stanley said that Stowe was "an incredible man of faith whom I loved dearly and inspired me profoundly." He also called Stowe his "spiritual father."[7]

His Grandfather, George Washington Stanley

An even greater influence was his preacher grandfather, George Washington Stanley (1876–1965), who was born near Siler City, North Carolina. George was a pioneer Pentecostal Holiness preacher who was instrumental in planting eighteen Pentecostal Holiness churches in Virginia and North Carolina, including the Dry Fork Church where Charles was born and the Danville church where he grew up. As an impoverished and illiterate young man, his grandfather was called to preach and learned to read by reading the Bible. George was raised and converted in a Baptist church but was soon expelled when he began to preach the Wesleyan doctrine of "entire sanctification." His first holiness influence was in a tent meeting with a Pilgrim Holiness preacher where he was sanctified in 1898. He never went to high school or college although he once considered attending W. B. Godby's Pilgrim Holiness Bible School in Cincinnati, Ohio. George Stanley preached

---

6. C. Stanley, *Wonderful Spirit Filled Life*, xi.
7. C. Stanley, *Courageous Faith*, 48.

his first sermon in 1902. Later he was licensed to preach in the Wesleyan Methodist Church.[8]

In 1906, George heard about the Pentecostal experience and soon was baptized in the Holy Spirit and spoke in tongues. Because of his tongues experience, he was excommunicated from the Wesleyan Methodist Church but continued preaching under his gospel tent. In time he came into contact with the Pentecostal Holiness people in Mount Olive, North Carolina. He was ordained in the North Carolina Conference of the Pentecostal Holiness Church in 1911 and became a powerful preacher, pastor, and church planter.[9] In time he bought a larger tent and evangelized wherever he could find an opportunity. Among the other strong Pentecostal Holiness churches he planted were the Buena Vista Church and the Natural Bridge Church in Virginia.[10]

Young Charles idolized his grandfather and loved to talk with him and glean wisdom from his years of ministry. He said of him, "[T]his is the most spiritual person I've ever talked to. He impacted my life profoundly. I was like a sponge soaking up everything he said." Charles described his grandfather as:

> …a quiet and easygoing man, but when he got to preaching, there was no stopping him. He was absolutely on fire, bold, fervent, and courageous for the Lord. The Spirit of God shook that small Pentecostal church and the people prayed loudly and long after he was done preaching the message. God worked through him in an awesome way.[11]

One thing his grandfather told him stuck with Charles Stanley for his entire life. It was, "Charles, if God tells you to run your head through a brick wall, you head for the wall, and when you get there, God will make a hole for it."[12] G. W. Stanley was a man who had dreams and visions and claimed the gift of healing. Once a girl born blind was healed after he said, "I demand that your eyes be opened." They both began to speak in tongues. He also promised that he would "trust God with my body" for healing. Although he suffered many maladies, he refused to take medicine for forty-five years.[13]

---

8. G. W. Stanley, *My Life's Experiences for God*, 4–8, 12.

9. See "Proceedings of the 12th Annual Convention of the Pentecostal Holiness Church of North Carolina, 1911," 6. He was listed as pastor of the Star Mission and the Maple Springs Mission.

10. In the Buena Vista revival, G. W. Stanley reported the following: 150 saved, 125 sanctified, 80 baptized in the Holy Spirit, 122 water baptized, and 146 joined the new church. See G. W. Stanley, *My Life's Experiences for God*, 25–27. Also see "The First 50 Years with the First Pentecostal Holiness Church, Buena Vista, Virginia, 1920–1970," n.d., n.p., IPHC Archives, Bethany, OK; and "History Highlights of the Natural Bridge Pentecostal Holiness Church: 50th Anniversary, 1919–1969," n.d., n.p., IPHC Archives, Bethany, OK.

11. C. Stanley, *Courageous Faith*, 50–51.

12. C. Stanley, *Courageous Faith*, 54.

13. G. W. Stanley, *My Life's Experiences*, 30–31.

Once, while trying to earn money to buy a tent, he had a vision of a town with a house on the corner. He was told to:

> …get on a train, go to a certain town, get off the train, and go to the south side of town. He showed me a house with rose bushes and trees in the yard. It was located on the corner of the street. The Lord showed me that I should go there, to go down the hall, and in the door to the left. There he showed me an old lady sitting in the corner. There was a handbag on the wall and there I would get the money to buy my tent.[14]

G. W. Stanley followed the directions exactly and when he entered the door, a woman handed him a bag with 300 dollar bills inside. Just the amount he needed to buy his first tent.

Life Changes

Charles Stanley's life changed drastically when his mother married John Hall when Charles was nine years old. Rebecca's new husband was a rude, bitter, and abusive alcoholic. Charles said about this situation, "I never felt completely safe walking into our home. I was never sure what he might do or what would set off his uncontrolled anger. So when I was in the house I wanted to be out of it." It was then that he would go down to the church basement where "I could pray all I wanted to—as loudly and for however long I needed to just as I learned to do in the Pentecostal Holiness Church. But down in that basement it was just me and God."[15]

After he was converted, young Charles definitely felt a call to preach, so he carefully studied and read his Bible looking forward to preaching his first sermon. That came when he was seventeen years old in the North Danville Pentecostal Holiness Church. He felt led to preach from Genesis 3 on the topic "Where Art Thou?" Before the service his mother noticed that he was concerned about speaking before such a large crowd, so she quoted a passage to him from Joshua 1:7–9 that was to follow him throughout his life. It ended with these words: "Be strong and courageous. Do not tremble or be dismayed, for the Lord your God is with you wherever you go." He remembered what happened next: "As soon as I walked up to the pulpit the message began to flow. God gave me the words to say in a manner that surprised and delighted me. I can't express the absolute joy I felt knowing that the Holy Spirit was in control and the Father was speaking through me."[16]

Soon after this, Charles was influenced by his high school girlfriend, Barbara Ann, to attend the nearby Moffett Memorial Baptist Church pastored

---

14. G. W. Stanley, *My Life's Experiences*, 16–17.
15. C. Stanley, *Courageous Faith*, 34.
16. C. Stanley, *Courageous Faith*, 72.

by David Hammock. He found many of his high school friends at the church and enjoyed the sermons of pastor Hammock. Charles explained his reason for becoming a Baptist: "[T]he Pastor of the Pentecostal Holiness Church, F. A. Dail, had retired and I was longing for a change. So I asked my mother if she approved, and she replied, '[I]f you can live as holy a life in the Baptist church as in the Pentecostal Holiness Church, then it's all right with me.'"[17]

Since he was called to preach Charles wanted to go to college to prepare for the ministry, but he had no money. The people in the Pentecostal Holiness Church had shown little interest in raising money for him. However, the kindly Baptist pastor arranged for Charles to receive a full-ride scholarship to attend the Baptist-related university in Richmond, from which he graduated in 1954. Here, despite the extremely liberal professors, his reluctant conversion from Pentecostalism to Southern Baptist theology occurred.[18]

Later in seminary in discussions with a fellow student, Charles referred to the Holy Spirit as an "it." He was sternly told that the Holy Spirit was a "He," not an "it." Later Stanley said, "I grew up in a church where He was never mentioned. My pastor didn't explain who He was or preach sermons about Him. In seminary I learned that the Holy Spirit was a 'He' and not an 'it.' Having been raised in the Pentecostal Holiness Church, I had always heard the Holy Spirit or the Holy Ghost referred to as 'it.'"[19] Yet he remembered seekers at the altars fervently praying for the baptism in the Holy Spirit with the expected Pentecostal sign of speaking in tongues. Also at Richmond he met his wife Anna Margaret Johnson and they were married in 1955. Later they both attended Southwestern Baptist Theological Seminary in Fort Worth, Texas.[20]

In time, Stanley rejected his Pentecostal upbringing with the strong emphasis on second blessing sanctification and the baptism in the Holy Spirit as a "third blessing." On the other hand, he became a strong proponent of the Baptist view on eternal security and the teaching that baptism in the Holy Spirit came at conversion without the evidence of speaking in tongues. In fact, he became a fervent cessationist despite his Pentecostal roots.[21] To complete his transition, Charles Stanley was ordained into the ministry of the Southern Baptist denomination on August 19, 1956, at the Moffett Memorial Baptist Church in Danville, Virginia.[22]

---

17. C. Stanley, *Courageous Faith*, 70.

18. C. Stanley, *Courageous Faith*, 74.

19. C. Stanley, *The Wonderful Spirit Filled Life*, 13–17.

20. C. Stanley, *Courageous Faith*, 79–84.

21. See C. Stanley, *Wonderful Spirit Filled Life*. In quoting the list of the gifts of the Spirit in 1 Cor 12:1–4 he omits tongues and interpretation of tongues, 127, and he agrees with Billy Graham that "there is only one baptism with the Holy Spirit in the life of every believer, and that takes place at the moment of conversion," 157–158.

22. C. Stanley, *Courageous Faith*, 74.

Baptist Pastorates and Deeper Experiences

For the next few years, from 1957 to 1969, Stanley pastored four Baptist churches where he honed his preaching style. They were: the Fruitland Baptist Church in North Carolina; Fairburn, Ohio; and later in Miami and Bartow, Florida. In 1957 while in Fruitland, Stanley felt a need for a deeper work of God in his life and began earnestly seeking to be filled with the Holy Spirit. Although he testified to being baptized in the Holy Spirit when he was converted, he believed that one could still be "filled" with the Spirit at any time. After much impassioned prayer while lying on his back, he suddenly experienced a "life changing moment" of being filled with the Holy Spirit. After "I had prayed, begged, bargained, and pleaded…I was overwhelmed with a sense of confidence and assurance.…I didn't see stars or hear a voice, I didn't speak in tongues."[23] He called it his "D-Day." "I wept, overwhelmed with joy that I no longer had to live the Christian life or do ministry in my own strength." He added, "[B]ut from that moment forward, everything in my life was transformed—my preaching, service, leadership, problem solving—everything." Even his wife noticed the difference. "It's like my husband is a different man," she said.[24]

Seven years later, in 1964, while pastoring the Miami First Baptist Church, Stanley had another vivid spiritual experience that Pentecostals would call a work of entire sanctification. He said, "For a long time I had a hunch that something was missing in my life but I couldn't put my finger on it. I had a nagging suspicion that there was more to the Christian life than I was experiencing but I didn't know where to turn for the answer." He went on to say that there were "several secret sins in my life. Things that no one knew about. Nothing out of the ordinary. But things I knew were displeasing to God."[25]

After reading a book by V. Raymond Edman, *They Found the Secret*, on how Hudson Taylor had an experience of "abiding in the vine," he said:

> When I finished the section on Hudson Taylor, I dropped to my knees there on the cold concrete floor and began to cry.…I was on my knees for almost three hours just crying and thanking God for opening my eyes to this wonderful truth. When I got up, I was a new man.… It was now Christ working through the Holy Spirit, producing character in me. What a relief! A huge burden was lifted off my shoulders that afternoon. And I walked out of my study a free man.[26]

---

23. C. Stanley, *Wonderful Spirit Filled Life*, 37–38.
24. C. Stanley, *Courageous Faith*, 119–20.
25. C. Stanley, *Wonderful Spirit Filled Life*, 55.
26. C. Stanley, *Wonderful Spirit Filled Life*, 59–60. This testimony of an experience of victory over sin was typical of what Pentecostal Holiness people experienced as a "second

Atlanta First Baptist Church

Armed with these deeper spiritual experiences, in 1969 Stanley reluctantly accepted a call to move to First Baptist Church in Atlanta to serve as the associate pastor to Roy McLain, a very liberal pastor by Baptist standards. He soon found that this church was a "hornet's nest" of unrest and division. His reception was poor and cold. The "Executive Committee," a group of seven lay leaders who had micromanaged the church for years, detested Stanley and was determined that he would not become the senior pastor when McLain retired. They particularly disliked his fervent conservative views and biblical preaching and pressured him to resign. When they learned of his Pentecostal roots they called him a "holy roller." They soon brought in other preachers to interview for the pastor's position. Stanley called them the "gang of seven" that "made me feel like an outcast at the church."[27]

Things came to a head on a Sunday morning in 1971 when Stanley arrived at the church to find that his opponents had put anti-Stanley leaflets on each seat. After the sermon, Stanley gave an altar call. He was surprised to see 300 opponents heading for the exits while 2,000 Stanley supporters came forward to the altar. It was a stunning and overwhelming victory for the embattled preacher. In a later Wednesday night business meeting when the church gathered to vote for a new senior pastor, the chairman of the Executive Committee spoke against Stanley's candidacy and used profanity in his speech. When Stanley intervened and said that this was improper language for the pulpit, the chairman slugged Stanley in the face. Stanley did not respond. Pandemonium broke out as strong men stormed the platform to defend their pastor. When the decision came, Stanley received sixty-five percent of the vote. His enraged opponents later left First Baptist to start another church after Stanley appointed new sympathetic leadership for the congregation.[28]

If ever a church was divided and grievously wounded, it was Atlanta First Baptist Church. However, in a short time the newly-united church began to grow immensely and soon had to buy more property in downtown Atlanta to hold the crowds. In 1972 Stanley started a new television ministry in Atlanta called *The Chapel Hour* that attracted even more people to the church. In 1990 Stanley organized a new national television ministry called *In Touch with Charles Stanley* that made him a nationally and internationally important figure. When the church grew to over 15,000 members, the old downtown property was too small to hold the crowds, so a search was made to find a larger campus. In 1992 the church moved into the immense former Avon

---

blessing" of entire sanctification. The only difference was that it came after Stanley was "filled with the Spirit" but not as a "second work of grace."

27. C. Stanley, *How to Handle Adversity*, 23–24. Also C. Stanley, *Courageous Faith*, 156–73.

28. C. Stanley, *Courageous Faith*, 161–70.

Southeastern Distribution Center in the Atlanta suburb of Dunwoody where a new sanctuary was remodeled to hold the huge crowds that came to hear him preach. It also became the set for the *In Touch* broadcasts.[29]

With his ever-increasing load of preaching, teaching, and his television ministry, Stanley became overwhelmed with his work. He confessed that after moving to Atlanta "I became married to the ministry and began to neglect my family. It took me several years to get things back in order."[30] This involved problems with his marriage to Annie and his relations with his son Andy Stanley, who had become a successful megachurch pastor in his own right. His marital problems came to a head when Annie obtained a divorce from Charles in May 2000, despite his efforts to heal their marriage. Andy strongly opposed the divorce. Despite the divorce, Stanley remained as pastor of First Baptist and never remarried.[31]

Retouching His Pentecostal Roots

With all his success as pastor of a megachurch and a major television personality, Stanley never forgot his Pentecostal roots. In most of his books he acknowledged his upbringing in the Pentecostal Holiness Church and wrote glowingly of his grandfather George Washington Stanley. In 2008 on the ninetieth anniversary of the Dry Fork Emmanuel Pentecostal Holiness Church, he came and preached in honor of his grandfather who helped found the church. He also visited the graves of his father and mother who lay buried in the church cemetery. Again, in 2018, he returned to celebrate the centennial of the church. Here he preached the Sunday morning sermon and renewed old acquaintances from his childhood days.[32]

Earlier, in 2017, he blessed Emmanuel College in nearby Franklin Springs, Georgia, a school he might have attended had he not joined the Baptist Church, by giving a large scholarship donation to the school. Also, in 2017, he celebrated his eighty-fifth birthday with a gala party in Atlanta. Attending this event were Dr. Douglas Beacham, the Presiding Bishop of the Pentecostal Holiness Church, and several other leaders of the denomination. As a token of appreciation for his courageous ministry, the Pentecostal Holiness Church presented pastor Stanley with a proclamation plaque recognizing his ministry at First Baptist Atlanta and showing support for his continuing worldwide ministry. In a rare stroke of ecclesiastical statesmanship, the tribute to Stanley was as follows:

---

29. C. Stanley, *Courageous Faith*, 173–82.
30. C. Stanley, *How to Listen to God*, 41.
31. C. Stanley, *Courageous Faith*, 204–12.
32. For photos of this event see, www.intouch.org/read/magazine/thepulpit/enduring-witness. [Editor's note: no longer available.]

International Pentecostal Holiness Church

Official Proclamation

WHEREAS, Today we celebrate the life of Charles F. Stanley of Atlanta, Georgia, the son of Charley and Rebecca Stanley and originally of Dry Fork, Virginia; who earned bachelor's degrees from the University of Richmond and Southwestern Baptist Theological Seminary, and master's and doctoral degrees in theology from Luther Rice Seminary, and

WHEREAS, Dr. Charles F. Stanley accepted Jesus Christ as his Savior, was born-again at age twelve, began his life of ministry at the young age of fourteen, and has faithfully preached the gospel for the past seventy-one years, serving in various national ministry positions, including twice as the president of the Southern Baptist Convention, and

WHEREAS, Dr. Charles F. Stanley has provided excellent leadership and vision by serving as senior pastor of First Baptist Church of Atlanta, Georgia, for forty-six years, and is deeply devoted to his congregation, and provides stable, passionate, Christ-centered leadership, and

WHEREAS, Dr. Charles F. Stanley is a New York Times best-selling author and is the founder and president of In Touch Ministries, an international ministry, which can be heard and seen on more than 2,600 radio and television stations and reaches millions of households around the world weekly with the mission "to lead people worldwide into a growing relationship with Jesus Christ and to strengthen the local church,"

THEREFORE, the Executive Committee of the Council of Bishops of the International Pentecostal Holiness Church, headquartered in Oklahoma City, Oklahoma, and its governing bodies mark September 25, 2017, Dr. Charles F. Stanley's 85th birthday, as an official day of recognition and celebration of his life and significant achievements. Dr. Stanley's living example demonstrates one can truly know the Father's will, obey the Holy Spirit's leading, and accept His sovereign plan for one's life. This example is recognized by the International Pentecostal Holiness Church and is celebrated in the presence of Dr. Charles F. Stanley on this special day. We, the Executive Committee of the International Pentecostal Holiness Church, extend our prayers and desire for God's richest blessing on Dr. Charles F. Stanley, his family, and his international ministry.

Presiding Bishop Dr. A. D. Beacham, Jr., IPHC General Superintendent

Bishop J. Talmadge Gardner, Executive Director of World Missions Ministries

Bishop Thomas H. McGhee, Executive Director of Discipleship Ministries, IPHC Vice Chairman, USA

Bishop Garry Bryant, Executive Director of Evangelism, USA

11

THE ROME STADIUM SPEECH

Vinson Synan

It is a high honor and joy to stand here as a Pentecostal and join with my Roman Catholic brothers and sisters from around the world to celebrate fifty years of Catholic Charismatic Renewal.[1] We Pentecostals are so thankful that Pope Francis was led of the Lord to call for this great and historic gathering. Today we are all truly one in the Spirit and one in the Lord.

I'll never forget one morning in 1972 when I went to the post office to check my mail. In the stack was a letter from Father Kilian McDonnell. He was inviting me to speak at the third annual Catholic Charismatic Conference, which would convene on the campus of Notre Dame University in June of 1972. It was daunting to think of speaking at Notre Dame, the intellectual and football capital of American Catholicism. When I was growing up, regardless of who Notre Dame played, we always rooted against the football team simply because they were Catholics. As a teenager, I'd become quite anti-Catholic. Indeed, I was probably more afraid of Catholics than of communists or rattlesnakes. Although I'd written about Catholic Pentecostals, I was still unconvinced that Catholics could receive a full Pentecostal experience as we had in established Pentecostal churches. I also felt sure that the Roman Catholic Church would not tolerate the renewal and that Catholics who spoke in tongues would soon be out of the church. It seemed inconceivable that the Pentecostal experience could ever be incorporated into the Catholic system. (The Catholic renewal was described as a "Surprise of the Holy Spirit" by Cardinal Suenens. A second surprise of the Spirit was how quickly the renewal was accepted by the Catholic Church.)

So, with deep foreboding, I boarded my plane to South Bend. When I arrived at the Notre Dame campus, I saw multitudes of people standing in line to register. They had expected 4,000 people that summer, but more than 12,000 came. I was informed that a small prayer meeting was being held in

---

1. Written and given orally by Dr. Synan upon request from the Vatican, June 2017. Used by permission and very special thanks to Hugh Morgan, *Hugh's News*, IPHC blog and online news archive. https://www.hughsnews.com/newsletter-posts/rome-stadium-talk-by-vinson-synan-ph-d/.

the basketball coliseum for early arrivals. As soon as I could, I hurried to my dormitory room, threw my luggage on the bed, and ran across the campus to see what would happen at this prayer meeting.

I'd never seen a living, breathing, tongues-speaking Catholic and I was quite excited about the prospect. I expected that maybe a few hundred people would come early that night. But to my surprise, I was shocked to see 8,000 people already at the coliseum. In order not to be "contaminated" with Catholicism, I went to the highest level of seats as far away from the platform as I could get.

Now, I'd read that Pentecostal Catholics were considered the "quiet Pentecostals." So I expected a quiet and decorous meeting. But when the priest on the platform called on everyone to "stand and praise the Lord," I was overwhelmed at the sheer volume of praise that filled the place. Everyone had their hands raised and many around me were speaking in tongues. This cacophony of praise soon turned into a beautiful four-part harmony that rose to a loud crescendo. A huge harmonious chord filled the place. As I looked at the priests, nuns, young backpackers, and older Catholics around me, I realized that they were singing in tongues. I, a "Classical Pentecostal," was the only one who wasn't joining in.

Suddenly, I was overcome with weeping as I sensed that these people were truly baptized in the Spirit and were singing like the "heavenly choir" at Azusa Street. In fact, this was the first time I'd heard a large group sing in tongues at one time. As I wept, it soon became almost impossible to breathe. So I ran to a restroom and literally sobbed before the Lord. As I tried to recover, I heard almost audibly the words: "This is real. I'm doing a new thing in the Catholic Church and it will spread over all the earth. You'll be a part of it and contribute to this great awakening. You must tell your own people what you've seen and lead them to pray for these Catholic Pentecostals."

You see, there is only one Holy Spirit; not a Pentecostal, or Protestant, or Catholic Holy Spirit. Jesus said about this: "You shall receive power when the Holy Spirit has come upon you and you shall be witnesses (martyrs) unto me in Jerusalem, in all Judea, and Samaria and to the uttermost parts of the earth" (Acts 1:8). When I promised the Lord that I would be obedient to this call, I realized that I would probably pay a great price among the people of my own denomination. Yet I felt assurance that the Lord would protect me and use me in a most unusual way to bless these newfound brothers and sisters in Christ. I really had no clue what this meant at the time. But I was so filled with the awesome presence of the Holy Spirit that I felt I could do anything.

During that week, I saw sights that were burned forever into my memory. All night, there were sounds of prayer and praise from prayer groups both inside the dormitories and those outside. During the day, hundreds of prayer circles assembled on the lawn as people prayed and ministered to one another. In my workshop session with Kilian McDonnell, more than 1,500 individuals filled the auditorium. The paper that McDonnell presented was the first proposed systematic theology for the Catholic Charismatic movement. It was soon published under the title "Baptism in the Holy Spirit as an Ecumenical Problem."

I also saw incredible sights in the plenary sessions. The crowd was overwhelmingly made up of young people, many who had hitchhiked and backpacked to get to South Bend. From the platform, a young man sang a solo in tongues and then sang the interpretation. The only instrumental music for the 8,000 people gathered was a flute, a guitar, and a tambourine. Some of the songs were new and exotic to me, coming from Catholic folk masses that had sprung up after Vatican II. But most impressively, they sang many songs from the Pentecostal tradition, including "Spirit of the Living God, Fall Fresh on Me" and the old camp meeting song "I Have Decided to Follow Jesus."

The leaders were so young. Most of them were in their early twenties and some were destined to play major roles in the renewal. Among those I met were Kevin and Dorothy Ranaghan, Bert Ghezzi, Steve Clark, Ralph Martin, and Bruce Yocum and Patty Gallagher (Mansfield). Most of these leaders were just finishing their graduate studies in theology at Notre Dame and had the dew of youth upon them. They were bubbling over with incredible enthusiasm for the revival that had engulfed them.

That was fifty years ago. So where do we go from here? Ancient Rome was famous for its great system of roads that carried Roman soldiers and merchants to the remotest reaches of the Empire.

Figure 5: During his visit to give this speech at the Vatican in June 2017, Dr. Synan met Pope Francis after speaking on Friday night before 35,000 people. Used by permission. Holy Spirit Resource Center, Oral Roberts University.

Now let us all become Spirit-filled anointed evangelists who take the dynamite power of the Holy Spirit from Rome to the uttermost bounds of the earth. So be it! Amen and Amen. Thank you.[2]

---

2. The end of this online post includes a comment by Hugh Morgan: "I want to thank Dr. Vinson Synan for being obedient to the voice of God. He walked through open doors that have positioned him to be a great blessing to the Renewal of the Holy Spirit in the

Catholic Church. It took moral courage for him as a leader in the International Pentecostal
Holiness to align himself with the Charismatic/Catholic Renewal in the 70s. He was invited
by the Pope to come and give his speech. He was there in Rome by divine appointment, and
I have been told that the crowd of 35.000 people gave Dr. Vinson Synan a standing
ovation." https://www.hughsnews.com/newsletter-posts/rome-stadium-talk-written-and-
given-orally-by-dr-vinson-synan-upon-request-from-the-vatican9079439.

Part II:

His Legacy Endures

12

ECUMENICAL BRIDGE-BUILDER AND MODEL OF VISIONARY SPIRIT-LED LEADERSHIP

Sally Jo Shelton

Abstract

H. Vinson Synan (December 1, 1934–March 15, 2020) was a key successor to David du Plessis, the latter known as "Mr. Pentecost" to Catholic and mainline Protestant leaders. Like du Plessis, Synan was a classical Pentecostal who dedicated much of his life to promoting the move of the Holy Spirit beyond the confines of his own classical Pentecostal denomination, the International Pentecostal Holiness Church. His call to this work came in 1972 at an annual Catholic Charismatic Conference held at Notre Dame University. When seeing some 8,000 participants singing in the Spirit, he came to the conviction that Catholics had indeed received the fullness of the Holy Spirit, or what classical Pentecostals call the baptism in the Spirit. This realization was life-changing. In addition to continuing to serve as a top church administrator later, as well as a church historian and author, teacher, and academic administrator, Synan collaborated with other Charismatic leaders to hold national conferences in the 1980s and 1990s, and then international conferences of Empowered21. After reviewing Synan's diverse accomplishments, this chapter analyzes the leadership style that Synan modeled, which was visionary, Spirit-led, and bridge-building. Although Synan remained true to his Pentecostal upbringing, he celebrated the outpouring of the Spirit on churches and denominations far different from his own and exhibited great humility and love in the process. Those who have benefited by his bridge-building are deeply indebted to Synan's work.[1]

Introduction

H. Vinson Synan (December 1, 1934–March 15, 2020) was unquestionably one of David du Plessis's key successors. Du Plessis (1905–1987), heralded

---

1. Reprinted with permission. Originally published as Sally Jo Shelton, "Vinson Synan: Ecumenical Bridge Builder and Model of Visionary Spirit-Led Leadership," *Spiritus: ORU Journal of Theology* 5, no. 2 (2020): 181–97.

as "Mr. Pentecost" due to his extensive ecumenical work beginning in 1947,[2] was one of the first classical Pentecostals after the Second World War actively to encourage mainline Protestant and Roman Catholic leaders to open their hearts and their churches to the move of the Spirit. Having received a call in 1936 through a prophetic message from Smith Wigglesworth, du Plessis had dedicated the second half of his life to serving as an unofficial Pentecostal ambassador to the rest of the Christian world, for eighteen of those years sacrificing his affiliation with the Assemblies of God USA to do so.[3] Although Synan did not engage with the World Council of Churches as du Plessis had, he did follow in du Plessis's footsteps in promoting the outpouring of God's Spirit on all Christians.

Figure 6: Synan at Indianapolis 1990. Used by permission. Copyright Holy Spirit Resource Center, Oral Roberts University.

By the grace of God Synan was able to lay aside the prejudice he had conceived in his youth against Catholics,[4] a bias he freely admitted, to recognize the authenticity of the outpouring of the Spirit on all Christians regardless of ecclesial or denominational affiliation. Once Synan recognized this surprising outpouring of the Spirit on what Pentecostals had tended to regard as ritualistic, dying churches, he responded first with tears and then, for the rest of his life, celebrated with joy, taking advantage of every opportunity to promote this unprecedented move of God.

To call Vinson Synan du Plessis's successor is to acknowledge the visionary, Spirit-led, bridge-building leadership whereby he, like du Plessis, came to serve the larger renewal that far exceeded the limits of his own denomination, the International Pentecostal Holiness Church (IPHC). However, before analyzing the leadership Synan exercised so effectively throughout his life and ministry, let us first review, as has been done to some

---

2. Others may well lay claim to successorship to du Plessis in his role as "Mr. Pentecost," Cecil Robeck being the first to come to my own mind.

3. David du Plessis, *The Spirit Bade Me Go: The Astounding Move of God in the Denominational Churches* (Plainfield, NJ: Logos International, 1970); David du Plessis with Bob Slosser, *A Man Called Mr. Pentecost* (Plainfield, NJ: Logos International, 1977).

4. Synan, *Charismatic Bridges* (Ann Arbor, MI: Word of Life, 1974), 22–23.

extent elsewhere,[5] his many accomplishments. Then the rest of the article will be devoted to a brief analysis of Synan's leadership, which, though typically Pentecostal in many ways, far exceeded that of most of the Pentecostal leaders of his time in the boldness with which he embraced the Charismatic movement, particularly the outpouring of the Holy Spirit among Catholics, and his efforts to build bridges of friendship and reconciliation with those of other traditions.

Achievements

Synan's lifework was multi-faceted, his leadership capabilities evident in virtually every task he undertook whether as pastor and church official, historian and author, teacher and academic administrator, or advocate of Christian unity and bridge builder, to say nothing of his personal roles as wise mentor, warm friend, and devoted family man. Whatever the level of his work—whether teaching a high school or seminary class, preaching in a small church of less than a hundred members or sharing the platform with Pope Francis, addressing over 30,000 Catholic Charismatics in Rome's Circus Maximus—Synan humbly but authoritatively proclaimed what the Spirit was saying to the church of his time.

Churchman

Synan's church work was widely diverse, including the establishment of an interdenominational, city-wide youth ministry patterned after the Jesus Movement. He served in the IPHC administration for twelve years, his highest offices being General Secretary and Assistant General Superintendent. At one point, he was called upon to oversee the trial of a bishop charged with misadministration. While others jockeyed for political power, Synan maintained a neutral stance, distancing himself from the fray, refusing to take advantage of the situation to advance his own position within the denomination.[6] His energy was particularly manifest during his tenure as Director of Evangelism when in the space of four years he oversaw the planting of over 150 new churches. He was also instrumental in helping to unite two Chilean churches—the Pentecostal Methodist Church of Chile and the Pentecostal Church of Chile—with the Pentecostal Holiness Church USA, thereby forming the IPHC.

---

5. See Daniel Silliman, "Died: Vinson Synan, Historian Who Saw Breadth of Pentecostalism," *Christianity Today* (March 17, 2020): n.p., https://www.christianitytoday.com/news/2020/march/died-vinson-synan-pentecostalcharismatic-historian.html.

6. Synan, *Where He Leads Me: The Vinson Synan Story* (Franklin Springs, GA: LifeSprings Resources, 2019), 145–47.

Educator

Synan was also a successful educator, beginning his teaching career first as a high school history teacher and then serving at Emmanuel College, an IPHC college in Franklin Springs, Georgia, teaching history and economics and heading the Social and Behavioral Science Department. He later taught at Southwestern College in Oklahoma City, where he also served as interim president for a brief period. Then, from 1990 to 1994, Synan was professor of Pentecostal and Charismatic history at Oral Roberts University (ORU) in Tulsa, Oklahoma, as well as Director of ORU's Holy Spirit Research Center. Moving to Virginia Beach, Virginia, in 1994, he became dean of the School of Divinity at Regent University, serving there for twelve years, and after retiring from the deanship, teaching there several more years. After his return to Oklahoma, he served a year as ORU's interim dean of the College of Theology and Ministry and then remained as Scholar in Residence, working with Billy Wilson, ORU's president, on Empowered21.

While dean at Regent, Synan had created a Ph.D. program in renewal theology, a project he had originally hoped to accomplish at ORU while there the first time. When Synan's return to ORU coincided with the establishment of its Ph.D. in theology program, he jumped at the opportunity to help ORU's new College of Theology and Ministry dean, Wonsuk Ma, and the assistant Ph.D. program director Eric Newberg in completing that process. Though suffering from serious ill health by that time, Synan took great delight in seeing his dream for an ORU Ph.D. program fulfilled when it was launched at the beginning of the fall of 2019, ORU's fully ATS-accredited doctorate in Spirit-empowered global Christian theology, with contextual theology being the first track offered.

Pentecostal Scholarship Promoter

Apart from his academic achievements, Synan's greatest contribution to the Pentecostal scholarly world was the founding of the Society for Pentecostal Studies (SPS). Synan had first discussed the idea with two of his fellow Pentecostal academics—Horace Ward and William Menzies—then worked with them to inaugurate the Society by holding a banquet for prospective members at the 1970 World Pentecostal Conference in Dallas, Texas. Synan demonstrated his flexibility and sensitivity by responding to a concern expressed by a church leader who questioned his welcome into the Society because he did not hold a graduate degree. As soon as Synan's team realized that the name originally chosen—The Society of Pentecostal Scholars— posed a potential barrier, they quickly changed the word scholars in the name to studies. Synan was elected SPS's General Secretary in 1970 and then President in 1973.

Upon its formation, the Society became the venue for the International Pentecostal/Roman Catholic Dialogue led initially by du Plessis and Fr. Kilian McDonnell, a prominent Catholic scholar, Synan himself participating in the earliest meetings. The Society rapidly became a venue for Pentecostal scholars from around the world, a catalyst for global Pentecostal research, and a hotbed of Pentecostal scholarship in the US. While other scholarly Pentecostal societies would later emerge,[7] SPS continues to play a major role. Having come from a background in which Pentecostals with advanced degrees had been few and far between, Synan lived to enjoy a day when Pentecostals with doctorates abound and in which Pentecostal scholarship continues to expand rapidly through SPS, the doctoral programs he helped to create, and beyond.

Historian and Author

Synan gained a global reputation as a church historian and author with the publication of his dissertation in 1971, *The Holiness-Pentecostal Movement in the United States*, retitled in its 1997 edition, *The Holiness-Pentecostal Tradition: Charismatic Movements in the Twentieth Century*. In this, his major work, Synan traced the origins of the Holiness-Pentecostal tradition back to the perfectionism of John Wesley and the subsequent Holiness and Keswickian movements. Due to a frustrating four-year delay in finding a publisher for the dissertation, Synan had the time to develop further the section that traced the beginnings of the Charismatic movement by writing a chapter on the Catholic Renewal, thereby expanding the book's influence far beyond those in the Pentecostal Movement to all those in the Renewal, especially Catholics. Throughout his lifetime, Synan wrote some two dozen monographs as well as numerous journal and magazine articles. Considering the many aspects of his work and the extensive travel he undertook, this prolific literary output speaks to Synan's lifelong energy and self-discipline, although he also credits Carol Lee, his wife of fifty-nine years, for her assistance as she had faithfully served as his editor, relieving him of the close work required to prepare manuscripts for publication.

Ecumenist

While Synan's life would be considered highly productive in light of his many achievements enumerated thus far, what makes him truly worthy of being called one of du Plessis's successors is the bridge-building role he played, promoting the move of the Holy Spirit among all the denominations, not just Pentecostals. Even before recognizing the authenticity of the move of the

---

7. e.g., European Pentecostal Charismatic Research Association

Holy Spirit among Catholics, Synan had heard of the Spirit's movement among the mainline Protestant denominations through the Full Gospel Business Men's Fellowship International (FGBMFI). What Synan saw when attending his first FGBMFI meeting in Charlotte, North Carolina, in 1970, helped lay the foundation for his understanding that God was doing things Pentecostals had never dreamed possible.[8]

After meeting Fr. McDonnell at the Pentecostal World Conference in 1970, Synan invited him to Franklin Springs, Georgia, to visit Emmanuel College there. Synan was fascinated as McDonnell told of the birth of the Catholic Charismatic Movement at Duquesne University in 1967 and its spread to Notre Dame, the University of Michigan, and beyond. Synan was deeply gratified to hear from McDonnell how grateful the Catholics were to Pentecostals for helping them rediscover the Pentecostal experience, which McDonnell called "a treasure of the Gospel and the church."[9]

Synan's call to ecumenical bridge-building came when, at the invitation of McDonnell, he attended the sixth annual Catholic Charismatic Conference at Notre Dame University in 1972. Whenever recounting this event, Synan enjoyed explaining how that from youth he had been "more afraid of Catholics than of Communists or rattlesnakes." (This down-home, humor-padded honesty is partly what makes Synan's message so compelling and his books so readable.) Apparently, at that point in his life, even though he had developed a friendship with McDonnell and written a chapter on the Catholic Charismatic Renewal for the published version of his dissertation, he was still not fully convinced of the authenticity of Catholics' experience of the Holy Spirit.[10]

Upon arriving on the Notre Dame campus, Synan heard that a preliminary prayer service would soon be held at the basketball coliseum. Not wanting to miss a minute—Synan's usual modus operandi—he rushed to the meeting, taking a seat as high in the stands as he could to distance himself from the crowd, and gazed down in fascination at the sight of some 8,000 Catholics raising their hands in praise and worship to God. Then, to his amazement, arose the sound of those 8,000 voices singing in the Spirit in four-part harmony. Suddenly, the realization that the Catholics had indeed received the baptism in the Spirit overwhelmed him, and he began to weep. Hardly able to breathe for the deluge of tears, he went to a restroom to regain his composure, but sobbed only harder. Then he heard God's message in his heart as clearly as though he had heard it with his ears:

> This is real. I am doing a new thing in the Catholic Church, and it will spread over all the earth. You will be a part of it and will contribute to this great

---

8. Synan, *Charismatic Bridges*, 19, 20.
9. Synan, *Charismatic Bridges*, 20, 21.
10. Synan, *Where He Leads Me*, 90.

awakening. You must tell your own people what you have seen and lead them to pray for these Catholic Pentecostals.[11]

Later that year, when given the opportunity to speak briefly at the annual IPHC conference, Synan gave the message that God had told him to share: that the Holy Spirit had indeed fallen on the Catholics as on the Azusa Street Pentecostals. At the time, he thought this announcement would be his "ecclesiastical swan song," the last he would be invited to speak on an IPHC platform. Instead, two days later, the IPHC delegates voted him the General Secretary of the church, placing him in the third highest administrative position in his denomination. While Synan found great joy in serving in the administration of his denomination as he was following in the footsteps of his father who had been IPHC bishop for many years, he never lost sight of the call to have an active part in promoting the Charismatic Renewal and was obedient to that call to the end of his life.[12]

Being elected to serve in IPHC administration in no way detracted from Synan's response to his call to promote the expansion of the Charismatic Movement. For some ten years Synan met annually with a Charismatic leaders group in Glencoe, a small town near St. Louis, Missouri. At these meetings, the leaders discussed issues and strove to resolve controversies that arose from time to time in the movement, the most well-known of which was called the "shepherding movement." Synan also served for some fifteen years as a member of the North American Renewal Service Committee (NARSC). As part of the NARSC planning committee, he helped to orchestrate the 1977 Charismatic Conference in Kansas City, which had some 50,000 in attendance, the largest gathering of Charismatics and Pentecostals held to that point, with Catholic Charismatics accounting for half the attendance.

Ralph Martin, in his preface to Synan's *Charismatic Bridges*, credits Synan for envisioning such a meeting for the purpose of "witness[ing]…to the world God's power to unite in love."[13] In reflecting on the 1977 event, Synan claimed that "the conference was not just a call for unity. It was a demonstration of the unity the Lord has already given." He considered it to be "one of the most significant religious gatherings in the history of this nation…[and] certainly the most important denominationally sponsored ecumenical gathering in our history." For Synan, "[T]he message of Kansas City is that the Charismatic renewal is the most vibrant, powerful force in Christendom today, and that this great force is not going to be fragmented but is going to move in the same direction."[14]

---

11. Synan, *Where He Leads Me*, 90.
12. Synan, *Where He Leads Me*, 90.
13. Ralph Martin, "Preface," in Synan, *Charismatic Bridges*, v.
14. Synan, "A Challenge to the Churches," *New Covenant* (October 1977): 11.

Under the aegis of the NARSC, Synan chaired three other major national Charismatic conferences: the New Orleans Congress on the Holy Spirit and World Evangelization (1987), the Indianapolis Congress on the Holy Spirit and World Evangelization (1990), and the Orlando Congress on the Holy Spirit and World Evangelization (1995).

In the ensuing years, Synan continued to promote the outpouring of the Holy Spirit on an even more global scale by working with Billy Wilson, who currently serves as ORU President, Global Co-chair of Empowered21, and Chair of the Pentecostal World Fellowship. Synan had worked with Wilson, first, on the Azusa Street Centennial (2006). Then later, he served as a leader and scholar participant in the Empowered21 conversations beginning in 2008. Despite health problems, he traveled with Wilson, visiting cities all over the world. He also served as chair of the scholars track for the first Global Conference on Holy Spirit Empowerment in the 21st Century held in Tulsa, Oklahoma, in 2010, and later the Empowered21 conference held in Jerusalem in 2015.

How fittingly climactic that in June 2017 Synan spoke to a gathering of some 30,000 Catholic Charismatics from 230 countries on the Golden Jubilee of the Catholic Charismatic Renewal, sharing the platform of Rome's Circus Maximus with Pope Francis, Billy Wilson, and other Charismatic leaders.

Synan's Leadership Style

Having reviewed Synan's many accomplishments, I will now analyze the kind of leadership he exercised, which was primarily visionary, Spirit-led, and bridgebuilding.

Visionary

As a faithful son who had closely observed the example of his father, Joseph A. Synan, bishop of the IPHC from 1950 to 1969, Synan naturally would have wanted to serve as the head of his denomination as his father had before him. However, God had a bigger plan for his life. The call of God on Synan's life went far beyond parochial churchmanship, transcending denominational ties and destining him for bigger things. Synan was able to respond to this call because he was willing to follow God's leading despite any loss to his personal ambitions or desires. In fact, in later years, when offered the opportunity to run for the top office in his denomination, he declined. He had long ago left behind that early desire, having answered God's call to serve the church in a much broader capacity.

Visionary leadership for Synan meant that he had the humility and courage to look beyond what he was familiar with and to allow God to broaden his horizons. It meant looking not only beyond his own denomination but beyond the Pentecostal Movement itself to see and acknowledge the move of the Spirit first among the Charismatics in the mainline Protestant churches and then among Catholics as well. The vision God gave Synan, like that of du Plessis, was the same as the early ecumenical vision of the Azusa Street revivalists, the vision of "the renewal of the entire church by the outpouring of the Holy Spirit before the second coming of Christ."[15]

To become a leader on a national and global scale required Synan to open his mind and heart to acknowledge and embrace the gracious largesse by which God was pouring out the Holy Spirit not only on classical Pentecostal folk but on all who called themselves Christian. It also required Spirit-inspired boldness to announce to his fellow Pentecostals this surprising move of God that far exceeded their imagination and to lead them in celebrating the fulfillment of the promise from the lips of Joel that Peter quoted on the day of Pentecost: "I shall pour out my Spirit on all flesh" (Joel 2:28; Acts 2:17).

Spirit-Led

The leadership style Synan modeled was Spirit-led leadership, the underlying principle on which it was based being that God is the true leader and that authentic human leadership is based on one's consecration to God. Such leadership is neither self-appointed nor self-directed, but divinely appointed and is contingent on sensitivity and docility to the Spirit. This kind of leadership can be exercised only by those who are humble and teachable, attentive to the voice of the Spirit not only as they hear it in their own hearts but also as the Spirit speaks through others.[16] This was seen in the life of du Plessis who held the call in his heart for some ten years after he had first heard it from Smith Wigglesworth, and in the life of Synan who responded to God's calling by tirelessly promoting the work of the Spirit among Charismatics, Catholic and otherwise, despite the prejudice against Catholics with which he had been burdened from youth.

As Synan acknowledged in the title of his most recent autobiography, *Where He Leads Me,*[17] spiritual leadership depends, first, on followership, submission of one's life to God's will. Unless a leader follows God's leadership, that person may lead—as he or she may have natural leadership abilities—but where that person leads may not be beside the still waters or in

---

15. Synan, "Charismatic Walls," *New Covenant* (April 1973): 1.

16. Raniero Cantalamessa, O. F. M. Cap., preacher of the papal household since the days of John Paul II, teaches that "humility must shine in renewal leaders and in anyone who ministers in some way. We need to let ourselves be challenged without immediately taking offense. We need to let ourselves be admonished and corrected by brothers and sisters." In *Sober Intoxication of the Spirit: Filled with the Fullness of God,* trans. Marsha Daigle-Williamson (Cincinnati, OH: Servant Books, 2005), 35.

17. Synan, "Charismatic Walls," 1.

the paths of righteousness to which the Good Shepherd calls his followers (Ps 23:3; John 10:11, 14).

For Holiness Pentecostals as well as those that came from the Keswick, or Higher Life, movement, whether or not submission to God's will begins with an instantaneous experience of sanctification, it is lived as a continuous consecration, a daily dying to self and a moment-by-moment obedience to the leading of the Spirit. Although Synan believed in sanctification as "a definite, instantaneous work of grace," as affirmed by the IPHC and other Holiness groups, he did not claim his every action or word to be totally aligned with the move of the Spirit, although that was indeed his earnest desire and firm purpose.[18] Those who knew him well can personally testify to his authenticity as a true follower of God who sought daily to attune every thought, word, and deed to that of the Spirit, although as we all know from our own self-knowledge, no one meets that standard perfectly.

The earliest modern-day Pentecostals understood leadership to be dependent on listening to and following the voice of the Spirit rather than relying on human leadership. William Seymour testified to the leading of the Holy Spirit whereby he was called to Los Angeles in his first article in the Azusa Street newsletter *Apostolic Faith*: "God put it in the heart of some of the saints in Los Angeles to write to me that she felt the Lord would have me come over here and do a work, and I came, for I felt it was the leading of the Lord."[19] Interestingly, in "Letter from Bro. Parham," the article that immediately follows Seymour's, an editor of the newsletter calls Charles Parham "God's leader in the Apostolic Faith Movement." However, in a later issue that statement is corrected:

> Some are asking if Dr. Chas. F. Parham is the leader of this movement. We can answer no, he is not. . . . We thought of having him to be our leader and so stated in our paper, before waiting on the Lord. We can be rather hasty, especially when we are very young in the power of the Holy Spirit. We are just like a baby—full of love—and were willing to accept anyone that had the baptism of the Holy Spirit as our leader. But the Lord commenced settling us down, and we saw that the Lord should be our leader. So we honor Jesus as the great Shepherd of the sheep. He is our model.[20]

The article then goes on to name Seymour as the human leader but describes him as "simply a humble pastor of the flock over which the Holy Ghost has

---

18. According to Synan's father, the conferral of sanctification does not guarantee "absolute perfection…angelic perfection…[or] 'sinless perfection'"; rather it is the beginning of "a life of devotion to all the will of God." In "Articles of Faith: amplification by Bishop Joseph A. Synan," art. 10, IPHC, n.d., n.p., https://iphc.org/beliefs/.

19. "Bro. Seymour's Call," *Apostolic Faith* (September 1906): 1

20. "Jesus Our Protector and Great Shepherd," *Apostolic Faith* (December 1906): 1.

made him overseer, according to Acts 20.28." From the earliest days of modern Pentecostalism, then, the Holy Spirit was the acknowledged leader.

At Azusa Street, greater emphasis was placed on unity and harmony than human leadership: "All work together in harmony under the power of the Holy Spirit."[21] Seymour described the basis of Christian unity in terms of the description of the expectant disciples on the day of Pentecost—"they were all with one accord in one place." For Seymour, "[T]he Apostolic Faith doctrine means one accord, one soul, one heart. May God help every child of His to live in Jesus' prayer: 'That they all may be one, as Thou, Father, art in Me and I in Thee; that they all may be one in us; that the world may believe that Thou hast sent Me.'"[22]

In acknowledging Seymour as the Spirit-appointed "humble pastor of the flock," the Azusa Street participants clearly considered him to be the leader of the revival, even though that leadership was challenged by Parham and later others. But clearly, from the beginning, Pentecostal leadership was considered authentic only if Spirit-appointed and Spirit-led and exercised with the evidence of the fruit of the Spirit, especially love and humility. Synan followed Seymour's leadership style, always seeking to be obedient to God's calling.

Bridge-Building

The first piece Synan wrote after his experience at the 1972 Catholic Charismatic conference was published as the lead article of the April 1973 issue of *New Covenant*, a Charismatic magazine edited by Ralph Martin. It was an exhortation to build Charismatic bridges rather than the walls of new denominations that would serve only to further subdivide the church.[23] Synan later used the article as the basis for his book entitled *Charismatic Bridges*. Bridge building then became the metaphor of choice for ecumenical leadership.

In contemplating bridge building as a metaphor for working toward Christian unity, what first comes to my mind are the six unforgettable words with which United States President Ronald Reagan addressed Soviet leader Mikhail Gorbachev in his 1987 Berlin Wall speech: "Mr. Gorbachev, tear down this wall!" He repeated it twice. Two years later the demolition began.

Vinson Synan, following the lead of the Holy Spirit, urged something similar to the classical Pentecostals and to the new Charismatics in the early 1970s. The language he used, however, was not one of destruction but of construction—his emphasis less on the tearing down of walls and more on

---

21. "Jesus Our Protector and Great Shepherd," 1.
22. William Seymour, "The Baptism of the Holy Ghost," *Apostolic Faith* (May 1908): 3.
23. Synan, "Charismatic Walls," 1–2.

the building of bridges. In reporting the move of the Holy Spirit on the traditional churches, Synan said:

> I have endeavored to build bridges of love and understanding between classical Pentecostals, the neo-Pentecostals, and the Charismatic Catholics. I realize fully the doctrinal and historical problems that still divide Christians who come from different backgrounds and traditions. Yet I have faith in the Holy Spirit that He will continue to break down those barriers in His own time and way.[24]

What was the origin of Synan's bridge-building metaphor? When recently finding Léon-Joseph Cardinal Suenens's book on rediscovering Jesus written two years before the publication of Synan's book on Charismatic bridges, I found that the Cardinal had also used the bridge-building metaphor:

> In the person of Jesus Christ, God purposes to re-establish communion between himself and all humanity, and thus by the dynamism of love that Christ sets in motion, to build bridges [my emphasis] among all nations, all races, all families, all human beings. In this way Christ serves as the principle of a vast network of reunion, the longitudes and latitudes of this zone of Christ extend[ing] to all human horizons [my translation].[25]

Could it be that Synan borrowed the building metaphor from Suenens? Or, perhaps, the Holy Spirit inspired both of these Charismatic leaders, the Catholic bishop and the Pentecostal churchman, to use the same metaphor. The difference was that, rather than expressing his thought in christological terms as Suenens had done, Synan interpreted bridge building pneumatologically, the Charismatic movement being the means by which the Holy Spirit was transforming the face of Christianity. Cecil M. Robeck, himself an eminent Pentecostal ecumenical leader, has employed that same metaphor in several articles including one in which he refers to David du Plessis as a bridge builder.[26] C. S. Lewis used the same metaphor when Aslan, his Christ figure in the *Chronicles of Narnia*, called himself the "great Bridge Builder."[27]

In envisioning ecumenical bridge building, Synan was thinking in terms not of orchestrating formal, structural unity but rather of encouraging spiritual unity. He sought to create opportunities for Pentecostals and Charismatics of different traditions to pray and worship together, share spiritual gifts, and develop friendships. Though each church would concentrate on the renewal of its own constituency, the underlying

---

24. Synan, "Charismatic Bridges," 27.

25. Léon-Joseph Cardinal Suenens, *Redécouvrir Jésus Christ* (Brussels: Éditions Foyer Notre-Dame, 1972), 34.

26. Cecil M. Robeck, Jr., "Pentecostals and Christian Unity: Facing the Challenge," *Pneuma* 26, no. 2 (Fall 2004): 338; "Taking Stock of Pentecostalism: The Personal Reflections of a Retiring Editor," *Pneuma* 15, no. 1 (Spring 1993): 38.

27. C. S. Lewis, *Voyage of the Dawn Treader* (New York: Macmillan, 1952), 215.

foundation was unity: "one body and one Spirit…one hope…one Lord, one faith, one baptism, one God and Father of all" (Eph 4:4–6). As Synan realized, "If there's ever going to be a healing of Christianity's divisions, it'll have to be God's work, because men cannot do it. Even when you're exactly alike [doctrinally and culturally], you can't get together; breaking down barriers must be the work of the Holy Spirit."

For Synan, the reason unity was so urgently needed was that the classical Pentecostal denominations were too small and growing too slowly to fulfill the Great Commission. To reach "the rapidly expanding world population," Synan asserted, "the Holy Spirit must use larger structures to bring change and renewal." Ironically, the Pentecostal who could not imagine the Holy Spirit falling on Catholics just a short time earlier was now pointing to the Catholic Church as the solution to global evangelism:

> Of course, the greatest structure in Christianity is the Roman Catholic Church, world-wide, but I never dreamed that such a thing could happen. To really meet the needs of this hour, the Roman Church would have to have a real renewal in the Holy Spirit and the hundreds of millions of Catholics around the world would have to be baptized in the Holy Spirit and begin to meet the spiritual needs of the world. It is happening, and it is having the effect of accelerating what we wanted to see done in the beginning [of the Pentecostal Movement] in a way we never could have foreseen. It's a move of the Holy Spirit. God has just gone ahead and done it, not making Pentecostals out of Catholics by making them join our church but by renewal just as the Holy Spirit renewed our church in the beginning.[28]

The quandary for honest ecumenical bridge builders is how to be truly open to the possibility of finding truth in other traditions and yet remain faithful to their own: How far can I go in appreciating what is good and true and beautiful in the teachings and liturgies of other traditions without compromising my own? Naturally, each tradition assumes that its own doctrines should not be compromised; however, eventually it becomes apparent that other traditions have elements of truth that our own has neglected or perhaps missed altogether. This is the dilemma with which all honest ecumenists struggle. That is why, despite the dialogue principle that participants remain within their own tradition,[29] ultimately each person must

---

28. "Sixth International Conference," 5.

29. "In the process of growing mutual understanding and trust, our stereotypes of one another diminish. In other words, we change, but the change is not compromise. . . . No one is called to compromise. Common witness is not a call to indifference or to uniformity. In fact, though division and separation are contrary to the will of God, the diversity within the unity of the one Body of Christ is a precious and indispensable gift which is to be recognized, valued and embraced." Joint International Commission for Catholic–Pentecostal Dialogue, "Evangelization, Proselytism and Common Witness: The Report from the Fourth Phase of the International Dialogue 1990–1997 between the Roman Catholic Church and

be allowed the freedom to obey should God call them to embrace another tradition because each is personally accountable to God.

Bernard Lonergan has articulated another side of the same dilemma. Ecumenists, with few exceptions, can go only so far in terms of expanding their horizons because eventually almost all reach a point where, regardless of their efforts to understand the other's perspective, they can go no further; they find themselves back almost to where they started: the other's doctrines are wrong, and their own are right. Once ecumenical leaders realize this natural, very human propensity, the only solution is prayer. Only the Holy Spirit can help them to bridge that seemingly impassable obstacle that separates them from seeing the truth in the other. As Synan said, only the Holy Spirit can unite us. Only the Holy Spirit can bridge these deeply embedded divisions and free us from the walls that divide us.

To my knowledge, Synan remained unwaveringly true to his Pentecostal roots even while at the same time acknowledging and rejoicing in the authenticity of the move of the Spirit in churches that differed so significantly doctrinally and liturgically from his own. While delighting in bridge building and enjoying worshipping and fellowshipping with his Catholic and mainline Protestant Charismatic brothers and sisters in the Lord, he apparently never considered conversion to any other tradition. From his perspective that would have been compromise. His perspective coincided fully with the Pentecostal stance articulated in the fifth phase of the International Pentecostal-Roman Catholic dialogue: "Pentecostals are cautious in regards to ecumenism. Al-though they recognize the work of the Spirit in other Christian traditions, and enter into fellowship with them, they are hesitant to embrace these movements wholeheartedly for fear of losing their own ecclesial identity or compromising their traditional positions."[30]

Even when, through a genealogical study, he came to the realization that the Synan family roots were in Catholic Ireland, not Protestant Ireland as his family had assumed, though delighted that Pentecostalism had come full

---

some Classical Pentecostal Churches and Leaders," n.d., §§119, 122, "Dialogue with Pentecostals," http://www.vatican.va/roman_curia/pontifical_councils/chrstuni/subindex/index_pentecostals.htm. Editor's update: (accessed September 2, 2025), https://www.christianunity.va/content/unitacristiani/en/dialoghi/sezione-occidentale/pentecostali/dialogo/documenti-di-dialogo/testo-in-inglese.html.

30. "On Becoming a Christian: Insights from Scripture and the Patristic Writings with Some Contemporary Reflections: Report of the Fifth Phase of the International Dialogue Between Some Classical Pentecostal Churches and Leaders and the Catholic Church (1998–2006)," Dialogue with Pentecostals, n.d., §171, http://www.vatican.va/roman_curia/pontifical_councils/chrstuni/eccl-commdocs/rc_pc_chrstuni_doc_ 20060101_becoming-a-christian_en.html. Editor's update: (accessed September 2, 2025), https://www.christianunity.va/content/unitacristiani/en/dialoghi/sezione-occidentale/pentecostali/dialogo/documenti-di-dialogo/testo-del-documento-in-inglese1.html.

circle in his family through the Catholic Renewal, he remained faithful to the classical Pentecostalism in which he had been raised.[31]

Conclusion

Vinson Synan was a beloved, highly respected figure not only within his own denomination, the IPHC, but also among Pentecostals worldwide, as well as among Charismatics, especially the academics and scholars. These groups each have their own special reasons for thanking God for this Pentecostal leader who had the vision to follow the Spirit's leading in building bridges that helped unite Pentecostals and Spirit-empowered believers around the world in joint witness to the incarnation of God in the person of Jesus Christ and the presence and power of the Holy Spirit whom God continues to pour out on all flesh to this day. Vinson Synan deserves special honor and gratitude from those who in their own journey to obey God have crossed the ecumenical bridge he so courageously helped to build.

Figure 7: Synan (top right) leads a conference with ministers hungry for God (above); Moscow, 1992, just after the fall of Communism. Used by permission. Copyright Holy Spirit Resource Center, Oral Roberts University.

---

31. Synan, *The Synans of Virginia: The Story of an Irish Family in America* (Xulon, 2003).

<h1 style="text-align:center">13</h1>

<h1 style="text-align:center">A PIONEER OF PENTECOSTAL STUDIES</h1>

Daniel D. Isgrigg

In the world of Spirit-empowered scholarship, few names are as well-known as that of Dr. Vinson Synan. In 1934, Harold Vinson Synan was born to Rev. J. A. Synan and Minnis Synan. His father was a prominent pastor and became a Bishop in the International Pentecostal Holiness Church (IPHC). In August 1951, Vinson surrendered his life to God, was sanctified, received a calling to ministry, and was filled with the Holy Spirit.

Though called to ministry, Synan was not content to go to Bible college like his brothers. He wanted a liberal arts degree. However, he decided to attend Emmanuel Bible College in Franklin Springs, Georgia with his twin brother Vernon in 1953. There he fell in love with preaching the Word and studying the scriptures.

In 1954, he received his license to preach and returned to Hopewell, Virginia, to serve as assistant pastor to his uncle, Lindsey Synan. Vinson was invited to preach in churches and youth meetings. People could tell he was following in his father's footsteps. In 1956, Bishop Oscar Moore ordained Synan in the IPHC. Shortly after, Synan took his first church in Fredericksburg, Virginia. In 1957, Synan met the love of his life, Carol Lee Fuqua. In 1960, they were married, but neither one believed their journey would take them around the world.

Because Bible college was not enough for Vinson, in 1956 he enrolled at the University of Richmond to work on a bachelor's degree. It was here that he got his first taste of being a historian. His bachelor's thesis was on the history of the Pentecostal Holiness Church from 1948–1958. Because of his father's position in the denomination, he was able to do archival research in the secretariat files of the IPHC. It was clear that Synan had a passion for the history of the movement.

After completing his B.A. degree in 1958, he felt a calling to education and began teaching history at Emmanuel College in Franklin Springs, Georgia. Synan went on to complete an M.A. from the University of Georgia in 1964 on the history of Emmanuel College, which was the flagship college for the IPHC, founded by G. F. Taylor. Synan's thesis became his first book in 1968 entitled *Emmanuel College: The First Fifty Years*. His passion for research and Pentecostal history led him to pursue a Ph.D. At first, he received an invitation from Oral Roberts to teach at Oral Roberts University (ORU), which was set to open in 1965. Roberts, a close friend of Vinson's father, even offered to pay for his Ph.D. if he would become one of the founding faculty. However, Synan felt that the IPHC was where he would make his career.

In 1965, Synan began his Ph.D. studies at the University of Georgia, where had a full ride and fellowship. He was encouraged by his faculty advisor, Horace Montgomery, to conduct a pioneering study on the social and intellectual history of the Holiness-Pentecostal tradition in the United States.[1] Montgomery, a renowned historian, encouraged him to conduct research in the archives of Emmanuel College. Montgomery also taught him to mine the treasures of historical details buried in the periodical literature of the early Pentecostal movement. This began a lifelong passion for the preservation of Pentecostal primary sources. In 1964, Synan was instrumental in forming a commission for an IPHC archive put together by himself, the first archivist, Dorothy Poteat, Rev. James Butler, and Harold Paul.[2]

Figure 8: Synan in the Holy Spirit Research Center at Oral Roberts University, 1966. Used with permission. Copyright Holy Spirit Resource Center, Oral Roberts University.

---

1. Synan, *Where He Leads Me* (Franklin Springs, GA: LifeSprings Resources, 2019), 69.

2. "IPHC Archives & Research Center," https://iphc.org/gso/archives-in-the-iphc-where-do-i-go-to-find-information-what-should-i-do-with-my-donation/.

As his research progressed, Synan sought out other archival collections with primary sources on the Pentecostal movement. At the time, there were few formal Pentecostal archives, and most were limited to informal record depositories of individual denominations. In 1966, Synan traveled to ORU to conduct research in the new Pentecostal collection in the Graduate School of Theology Library (later called the Holy Spirit Research Center). ORU's special collection was the archive for the broader Pentecostal and Charismatic movement. The first librarian over the collection was Juanita Walker, who served previously as a librarian at Emmanuel College. As Synan was exposed to primary sources of the broader Pentecostal tradition, the experience confirmed that his historical work should transcend the IPHC and focus on the movement as a whole. He showed remarkable acumen and completed his dissertation in 1967, less than two years.

With Montgomery as his faculty advisor, Synan was encouraged to look at Pentecostal history through a social-intellectual lens. This led him to focus on the history of Black Pentecostalism, a major contribution in his dissertation. In exploring the Black roots of Pentecostalism, Synan was one of the first Pentecostals to contribute to conversations about race and Pentecostalism. His chapter on "Negro Pentecostals" was the first to document the histories of the United Holy Church of America and C. H. Mason's Church of God in Christ (COGIC). Synan also highlighted the early interracial impulses in the movement and discussed how Jim Crow and segregation led to racial divisions. Synan was the first to suggest an early arrangement between white ministers who formed the Assemblies of God and Black leadership of the COGIC, although this suggestion has been questioned recently.[3] No doubt, the social aspects of the Pentecostal movement would emerge as a dominant theme in research in the coming years.

Upon completing his dissertation in 1967, Synan expanded it for publication with Eerdmans in 1971 as *The Holiness-Pentecostal Movement in the United States*. S. David Moore comments that this book was "catalytic" to the birth of the field of Pentecostal Studies.[4] Synan was quickly recognized as the foremost voice for Pentecostalism in the country. As James Goff comments, every scholar knew the work of Vinson Synan.[5] He was invited to many college campuses to give lectures introducing the growing phenomenon of

---

3. Synan, *The Holiness-Pentecostal Movement in the United States*, 169. For a rebuttal of this narrative created by Synan see Daniel D. Isgrigg, *Aspects of Assemblies of God Origins* (Eugene, OR: Pickwick, 2024), chapter 2.

4. S. David Moore, "Vinson Synan: Pentecostal, Historian, and Bridge Builder," in *Renewal History and Theology: Essays in Honor of H. Vinson Synan*, ed. S. David Moore and James M. Henderson (Cleveland, TN: CPT Press, 2014), 8.

5. James R. Goff, Jr., "Probing the Past, Fueling the Future," in *Renewal History and Theology*, ed. S. David Moore and James M. Henderson (Cleveland, TN: CPT Press, 2014), 39.

the Pentecostal movement. Up until this time, the Pentecostal movement had been ignored by the broader academic community. Most of his fellow Pentecostal historians, such as William Menzies and Klaude Kendrick, focused more on denominational histories rather than the movement as a whole. But Synan's book was focused on the Holiness roots, interracial beginnings, and various branches of the Pentecostal movement. This made his work appeal to an ever-growing number of scholars who were curiously observing the movement.

While recognized for his broader contributions, Synan continued to use his gifts to document history of his church, the IPHC. In 1973, he published *Old Time Power: A History of the Pentecostal Holiness Church.* He quickly realized that he could flourish in this space and advance knowledge in the tradition he loved. Synan continued to serve the IPHC in various capacities including professor at Southwestern College (1975–1977), an IPHC institution, and later as interim President, in 1980. In 1973, he was selected to serve as IPHC General Secretary, a position he held until 1977. He was then elected to the office of Assistant General Superintendent from 1977 to 1981 and Director of Evangelism from 1981 to 1985. At each stage, he maintained one foot in the church and one foot in the academy.

Synan was among the first generation of Pentecostal scholars who completed their doctoral work in the 1960s. In 1970, he teamed up with Menzies and Horace Ward, two other pioneering Pentecostal scholars, to establish the first Pentecostal academic society: the Society for Pentecostal Scholars (SPS; later changed to the Society for Pentecostal Studies). Within SPS, Synan served as the first General Secretary from 1970–1972, then President-elect in 1973, President in 1974, and Executive Director from 1980–1983.

Figure 9: Announcement of Synan's election to the General Secretary of SPS in *The Advocate,* January 2, 1971. Used with permission. Copyright IPHC Archives. Courtesy of Consortium of Pentecostal Archives.

He published the first member-based newsletters and also, in 1975, the first edited volume of essays from an SPS conference entitled *Aspects of Pentecostal/Charismatic Origins*. Goff comments that this book was a watershed moment as it featured critical evaluations of different perspectives on Pentecostalism by some of the most notable Holiness, Pentecostal, and American religious scholars.[6]

In the 1970s, Synan's influence shifted from the Pentecostal movement to the larger Charismatic Renewal taking place in the U.S. During the 1960s-1970s, members of mainline denominations began to receive the baptism in the Holy Spirit. Renewal leaders in the denominations sought out Pentecostal leaders who could help their communities understand and promote the experience. As one of the most recognized Pentecostal scholars, Synan was invited by many of these communities to lecture and preach at their conferences. One such gathering was with the Charismatic Catholics. In 1972, Synan was asked to speak at a conference of over 12,000 Charismatic Catholics at the University of Notre Dame. As he witnessed Catholics receive the outpouring of the Spirit in those services, he knew God was calling him to embrace the movement and help in any way he could.[7] This led to Synan being invited to join Pentecostal ecumenist, David du Plessis, in a Catholic-Pentecostal dialogue in Rome. These experiences helped to abate prejudices against Catholics that he himself had and were shared by many in the Pentecostal movement.

Over the next few years, Synan used his position as General Secretary in the IPHC to help build bridges between the Charismatic Renewal and the classical Pentecostal movement. In 1974, he wrote *Charismatic Bridges*, a volume that celebrated the unifying work of the Spirit in the Charismatic Renewal. In 1977, Synan was asked to work with leaders of various Charismatic Renewal groups to hold a joint Charismatic conference in Kansas City, Missouri, at Arrowhead Stadium. That weekend, over 50,000 people gathered in the largest ecumenical gathering of Spirit-filled believers. As believers from all traditions lifted their hands and voices in praise, it was clear that the Holy Spirit was bringing a new unity within the church.

The success of the Kansas City conference led to the formation of the North American Renewal Service Committee (NARSC), an organizing body to unite Pentecostal-Charismatic Renewal groups. Synan was asked by various Renewal leaders to serve as chairman. He and Kevin Ranaghan worked closely together to organize conferences on renewal throughout the 1980s. In 1987, the North American Congress on the Holy Spirit was held in the New Orleans Superdome with over 40,000 people in attendance. Other conferences were held in Indianapolis (1990), Orlando (1995), and St. Louis

---

6. Goff, "Probing the Past, Fueling the Future," 39.

7. Synan, *Where He Leads Me*, 89–98.

(2000). As a bridge builder in the movement, Synan was invited to speak worldwide, including in dialogues between Pentecostals and Charismatic Catholics at the Vatican in Rome, where he met Pope John Paul II in 1993.

Having spent two decades in denominational service and ecumenical work, Synan decided to return to academia. In 1990, he accepted a position at Oral Roberts University as Professor of Pentecostal/Charismatic History and Director of the Holy Spirit Research Center. In 1992, he published a history of the Full Gospel Business Men's Fellowship International (FGBMFI) called *Under His Banner.* In it, he highlighted the impact that FGBMFI had made in spreading the Pentecostal experience beyond Pentecostalism. He noted that, in 1990, not a single thesis or dissertation had explored the importance of this movement of laypersons in bringing renewal to the church.[8]

During the early 1990s, Synan continued his ecumenical work with NARSC. One aspect of his work was to help historians and demographers to craft profiles of Pentecostal-Charismatic Christianity. In 1992, Synan published *The Spirit Said "Grow,"* a demographic profile of the growth of the Pentecostal-Charismatic movement. Synan harnessed the work of church growth expert C. Peter Wagner, and *World Christian Encyclopedia* editor David Barrett, to draw attention to the astounding statistics emerging from the spread of the movement. The *Spirit Said "Grow"* also introduced a taxonomy of Spirit-filled believers dividing them into Classical Pentecostals, Charismatics, and "Third Wave" categories. Statistical growth in all three categories proved that not only was Pentecostalism an explosive force, but it was a global (non-white) movement.

As the 1990s progressed, Pentecostalism became a force the broader world was paying attention to. What was left was for Pentecostal-Charismatic communities to take up the task of fostering Pentecostal scholarship. Synan came to ORU in 1990 with the hope of pioneering a Ph.D. program in Pentecostal and Charismatic studies. This initiative was originally part of a plan to relaunch ORU's seminary in 1977 under James Buskirk. However, the financial situations that hindered ORU in the 1980s were still a reality in the early 90s, and there seemed to be no progress during Synan's short stay. Still, he made a significant contribution to reviving the Holy Spirit Research Center collections in hopes of supporting original research in Pentecostal history through a future ORU Ph.D. program.

In 1994, Synan was contacted by Regent University to become Dean of the School of Divinity. Alongside leading the school, in 1995 he realized his dream of starting the first Ph.D. program focused on Renewal Studies. Over the next decade, Synan built a world-class School of Divinity with an outstanding faculty known for Pentecostal scholarship. He also started a

---

8. Synan, *Under His Banner*, 12.

Doctor of Ministry program. Regent gathered students from around the world to research and publish studies on the global Spirit-empowered movement. While serving as Dean, Synan traveled as a global ambassador for the Spirit-empowered movement.

Synan wrote twenty-five books on the Pentecostal-Charismatic movement in his lifetime. His best-selling book was the massive 500-page volume, *The Century of the Holy Spirit,* which chronicled the remarkable story of the Pentecostal-Charismatic tradition. This book presented the insights he had dedicated his life to bringing to light. He also wrote *An Eyewitness Remembers the Century of the Holy Spirit* in 2010. For Pentecostals, Synan convinced the movement of the significance of their history. For the outside world, he convinced religious scholars that Pentecostalism was reshaping global Christianity. No doubt, Synan's scholarship was instrumental in establishing Pentecostalism as a significant global movement within the broader field of religious studies.

In 2006, Synan announced his retirement from Regent University and a symposium was held. The papers from that symposium were published in 2014, in honor of his 80th birthday, as a volume entitled *Renewal History and Theology: Essays in Honor of H. Vinson Synan,* edited by S. David Moore and James M. Henderson.[9] Synan also received an honorary doctorate from Regent in 2008. He was named Dean Emeritus and continued to teach part-time at Regent. In his time there, he not only built a world-class Ph.D. program, but he recruited many young Pentecostal scholars to join the faculty. Many of them have since become prolific scholars and leaders in the Pentecostal academy. He also mentored students and supervised countless dissertations on the history and theology of Renewal movements globally.

The next phase of Synan's influence came as he was recruited to advise the planning of the 2006 Azusa Centennial Celebration organized by William (Billy) Wilson.[10] The celebration included a large conference featuring Spirit-empowered leaders from around the world. Over 50,000 people from over 100 nations attended to celebrate the legacy of this outpouring of the Holy Spirit. This celebration planted the dream in Wilson to create a global network of Spirit-empowered believers. From 2006–2008, Synan was invited to join Wilson in discussing with global leaders about forming a relational network called Empowered21. Alongside the discussions with global leaders, Synan hosted meetings with international scholars to discuss the future of the Spirit-empowered movement. The papers and research presented at those discussions became the 2011 edited volume, *Spirit-Empowered Christianity in the Twenty-First Century.*

---

9. S. David Moore and James M. Henderson, eds. *Renewal History and Theology: Essays in Honor of H. Vinson Synan* (Cleveland, TN: CPT Press, 2014), 8.

10. Vinson Synan and William M. Wilson, *As the Waters Covers the Sea: The Story of Empowered21 and the Movement it Serves* (Tulsa, OK: Empowered Books, 2021).

In 2010, Wilson convened the first Global Congress on the Holy Spirit on the campus of Oral Roberts University to launch the Empowered21 network (E21). The conference drew over 10,000 people as leaders, scholars, and lay people gathered to discuss Spirit-empowered Christianity in the twenty-first century. Synan led a scholars track of 210 workshops where global scholars and ministers presented papers on issues related to Spirit-empowered theology, missions, ministry, and leadership. In the next few years, Synan directed annual scholars consultations in Sydney, Australia (2013), Quito, Ecuador (2014), and Jerusalem (2015). The latter was a Global Congress where Spirit-empowered scholars from every region of the world met and can be seen in photos with Synan, reading papers together in halls and archways. These conversations resulted in a four-volume regional series edited by Synan and Amos Yong entitled *Global Renewal Christianity: Spirit-Empowered Movements Past, Present, and Future.*

When Synan was finally enjoying retirement in Virginia, a call came from Oral Roberts University. Wilson had been elected to serve as the fourth president of ORU and invited Synan to join its Board of Trustees. Accepting the invitation, Synan continued organizing the 2016 scholars consultation of E21 in London. From this gathering, he edited and published *The Truth About Grace.* The publication of this volume began a precedent of E21 scholars consultation volumes highlighting global scholars and publishing new research on the global Spirit-empowered movement.

As he contributed significantly to E21, another crucial moment came in 2016, when Synan was asked to serve as Interim Dean of the College of Theology and Ministry at ORU. Wilson recruited Synan to serve as the chair for the search for a new dean. Having already felt that he wanted to move back to Oklahoma to be closer to his children, Synan accepted the role, knowing it was temporary. Eventually, Wonsuk Ma accepted the role as Dean, and Synan transitioned to a new role of Scholar in Residence in 2017. Synan assisted Ma and Eric Newberg in starting ORU's Ph.D. program in Global Contextual Theology and served as the Program Director for one year. Finally, nearly 30 years after his initial professorship and attempt to start a Ph.D. program at ORU, he was able to see it become a reality.[11]

In this new role, Synan could return to research and writing. In 2017, he published a biography of B. H. Irwin and the Fire Baptized Holiness Church with Dan Woods. He also partnered with Wilson to co-author a new book on the story of Empowered21 called *As the Waters Cover the Sea.* Concurrently, Synan began working on his memoirs of his many journeys as a Pentecostal minister, scholar, ecumenist, and family man. In 2019, his life story, *Where He Leads Me: The Vinson Synan Story,* was released. It was his twenty-fifth book.

---

11. Sally Jo Shelton, "In Memoriam: Vinson Synan: Ecumenical Bridge-Builder and Model of Visionary Spirit-Led Leadership," *Spiritus* 5, no. 2 (Fall 2020): 181–97.

In 2019, Synan faced significant health challenges but continued serving as Scholar in Residence at ORU. Amid several health episodes, he made his final trip to the Society for Pentecostal Studies in Washington, D.C., in March 2019. His presence there was providential. For many SPS attendees, this moment became a heartfelt farewell to a beloved friend, mentor, and professor whose inspiring influence on the Pentecostal community would be cherished forever. On March 15, 2020, Synan passed away at the age of 86. His dear wife Carol, who had been his companion on all of these journeys, passed away a year later on March 18, 2021. They are both buried in Virginia.

14

REFLECTIONS ON VINSON SYNAN'S MINISTRY IN KOREA AND ASIA

Younghoon Lee

Dr. Vinson Synan (1934–2020) was one of the most influential Pentecostal theologians of the twentieth century. A distinguished scholar from the International Pentecostal Holiness Church (IPHC), he played a pivotal role in laying the theological foundations of the Pentecostal movement in the United States and spreading its influence across the globe. He served as the Dean of the School of Divinity at Regent University and, in 1970, founded the Society for Pentecostal Studies (SPS), dedicating himself to ensuring that Pentecostalism would be recognized and respected as a legitimate academic discipline. Dr. Synan also served as a vital bridge between classical Pentecostalism and the Charismatic movement, the Catholic Charismatic Renewal, and Pentecostal communities in Latin America and Asia. Due to his prolific writing and international engagement, he came to be known as the historian of the Pentecostal movement.

Dr. Synan showed a particular interest in the Pentecostal movement in Asia, especially in Korea through connection with Yoido Full Gospel Church (YFGC). Having visited Korea multiple times since the 1990s, he recognized the explosive growth and dynamic spiritual movement within YFGC as a living model of global Pentecostalism, offering an optimistic outlook on the future of the movement in Asia. After the establishment of the International Theological Institute in 1991, Dr. Synan frequently visited Korea as a keynote speaker for academic seminars. During the early to mid-1990s, when I served as the president of the Institute, our academic collaboration deepened significantly.

Through this reflection, I seek to revisit my personal relationship with Dr. Vinson Synan and to consider how he journeyed alongside and collaborated with YFGC and the Pentecostal movement in Korea.

139

Meeting in 1970

The relationship between Dr. Vinson Synan and YFGC dates back to 1970. From November 3 to 8 of that year, the Ninth Pentecostal World Fellowship was held in Dallas, Texas, USA. Dr. Synan played a key role in organizing the event, and it was there that he met Dr. Yonggi Cho for the first time. On November 6, during the conference, a special gathering of 139 scholars and leaders was convened to discuss the theology and history of Pentecostalism. This conference would later serve as the catalyst for the formation of SPS. With financial support from Dr. Cho, Dr. Synan, together with Dr. William Menzies, took the lead in founding SPS. From that point forward, Dr. Synan participated in every annual meeting of the Society, dedicating himself wholeheartedly to the academic development of Pentecostal studies.

At that time, although YFGC had already become one of the most prominent megachurches in Korea, its theological contributions had not yet gained significant international recognition. However, during his scholarly research, Dr. Synan came to view YFGC as a model of Spirit-empowered ministry and lifted it up as a prime example of the worldwide movement of the Holy Spirit.

Mentorship at Temple University

While pursuing my doctoral studies in philosophy of religion at Temple University in the United States, I was writing a dissertation on the topic, "The Holy Spirit Movement in Korea: Its Historical and Theological Development." Dr. Synan, serving as an external adviser, gave me substantial guidance throughout my research. We corresponded frequently via email and occasionally met in person to discuss academic matters. He provided me a clear picture of the Pentecostal-Charismatic movement, and I remain deeply grateful for his teaching and wise counsel to this day.

1994: Collaboration with the Korean Church Begins

The period from 1994 to 2006, when Dr. Synan served as Dean of the School of Divinity at Regent University, marked the height of his collaboration with YFGC. During this time, through the International Theological Institute, where I was serving as president, we worked closely in various areas including theological education, academic publishing, scholarly exchange, and the establishment of Korean-language extension programs for Regent University's Master of Divinity (M.Div.) and Doctor of Ministry (D.Min.) degrees. These collaborative efforts significantly deepened our academic and personal relationship.

In December 1994, Dr. Synan visited Korea at the invitation of the International Theological Institute and delivered a special lecture on the history and challenges of the global Pentecostal and Charismatic Movement. In his address, he recognized YFGC as one of the most influential churches in the world and emphasized the restoration of the gifts of the Holy Spirit as an urgent task of our time. He actively supported the establishment of a continuing education program for pastors. Developed in collaboration with the International Theological Institute, and based on Regent University's curriculum, this program significantly expanded access to internationally accredited theological training for Korean pastors.

During this period, the establishment of the Master of Divinity (M.Div.) and Doctor of Ministry (D.Min.) programs at Regent University, in cooperation with YFGC and the International Theological Institute, was also made possible through Dr. Synan's enthusiastic support. He personally contributed to the development of the curriculum and delivered lectures on several occasions, playing a key role in the academic formation of Korean pastors. Through this program, approximately 450 Korean pastors, including Rev. Youngmo Ryu, the emeritus pastor of Hansomang Presbyterian Church, obtained advanced degrees. Many of them later became professors in seminaries or leaders within their denominations, making significant contributions to the theological advancement of the Korean church.

1995: International Theological Symposium

In August 1995, Dr. Synan and his wife, Carol, visited Korea once again as guest lecturers for the International Theological Symposium. For several days from August 11, my wife and I had the opportunity to travel with them to Jeju Island. Coincidentally, August 13 marked their wedding anniversary, and they often recalled this journey as an unforgettable experience. Although the weather was quite hot at the time, Dr. Synan and Carol were deeply impressed by the breathtaking scenery of Jeju's skies and seas, repeatedly expressing their joy and wonder. During that trip, we shared not only personal stories but also meaningful theological conversations, forming lasting memories. My wife still recalls how deeply moved she was by Dr. Synan's humble and sincere character.

On August 21, Dr. Synan delivered a keynote lecture at the Fourth International Theological Symposium held at Yonsei University, titled "Prospects and Challenges of the Twentieth-Century Pentecostal Movement." In this lecture, he offered a compelling analysis of how the Pentecostal movement was reshaping the global landscape of Christianity. He highlighted the pivotal role that YFGC had played in this process. With nearly 1,000 scholars, pastors, and seminary students in attendance, this symposium served as a turning point for Pentecostal theology to gain recognition as a legitimate and influential theological stream within the broader Korean theological academy.

At the time, I believed that it was not only important to invite Dr. Synan to Korea for lectures, but also essential to introduce his work to the Korean theological community through translation and publication. As a result, one of his representative works, *In the Latter Days*, was translated into Korean and published in 1995 under the title *The Current Status of the Twentieth-Century Pentecostal Movement* 20세기 성령운동의 현주소』, coinciding with his visit to Korea. In the preface to the Korean edition, Dr. Synan wrote:

> I pray that this book will greatly impact the Korean Church. Based on my experience in researching the history of the global Pentecostal-Charismatic movement, I sincerely hope that the Korean Church will, through the unifying work of the Holy Spirit, break down denominational walls and embrace a future of mutual understanding, reconciliation, and unity."

1996: Visit to Hansei University and the Kukmin Daily

In the spring of 1996, Dr. Synan visited Korea once again, this time accompanied by fifteen delegates from Regent University, including its president. During this visit, they explored possible avenues of collaboration with Hansei University and the Kukmin Daily. These two institutions, established by YFGC as platforms for gospel communication through education and media, served as vital instruments of cultural engagement and spiritual mission. Given that Regent University itself was closely affiliated with the Christian Broadcasting Network (CBN) and had initially been named CBN University, this meeting underscored a shared understanding of the theological and communicative roles of Pentecostal higher education and Christian journalism in both the United States and Asia.

1997: The Asia Pacific Theological Association Forum

In February of the following year, Dr. Synan presented a lecture titled "The Pentecostal/Charismatic Movement in the Twentieth Century" at a theological forum hosted by the Asia Pacific Theological Association. The forum took place at Asia Pacific Theological Seminary (APTS), affiliated with the Assemblies of God, located in Baguio, Philippines. Dr. Synan provided a sweeping overview of the Pentecostal and Charismatic movements over the past century and offered profound insights into their future trajectory. At the same event, I presented on the topic, "Yoido Full Gospel Church and the Movement of the Spirit in Korea," highlighting the influence of the Holy Spirit movement centered around YFGC on the Korean church.

During the three-day forum, from February 4 to 6, I engaged in meaningful dialogue with Dr. Synan and Dr. Wonsuk Ma, then Academic Dean of APTS, concerning the revival of the Asian church. Dr. Synan expressed deep admiration for the remarkable growth of the Korean church and emphasized the need for Asian missions to expand further into the developing world, including China, which had begun opening its doors to capitalist markets, as well as Southeast and Southwest Asia. His perspective deeply resonated with us, especially since YFGC was then in the process of reshaping its missions strategy to prioritize indigenous leadership in the Global South.

1998: Asia Pacific Theological Forum and 18th Pentecostal World Conference

The year 1998 marked one of the most active seasons of Dr. Synan's engagement with the ministry of YFGC and the Pentecostal movement in Asia. On May 18, the anniversary of the church's founding, Dr. Synan served as a keynote speaker at the Seventh International Theological Conference held in the newly completed seminar hall of the Kukmin Daily headquarters (now CCMM Building).

In his presentation on the topic "Korean Christianity: Yonggi Cho and the Yoido Full Gospel Church," he observed that Korea, which had shown strong resistance to the gospel just half a century ago, has now experienced a remarkable spiritual revival. He described this transformation as "the miraculous work of the Holy Spirit" and "an incredible missionary success." He particularly emphasized that at the center of this revival was the Pentecostal movement of YFGC. His detailed and appreciative analysis of Korean church history demonstrated his deep interest in the development of the Asian church. He also emphasized that Asian churches, including YFGC, had a substantial mission for global revival in the twenty-first century. In the same conference, I presented a paper entitled, "Faith and Theology of Yoido Full Gospel Church," examining the theological significance of the church's contribution to the Korean Pentecostal movement.

Later that year, from September 22 to 25, the Eighteenth Pentecostal World Conference was held in Seoul, organized by YFGC. This large-scale gathering, hosted at the 70,000-seat Jamsil Olympic Main Stadium, was a deeply significant event in the history of the global Pentecostal movement. As the Pentecostal movement, which began in 1901, approached its centennial, it was deeply meaningful to me that that celebration would take place in Seoul.

Academic seminars were also held during the conference, involving prominent Pentecostal scholars from around the world. Under themes such as "In the Korean Context," "In the Asian Context," and "In the Non-Asian Context," these sessions provided a unique opportunity to reexamine the global Pentecostal movement through Korean and Asian lenses.

At this conference, Dr. Synan delivered a lecture on theological tendencies within Pentecostalism, emphasizing that the gifts of the Holy Spirit must continue to be manifested in the twenty-first century and that a solid theological foundation must be established to support their ongoing operation. He also remarked that it was deeply encouraging for the centennial of modern Pentecostalism to be held in Seoul. In particular, he compared the fervent prayers of the believers who filled Jamsil Olympic Stadium to those of the 120 disciples who waited for the Holy Spirit in the Upper Room, offering high praise for the dynamic work of the Spirit taking place in Asia. At the concurrent meeting of the Asian Pentecostal Society, Dr. Synan offered a special prayer, fervently interceding for the continued spread of Pentecostal revival throughout Asia. His heartfelt prayer testified to the depth of his commitment and affection for the Asian church.

Figure 10: Synan (second from left) meets with Rev. David Yonggi Cho and wife Kim Sung Hae, and Rev. Younghoon Lee (far right), Seoul, Korea (Lyle Story, far left). Used with permission. Copyright Holy Spirit Resource Center, Oral Roberts University.

2000: Korean Translation Work

In November 2000, Dr. Synan's seminal work, *The Holiness-Pentecostal Tradition: Charismatic Movements in the Twentieth Century*, was translated into Korean and published under the title *A History of the Holiness-Pentecostal Movement Worldwide* 『세계 오순절 성결운동의 역사』. The book was co-translated by Dr. Myungsoo Park and myself, and has been recognized as a groundbreaking study that reexamines the historical significance of the Pentecostal movement within church history. In this work, Dr. Synan locates the origins of Pentecostalism within the historical trajectory of the Wesleyan-Holiness tradition, offering a profound insight into Pentecostalism as part of the mainstream narrative of Christian history. Above all, the book presents a systematic analysis of how Pentecostalism expanded across the globe, including Asia, making it an invaluable resource from a missiological and historical perspective.

2006: Young San International Theological Symposium

In May 2006, Dr. Synan once more traveled to Korea to participate in the Young San International Theological Symposium held at Hansei University. There, he delivered a keynote lecture titled, "Roots of Yonggi Cho's Theology of Healing," in which he offered a comprehensive analysis of the theological and historical influences that shaped Dr. Cho's healing ministry. He highlighted the complex interplay between the early Azusa Street Revival, the theology of Oral Roberts, and the historical realities of war, poverty, and national suffering in Korea, which together provided a unique emotional and spiritual impetus for Cho's theology. This presentation, which showcased Dr. Synan's keen historical-theological insight, served as a meaningful attempt to demonstrate how a ministry that began in a small Asian nation could be reexamined within the broader context of the global Pentecostal movement. Following the symposium, Dr. Cho, Dr. Synan, and I shared a meal at a Chinese restaurant in Yoido, where we engaged in deep conversation about the theology of healing. It was a rare and valuable moment in which spirituality, intellect, pastoral experience, and scholarship were beautifully interwoven. On that Sunday, Dr. Synan also preached at YFGC on Luke 24:49 and Acts 1:5 under the title "The Father's Promise," emphasizing that the Pentecostal spirituality of being filled with the Holy Spirit remains central to Christian faith today.

Conclusion

It is nearly impossible to capture the full breadth of Dr. Synan's theological contributions, academic writings, and influence on the Korean and Asian churches in a brief article such as this. Nevertheless, his theological legacy may be summarized in three major points.

First, Dr. Synan was a leading historical theologian who placed the Pentecostal movement within the broader continuum of Christian history. By tracing its roots to the Wesleyan-Holiness tradition, Pietism, and even to pre-Reformation Catholic spirituality, he demonstrated that Pentecostalism was not a sudden or isolated phenomenon, but rather a movement deeply grounded in the historical development of the church.

Second, he meticulously documented the global expansion of the Pentecostal movement, particularly its spread across the Global South including Asia, Latin America, Africa, and the former Communist bloc. Through this, he illuminated the global historical significance of Pentecostalism.

Third, he was a forward-looking theologian who envisioned the future of Pentecostalism centered on the Global South. With keen insight, he called the church to preserve the core essence of Pentecostal faith in the midst of the ever-changing tides of culture and history.

Above all, Dr. Synan carried a deep affection for the Korean and Asian churches. His thought and practice were completely devoid of Western ethnocentrism or cultural superiority. Instead, he embraced the revival of the Asian church as a genuine work of the Holy Spirit and offered sincere encouragement and theological support. He sought to empower Korean and Asian churches to recognize their identity and stand confidently upon their theological foundation. For this reason, Dr. Synan must be remembered as a crucial bridge-builder between the rising churches of the Global South and the long-established churches of the West.

In March 2020, my teacher, mentor, and senior in Pentecostal theology, Dr. Vinson Synan, was called home to be with the Lord. It is now our task to reflect on his theological legacy and burning passion, and to consider how we might carry forward the vision he so faithfully pursued. This, I believe, is the most fitting tribute we can offer to his memory.

15

VINSON SYNAN'S FORAY INTO AFRICAN PENTECOSTAL-CHARISMATIC MISSIONS

Kunle Ogunkolati

Introduction

Vinson Synan left an indelible mark on African Pentecostalism through his writings and intercontinental ministry engagements.[1] In July 1984, during his first visit to Nigeria, he was introduced to Deeper Life Bible Church by Segun Shafe,[2] the Vice Principal of the International Bible Training Center in Lagos, Nigeria. This visit shaped both the church and training center, and impacted the General Superintendent, Pastor William Kumuyi, at the Old Gbagada Headquarters' Church in Lagos.[3] I was part of that congregation at the Old Gbagada Church the night that Shafe welcomed Dr. Synan to speak and teach approximately 3,000 people. His message introduced a new paradigm for mission engagement and Pentecostal holiness that still has ripple effects today.

Encouraging IBTC

The International Bible Training Center (IBTC) was established about four years before Vinson Synan's visit to Nigeria. As an academic institution, the school aimed to equip West African pastors for regional evangelism, becoming an influential center. Deeper Life Bible Church (DLBC) had two training arms: one focused on local evangelism for domestic growth, and the other providing regional pastoral and evangelistic training for individuals from West Africa. Vinson Synan recognized these two schools as bifocal

---

1. J. Kwabena Asamoah-Gyadu, Vinson Synan, and Amos Yong, eds., *Global Renewal Christianity: Spirit-Empowered Movements Past, Present, and Future: Africa*, vol. 3 (Lake Mary, FL: Charisma House, 2016).

2. Segun Shafe, Vice Principal of International Bible Training Center and founder of Banner of Grace Church, Nigeria; personal interview with author, 2025.

3. William Kumuyi was the founder of Deeper Christian Life Ministry in 1973 with fifteen people at the University of Lagos.

institutes for equipping and establishing mission arms of DLBC and offered insights during his week-long stay.

Alex Akpojovor, the protocol officer and full-time worker at Deeper Life Bible Church, recalls Dr. Synan's visit and ministry at the Thursday Evangelism School in 1984. He remembers that Dr. Synan shared a series of messages with DLBC and had several meetings with Pastor Kumuyi throughout the week. "Several times, we brought Dr. Synan from the Sheraton Hotel, Ikeja Lagos, to meet with Pastor William Kumuyi at the International Bible Training Center where he resides," said Akpojovor. "They discussed and shared ideas about the goal and vision of Deeper Life, particularly focusing on retreats or camp meetings as effective means of impacting lives and helping people become fully committed disciples of Christ."[4]

Empowering Missional Vision

One of Synan's main accomplishments in his ministry was encouraging and strengthening missional vision. Synan's visit happened to coincide with Deeper Life Bible Church's strategic missionary vision for Africa that was to mark the first mass posting of missionaries to the continent. Synan emphasized that, "The church, as the body of Christ, has a single calling to be the light of holiness to the world through propagation and proclamation of the gospel." This deeply resonated with DLBC's Thursday Bible School's focus on training believers to reach the world. Synan stressed that, "The gospel is an imperative" for the church, as is the Great Commission to preach it to every creature. During the Sunday worship service at Gbagada, Synan declared, "In the midst of plurality of religion, we have singularity of redemption." This message countered the multifaceted African perspectives on salvation that often seek God through various sources apart from Jesus Christ, the Light of the World. Synan emphasized that the church must proclaim the unequivocal truth of Jesus Christ as the only Savior, regardless of opinion. Following, Itiowe affirmed that Synan's influence undoubtedly catalyzed DLBC's missionary expansion initiatives.[5]

Empowering Holiness & the Second Blessing

Vinson Synan also commended Deeper Life's vision and practice of holiness as unique in Africa. Synan stressed that holiness was a pivotal doctrine of the early church and is essential for today's church—not something to be

---

4. Alex Akpojovor, Former Secretariat and Protocol DCLM, Nigeria; personal interview with author, 2025.

5. Alfred Itiowe, Global Mission Director, Deeper Christian Life Ministry and Founder, Old Path Revival Ministries, Nigeria; personal interview with author, 2025.

compromised for numerical growth or cultural relevance. He spoke about Pentecostal holiness in particular, encouraging Pastor Kumuyi in his pursuit of holiness coupled with the gifts of the Holy Spirit. Then, during the Sunday worship service, Vinson Synan taught on Pentecostal holiness and heritage from the Azusa Street Revival, saying:

> I am from America, and I want to share with you what we do in America, which can be of help and encouragement to the Deeper Life Bible Church. The story of holiness is rooted in the Bible, believed and practiced by the apostles, which resulted in the early church revival. This biblical emphasis on holiness and power was restored in its fullness with the emergence of the Azusa Street revival in 1906.

After sharing on Azusa Street, Synan taught with vigor on holiness, emphasizing entire sanctification as the second work of grace subsequent to salvation by faith in Christ. Years later, Deeper Life Bible study leader Samuel Ogun admitted that many of those in that audience were initially skeptical about Dr. Synan's ministry. They perceived the West as having a diluted form of Christian faith compared to faith in the totality of the Word of God that Deeper Life leaders preached and believed.[6] But Synan's message on entire sanctification and holiness of heart, in the context of strong doctrinal belief, changed the image of Western Christianity as superficial with the light beaming from his impartation.

Empowering Pentecostal Revival in Nigeria

By the end of the week, Itiowe claims that Synan's visit had provided a framework for Pentecostal revival that came to Nigeria and West Africa a year later, in 1985, and to Deeper Life Bible Church in particular.[7] During his visit, Synan shared more with Kumuyi about Azusa Street, which motivated Kumuyi to seek the Lord for greater spiritual breakthrough. Prior to this, Kumuyi was seeking connections, open doors for ministry, and international credibility. He was looking for like-minded individuals to collaborate with, expand the reach of the holiness gospel to other countries, and support the teaching of holiness in Nigeria. In Vinson Synan, he found a valuable ally. After the visit, Kumuyi explained the significance of Synan's visit to the church as strengthening his convictions about the importance of ministry with ministers and ministries of like passion. Within the year, Kumuyi organized the Great Miracle Crusade at the National Stadium in Lagos. The crusade drew over 100,000 attendees daily, with thousands experiencing new birth, miracles, signs, and wonders.

---

6. Samuel Ogun, First Agege Lagos Bible Study Leader, Deeper Christian Life Ministry, personal interview with author, 2025.

7. Itiowe, personal interview.

This Pentecostal revival has since marked the emergence of an indigenous Pentecostal movement in Nigeria and West Africa. Similar to Azusa, this movement featured Pentecostal phenomena and sparked a new wave of evangelism across indigenous denominations in Nigeria and Africa, leading to missionary efforts in less evangelized countries such as Western Sahara, Mauritania, Djibouti, and Gambia. The revival has since been characterized by the restoration of God's power, transformation of lives, and a return to the apostolic era with prophetic manifestations of God's presence. The sowing that Synan did in 1984 encouraged Isaiah Lawon, then State Overseer of Deeper Life Bible Church in Ibadan, Oyo State, to deem Synan a friend of the church in Nigeria, and Deeper Life Bible Church in particular.[8]

Spirit-Empowered Legacy

I mentioned coming to know Dr. Synan when he spoke for that week in 1984. At the time, I was an undergraduate and president of the Deeper Life Campus Fellowship, University of Ife, (Now Obafemi Awolowo University, Nigeria). I saw his visionary leadership for a redeemed Africa through empowering African leaders to evangelize their native lands. His process entailed the passing of the relay baton from visionary leadership to indigenous churches and laying the groundwork for reverse mission in the global North from the Majority World.[9]

His messages and writings shaped my ministry and missions approach, which has now been passed down to four generations since 1984. For example, he inspired me to rediscover the art of presenting academics and the gospel in a way that resonates with intellectuals. This helped me raise trained and empowered students like gospel armies who could impact their world for Jesus Christ. Now some of them are global leaders—in Africa, Europe and North America—with their foundation rooted in the Christian leadership training they received in Ile-Ife, Nigeria.[10] New mission concepts from Synan's teachings led to initiatives like Meine Freude (1984), Perfugium (1985), and Campus Success Confab (1986),[11] which continue to have a lasting impact. Some of these leaders have become Region Overseers in DLBC, serving in cities like London, Manchester, Milton Keynes, Brussels,

---

8. Isaiah Dayo Lawon, East Africa Mission Director, Deeper Christian Life Ministry and Founder, Full Stature Mission International, Nigeria; personal interview with author, 2025.

9. Allan Anderson, "The Spirit and the African Spiritual World," in Global Renewal Christianity: Africa, vol. 3, ed. Vinson Synan, Amos Yong, and J. Kwabena Asamoah-Gyadu, (Lake Mary, FL: Charisma House, 2016), 304–20.

10. Kunle Ogunkolati, *Mobilization of lay Persons for Christian Mission: A Case Study of Selected Pentecostal Churches in Southwest Nigeria* (Ph.D. diss., Lagos, 2023).

11. Martin Dada, personal interview with author, 2025. Former Building Engineer, Deeper Life Bible Church, IBTC. University of Lagos, Building Department.

New York, Chicago, North Carolina, and Dallas.[12] This demonstrates the profound influence one person can have, generating hundreds of impactful outcomes.

Shafe likewise attests that Synan's teachings had a lasting impact on the IBTC and Deeper Life Bible Church's development and growth[13] In August 1992, Synan returned to Ayobo, Lagos to attend a church growth conference. At that time, Femi Afolabi, the publication manager of Women Mirror, by Deeper Christian Life Ministry, quoted Dr. Synan on this second visit:

> I'm excited to be here at Deeper Life Bible Church, Nigeria. This is the first time I have seen a church in Africa that believes the same things we do in America – teaching salvation, sanctification, and baptism in the Holy Ghost in the same way we do in IPHC, America. You have made me realize today that we are one in Christ, regardless of our color, culture, or calling. Jesus Christ is both Lord and Savior over His Church, whether in America or Africa, and specifically in Nigeria…[14]

He continued,

> Many denominations fear that standing on holiness will limit their followers, but what I see today in Deeper Life Gbagada disproves this fear, given the thousands of people in this congregation and worship service. Holiness is not about interpretations but about beliefs and traditions grounded in the scriptures. What's remarkable is that what I've seen today isn't different from what I've experienced in the West.[15]

He was a glorious encourager and bridge builder. And he was caring, personally. Hospitality was a hallmark of compassion for Dr. Synan. During his departure from Nigeria, at the airport, he gave Alex Akpojovor two envelopes—one for him and the other for Pastor Kumuyi. When Alex shared the envelopes with Kumuyi, the pastor opened them and instructed Alex to keep the one meant for him (Alex) but put his (Kumuyi's) envelope in the church's offering box. These gifts highlighted Dr. Synan's spirit of giving and care, especially about member care in ministry. Not everyone exhibits such hospitality, especially to ministers who may not be well-known.

Conclusion

I have highlighted how Vinson Synan significantly enriched the rapidly growing ministry of Deeper Life Christian Ministry in Lagos, Nigeria and of

---

12. Sunday Oyediran, personal interview with author, 2025. National Coordinator, Deeper Life Campus Fellowship, Nigeria/Africa.

13. Segun Shafe, personal interview with author, 2025.

14. Femi Afolabi, personal interview with author, 2025. Christian Women Mirror Publisher, Deeper Christian Life Ministry.

15. Afolabi, interview.

Pentecostal-Charismatic Christianity more broadly in Africa. As a prominent voice, he reinforced the new wave of Pentecostal holiness in Africa during its early stages of revival. He also thoroughly believed in the Global South's potential, having apocryphally said that Africa is a weapon for Jesus in global evangelization. Dr. Synan's work and personal encouragement provided a blueprint for renewing the vision of African congregations in contextual missions. His contributions as a Pentecostal scholar overall played a crucial role in shaping theological foundations and catalyzing revival in African Pentecostal-Charismatic Christianity.

Part III:

In Memoriam

In Memoriam
H. Vinson Synan, Ph.D.

December 1, 1934–March 15, 2020

International Pentecostal Holiness Church Tribute to Vinson Synan

Hugh H. Morgan

HARTWELL, VA[1] (March 17, 2020) – One of the greatest tributes (In Memoriam) in all of English history was the one written by Alfred Lord Tennyson about his friend, Arthur Henry Hallam. I do not have the linguistic ability to approach such a poem. But with the gift of writing God has given me, I will use it now for His glory and to honor my highly esteemed friend and brother in Christ, Vinson Synan.

As I thought about my longtime friend, Vinson Synan, I wondered how I would say in a few words what a servant of Jesus Christ has meant to me for more than half of a century. There are three men in history—Vinson Synan, Billy Graham, and Hugh Morgan—who had one thing in common. They were married to their respective wives on August 13. Billy and Ruth Graham were married in the late 40s, while Vinson and Carol Synan, and Hugh and Melvine Morgan were married the same year: 1960.

In the providence of God, our paths met at different times in the course of history. It was at the General Conference in Roanoke, VA that God gave me the privilege to nominate Vinson to be the General Secretary of the Pentecostal Holiness Church. It was Charlie Bradshaw who approached me and asked me if I would nominate Vinson Synan to be the next General Secretary. He said he was not going to run for that office. He suggested that I wear my Air Force uniform as a chaplain when I mentioned him. I told Charlie I would pray about it and ask Vinson if I may nominate him.

Of course, it was a surprise to Vinson, but he allowed me to nominate him, and we both trusted that if it were God's will, Vinson would be elected. Sure enough, he was elected. Well, the rest is history. Vinson was elected and served the church not only as the General Secretary (1973–1977) but later was elected as Assistant General Superintendent of the Pentecostal Holiness Church (1977–1981), and Executive Director of Evangelism (1981–1985).

Little did I know that the church (IPHC) leadership, namely Bishop J. Floyd, would call me and ask if I would consider resigning my commission as an Air Force chaplain and come to Oklahoma City to be the third President

---

of Southwestern College, now Southwestern Christian University. Melvine and I prayed and fasted about it, and finally God led me, with Melvine's blessings, to accept the offer as God's will for our lives.

It was there at the college that Vinson and I worked together, as he was a professor of history and served on my executive board. We, and our families, all attended Muse Memorial Church, the large church across the street from the college. Over the years, Vinson and I kept in touch and I was privileged to promote and advertise his many books and various speaking engagements. Until his death, we were in contact. When he was no longer able to speak, I communicated with Carol Lee, his wife, by phone.

I am grateful for the significant contribution of Mark Taylor, a son-in-law who married Virginia, a daughter of Vinson and Carol Lee. I have known Mark since he was in high school and in musical dramas like "Oklahoma." I followed his college years at Oral Roberts University when he was a lead singer in the World Action Singers. His parents, Dr. James and Mary Taylor, were dear friends of mine.

As we remember Vinson, we pray for the family and the grace of Christ to be with you all at this time.

In Appreciation

Kevin M. Ranaghan

On the vigil of Pentecost, my wife Dorothy and I continued our pandemic stay-at-home lifestyle.[1] Yet we experienced two outstanding Pentecostal events. With over 200,000 Catholic Charismatics (and I suppose Protestant and Orthodox Charismatics as well) we participated in the worldwide Pentecost streaming celebration hosted by CHARIS [Catholic Charismatic Renewal International Service]. But just prior to it, we were blessed to participate in the memorial celebration of the life and work of Harold Vinson Synan, streamed from the chapel at Oral Roberts University in Tulsa, Oklahoma. These two events are wonderfully connected in our "one current of grace."

It has been a privilege and a blessing for me to have known and worked with Dr. Vinson Synan since the early 1970s. He was a lifelong member of the International Pentecostal Holiness Church, with roots in the Azusa Street Revival. He was the son of a Pentecostal bishop and was the general superintendent of the denomination. Early on he was inclined to a life of academic scholarship, pursuing studies in theology and history. He was part of the first generation of Pentecostal scholars, a career path not always appreciated by older Pentecostals. Vinson authored twenty-five books and edited others. He taught undergraduate and graduate students at Oral Roberts University (ORU), served as Dean of Divinity at Regent University and returned to ORU to establish the Ph.D. program in theology. Along with Dr. William Menzies and Msgr. Peter Hocken, he founded the Society for Pentecostal Studies in 1970.

In the early 1970s, we began to work together and became friends in Christ. Vinson was always a thoroughly committed Pentecostal. Still, he was excited by the spread of baptism in the Holy Spirit among mainline Protestants and almost overwhelmed by the early Catholic Pentecostal movement. He was both shocked and filled with joy at what for him was a totally unexpected development, so he added to his role as a preeminent historian, that of being a leading Pentecostal ecumenist. He embraced Catholic and Protestant Charismatics as brothers and sisters in Christ. He

---

1. Used with author's permission.

shared his Pentecostal wisdom and was eager to learn what the Holy Spirit was doing with others.

For example, it was at a Continental Conference on the Charismatic Renewal in the Catholic Church held in the University of Notre Dame in the early 1970s that he first witnessed the long-forgotten Pentecostal practice of singing in tongues. He shared in the leadership of ecumenical committees too numerous to mention, was one of the leaders of the Conference on the Charismatic Renewal in the Christian Churches held in Kansas City in 1977, and then chairman of the NARSC (North American Renewal Service Committee) which held subsequent ecumenical conferences in New Orleans, Indianapolis, Orlando, St. Louis, and elsewhere. He never tired of building bridges through relationships with church leaders around the world, including at the Vatican. In fact, many people considered him to be the successor of David du Plessis a second "Mr. Pentecost."

At heart, Vinson was always a pastor, a spiritual father and mentor, the devoted husband of his wonderful wife Carol Lee, a beloved father and grandfather. Always a quiet and gentle southern gentleman, Vinson Synan, historian, theologian, ecumenist and charismatic leader made innumerable contributions to the Catholic Charismatic Renewal which drew 200,000 of us to our CHARIS Pentecost celebration. May Jesus welcome him to glory!

IN HONOR OF DR. VINSON SYNAN

Matteo Calisi

Dr. Vinson Synan was not only an esteemed scholar and protagonist of the contemporary Pentecostal movement, but also a fraternal presence for many of us Catholic Charismatics who shared paths of dialogue and collaboration with him.

For several decades he participated in numerous meetings—congresses, academic conferences, ecumenical seminars, and appointments of the Catholic Charismatic Renewal, both in the United States and in Italy and the Vatican, always contributing with competence, clarity and a spirit of communion. Over time, relations of mutual esteem and friendship were consolidated, nourished by a common passion for Christian unity. Many remember the meetings they lived together and the spiritual fraternity that was born from them.

Among these moments, the interventions he gave in the dialogues between Catholics and Pentecostals promoted by the Italian Charismatic Consultation in Rome and Bari since the early 1990s remain significant, as well as the conference at the Catholic Charismatic Congress at the San Nicola Stadium in Bari on Pentecost in 1992, on the occasion of the twenty-fifth anniversary of the Catholic Charismatic Renewal. Since the 1990s, Vinson Synan has fostered the encounter between leaders and scholars of different Christian traditions, involving them in ecumenical environments such as the North American Renewal Services Committee (NARSC), the International Charismatic Consultation on World Evangelisation (ICCOWE), and the Charismatic Leaders Fellowship (formerly the Charismatic Concerns Committee, Glencoe, Missouri).

In this perspective, in April 2010, at Regent University, he organized an ecumenical forum for the 50th anniversary of the birth of the Charismatic Renewal, with the participation of numerous Christian leaders of different denominations: Rev. Pat Robertson, Francis McNutt, Rita Bennett, Patti Gallagher Mansfield, Larry Christenson, Scott Kelso, Matteo Calisi, and Vinson Synan himself.[1]

---

1. See Sarah H. Dolan, "School of Divinity Celebrates 50th Anniversary of Charismatic Renewal," March 10, 2010, Regent University, http://www.regent.edu/news_events/?article _id=626&view=full_article.

He also collaborated on the initiatives that would later lead to Empowered21, promoting international preparatory meetings and encouraging the participation of representatives from various ecclesial contexts that included Catholic Charismatic leaders. In April 2010, a meeting of the Catholic Fraternity of Charismatic Covenant Communities and Fellowships and an ecumenical Roundtable of United in Christ International took place at the Graduate Center of Oral Roberts University. Catholics, Pentecostals and Orthodox Charismatics participated; Vinson Synan and Billy Wilson were among the keynote speakers. On that occasion, Synan also invited Catholics to contribute reflections on the future of the Catholic Charismatic Renewal to the volume *Spirit-Empowered Christianity in the Twenty-first Century*, published by Charisma House.[2]

In 2017 he agreed to speak at the Kairòs ecumenical meeting organized in Kansas City, Missouri to commemorate several significant anniversaries for the Church in the world: the 500th anniversary of the Protestant Reformation, the 50th anniversary of the Catholic Charismatic Renewal, the 50th anniversary of the Messianic Movement, and the 40th anniversary of the meeting of the first conference in Kansas City. Leaders present at the historic event joined the celebration, including Charles Simpson and Larry Christenson.

The Historian and the Ecumenist

An attentive scholar and convinced ecumenist, Synan showed a particular interest in the Charismatic experience in the Catholic Church. He was among the first Pentecostal scholars to consider the Catholic Charismatic Renewal not as an anomaly or syncretism, but as an authentic historical-theological event: a Charismatic irruption within a non-Pentecostal Church.

He interpreted this experience as a genuine work of the Spirit in the contemporary Church and documented the progressive change in Pentecostals' outlook on Catholics and on the reforms of the Second Vatican Council. He also highlighted how the Catholic Charismatic Renewal became one of the rarest and most real spiritual bridges between churches in the twentieth century, a sign of the overcoming of the confessional boundaries of Pentecostalism. He did not consider it a "Protestantization" of Catholicism, but the global spread of the Pentecostal experience: an authentic, historically decisive, theologically interpretable, and ecumenically fruitful phenomenon. He observed how, on the level of experience, Catholics and Pentecostals shared prayer in tongues, testimonies of healing, and experience of the outpouring of the Spirit. He interpreted baptism in the

---

2. Matteo Calisi, "The Future of the Catholic Charismatic Renewal: The Dawn of a Charismatic Awakening in the Catholic Church," in Synan, ed., *Spirit-Empowered Christianity in the Twenty-First Century* (Lake Mary, FL: Charisma House, 2011), 60–105.

Spirit not in opposition to the sacraments, but as an actualization of the grace already received: a different theological framework for the same spiritual event.

With over 150 million members, the Charismatic Renewal represents the largest lay renewal movement in modern Catholic history. For Vinson Synan, it constituted significant proof that charisms do not belong to a single ecclesiology but are an essential part of the "Pentecostalization of world Christianity."

He loved to repeat that the twentieth century was not the century of Protestants, but the century of the Holy Spirit.

A Man of Communion

Vinson Synan felt fully at home in the circles of the international Catholic Charismatic Renewal, including the Vatican—already at the time of Cardinal Léon Joseph Suenens, promoter of the "Catholic Pentecostal movement." Also, in the following years, he offered teachings in the meetings of the International Catholic Charismatic Renewal Services and, until the last years of his life, at CHARIS on Pentecost 2019 in Rome.

Many testify to how he encouraged paths of reconciliation between Christians, fostering relationships between Pentecostal, Charismatic, and academic environments, including Regent University and Oral Roberts University. He generously invited friends and collaborators to contribute to his publications and valued the work of others with sincere esteem.

His death leaves a real void for those who shared his commitment to Christian unity. However, the memory of his teaching, his service and his vision remains alive: a testimony of dialogue, faith and communion that continues to bear fruit.

SOCIETY FOR PENTECOSTAL STUDIES CELEBRATES THE LIFE OF FOUNDER DR. VINSON SYNAN

The Society for Pentecostal Studies[1] mourns the loss of Dr. Harold Vinson Synan and expresses our condolences to the Synan family. Historian, author, theologian, educator, leader, evangelist, church planter, pastor, mentor, family, and friend are but a few words many are using as they express their heartache in the passing of someone so special and influential […].

Dr. Vinson Synan, Dr. William Menzies, and Dr. Horace Ward were instrumental in founding the Society of Pentecostal Studies in 1970, following a discussion on the state of Pentecostalism during the ninth Pentecostal World Conference. The intention of "[serving] the church world by providing an authoritative interpretation of the Pentecostal movement," created a carefully drafted focus that guided others toward bringing attention to Pentecostal scholarship and is evidence of only the beginning of the legacy within Pentecostalism that Synan would continue to forge. Synan writes the full details of this experience and the events surrounding it in his paper presented at the 34th SPS Annual Meeting.[2]

Within the Society, Synan served as the first General Secretary (executive director) from 1970–1972. He went on to serve as President-elect of the society in 1973 and then President in 1974. His commitment to both education and Pentecostalism are evident in the early themes of the annual conferences: "Following the Spirit of Truth" (1970), "Higher Education Within the Pentecostal Perspective" (1971), "Perspectives on the New Pentecostalism" (1972), "Aspects of Pentecostal Origins" (1973), and "The Third Force and the Third World" (1974). Synan served a second term as executive director from 1980–1983 […].

As a prolific writer, Synan published more than twenty books on Pentecostal and Charismatic history and theology, in addition to numerous articles, papers, and public presentations. His love of writing never waned.

---

1. Used with permission from the Society of Pentecostal Studies, March 17, 2020.. Slightly adapted to highlight SPS work. Original note reads: "Thanks to Drs. Lois Olena, Dale Coulter, Kim Alexander, and David Roebuck for their assistance and contributions to this article."

2. Synan, "The Beginnings of the Society for Pentecostal Studies: Plenary Session," (34th Annual Meeting, 2004), https://sps-usa.org/download/history/synan_sps_beginnings.pdf.

Synan describes his 1971 book, *The Holiness-Pentecostal Movement in the United States* as the turning point in his career. This book was later revised and published again in 1997 as *The Holiness-Pentecostal Tradition*. This book gained immediate attention and was recognized in 1998 as number 15 in *Christianity Today's* book of the year list.

Following the original 1971 publication, he was invited by Fr. Kilian McDonnell to attend a Catholic Charismatic conference at the University of Notre Dame in 1972. When Synan arrived, he attended a prayer meeting in which he heard thousands of Catholic Charismatics speaking and singing in tongues. Synan felt that he was hearing the "heavenly choir" that had marked the early Pentecostal revival at Azusa and beyond. Overcome with the Spirit, he wept and repented, hearing God say, "This is real. I'm doing a new thing in the Catholic Church and it will spread over all the earth. You'll be a part of it and contribute to this great awakening. You must tell your own people what you've seen and lead them to pray for these Catholic Pentecostals." Synan became a member of the first team for the International Pentecostal-Catholic Dialogue in 1973. In 2017, he addressed thousands gathered in Rome for the fiftieth anniversary of the Catholic Charismatic Renewal.

Dr. Synan's work and ministry led him to be a forerunner in multiple shifts within Pentecostalism. He was quick to step over traditional social barriers between denominations, race, and gender. He was at the forefront of the Neo-Pentecostal and Charismatic movements across the globe with David J. du Plessis. In particular, he was part of a pre-Lambeth Conference of Anglican Charismatics in 1978, where approximately 40 bishops attended, including some African Archbishops. He also met George Carey, who went on to become Archbishop of Canterbury from 1991–2002. He, along with Dr. Ithiel Clemmons and Bishop Bernard Underwood, was involved in the Memphis Miracle meeting in 1994 that dismantled the all-white PFNA and organized the new and inclusive body known as the Pentecostal and Charismatic Churches of North America (PCCNA).

He became one of the key leaders of the global Charismatic movement. He was part of the International Congress of Anglican Charismatics that convened in Canterbury Cathedral in 1978. He also had audiences with Pope John Paull II and Pope Francis. Through all of this, Synan tried to embody his vision of building Charismatic bridges instead of barriers […].

Giants within the Christian faith cannot be summarized. The imprint of Dr. Vinson Synan is global. Yet, his leadership and influence never overtook his humility and deep desire to mentor young scholars. His masterful ability to tease out the potential in others is widely evident in the generations of leaders who nod to their relationship with Synan as instrumental. We are grateful to his wife, Carol, and their four children for so graciously supporting his life work and ministry. The lives he reached are immeasurable.

Regent University Celebrates the Life of Theologian Dr. Vinson Synan

"Dr. Vinson Synan was a powerhouse minister whom God used to bring His people together and grow His kingdom," said Dr. M. G. "Pat" Robertson, founder, chancellor, and CEO of Regent University.[1] "He was also a world-class scholar who recorded God's mighty works and trained new generations of ministers as dean of the Regent University School of Divinity."

Synan graduated in 1967 from the University of Georgia, earning a Ph.D. in American Social and Intellectual History. As a distinguished and prolific scholar and educator, he was an eminent historian of the Pentecostal and Charismatic movements, publishing numerous books, articles, scholarly papers, and giving many presentations on the subjects of history and theology germane to his Pentecostal heritage and his interest in spiritual renewal of the church.

"Today, the Regent University School of Divinity is known as a center for research on revivals and renewal movements," said Dr. Corné J. Bekker, Dean of the Regent University School of Divinity. "We are indebted to Dr. Synan for not only establishing and nurturing the robust research stream in church history at Regent, but his love for God's church continues to inspire us to serve the body of Christ in faithfulness and humility."

Following the Pentecostal World Conference in 1970, Synan was instrumental in forming the Society for Pentecostal Studies (SPS) and was elected as the society's first general secretary. He also served, over several years, as the society's newsletter editor. As a leader in the Pentecostal Holiness Church he served as General Secretary, then Assistant General Superintendent, and later as Director of Evangelism, inclusive of the years 1973 to 1985.

A distinguished scholar of the Holy Spirit's renewal of the church, Synan was magnanimous in his acceptance and love for all Christians. With a gracious spirit, Synan embraced the body of Christ in all its diversity. He touched and influenced countless lives as a pastor, denominational leader, scholar, teacher, and mentor.

---

1. Used with permission. Available at https://www.regent.edu/news/regent-mourns-the-loss-of-theologian-dr-vinson-synan/.

One of Synan's greatest accomplishments was his dedication in joining with other Christian leaders in opening the door to dialogue, building understanding, and fostering honor and mutual respect among leaders and participants in the Pentecostal and Charismatic movements. He has been recognized for his instrumentality in building relationships with leaders in the Roman Catholic church relative to spiritual renewal in both the Protestant and Roman Catholic traditions.

Synan served as Dean of Regent University School of Divinity from 1994 to 2006 and achieved emeritus status while he continued his contributions to teaching and mentoring. While serving as the dean, Synan was instrumental in supporting and encouraging the emerging educational resource of online learning programs and courses. As a strong advocate for women's roles in ministry, Synan initiated the hiring of the first female faculty members at the School of Divinity.

During the 100th Anniversary year of the Azusa Street Revival, Synan initiated a special event at Regent to celebrate this auspicious landmark in church history. Faculty and students collaborated in presenting a dramatic presentation in which the testimonies of Azusa Street participants were recreated as dramatic readings by students dressed in period costumes.

Dr. and Mrs. Synan were known for their gracious hospitality, often inviting faculty and staff, with their respective spouses, to visit their beautiful home to enjoy times of worship, fellowship, and sharing in community meals. Vinson was always willing to joyfully lead worship at these times and during faculty meetings as he accompanied songs of praise with his guitar.

He was intensely interested in supporting the scholarship of both faculty and students and generous in his mentoring of those who needed scholarly guidance. With his leadership, the School of Divinity progressed to new levels of moving forward in its vision and mission to the glory of God.

During the final phase of his prolific career, Synan and his wife moved to Oklahoma, where they would experience the joys of nearby family. With that move, Synan continued in educational leadership as interim dean of the College of Theology and Ministry at Oral Roberts University, later serving as Scholar in Residence. In 2017, he presented a moving address in Rome at the occasion of the 50th anniversary of the Catholic Charismatic Renewal.

In 2018, Synan, as a son of the Commonwealth of Virginia, was named to the Historical Hall of Fame of the Virginia History Series, a nonprofit devoted to the collection, organization, presentation, and dissemination of information about Virginia's history. Synan served the global Church and academy with great faithfulness. He will be greatly missed at Regent University, but his legacy continues with eternal impact.

MEMORIAL SERVICE
ROCK CHURCH, VIRGINIA

June 20, 2020

Pat Robertson

Today I want you to know that I mourn the passing of my dear friend, brother Vinson Synan.[1] Vinson was chosen by the Lord to chronicle the rise of the Pentecostal-Charismatic movement. He wrote the definitive book of the Pentecostal-Charismatic movement in the world, and his book is a classic. In addition, when he was here at Regent University, as Dean of the School of Theology, he introduced a doctoral program on Charismatic studies. He brought several of the most distinguished faculty members, and his work was legendary.

But there was always a little humorous side to Vinson that some of you might not know. During Thanksgiving, I had asked how I could do something for international students who were here and didn't have a place to go for the holiday. I asked Vinson if he would get me ten people from the divinity school whose families were overseas but that I could invite to share Thanksgiving with us. I also said, you and your wife need to be there. So he came, his wife came, and the students came. We had a lovely Thanksgiving meal together. Afterwards, we gathered in my living room, and Vinson had brought his guitar. I said, "Ok, now, we're all going to sing. Here is the dean of our School of Theology, Dr. Vinson Synan. He's got a Ph.D., and he's an author…" and so forth. Vinson takes his guitar out and he, as Dean, and I, as Chancellor, started singing marvelous songs like "The Wreck of Old 97" and "Wreck on the Highway" with these great classic lines: "When whiskey and blood run together/ I didn't hear nobody pray." Vinson and I were just singing and the students were listening. Of course I couldn't sing nearly as well as Vinson, but how much fun it was to sing all these country western songs and classics while students were there, listening to Vinson.

---

1. This tribute is excerpted from the memorial service at Rock Church, Virginia on June 20, 2020. Speakers included Rev. Craig Walker, John and Robin Blanchard, Bishop Dr. Doug Beacham, Bishop Dayton Birt, Archie Burt, Bishop Anne Gimenez, and from Regent University: Drs. Kim Alexander, Corne Bekker, Timothy Cremeens, and Pat Robertson, who closed this gathering via video (during the coronavirus pandemic).

Vinson was an amazing person. The thing he wrote in his book that I thought was so important was that he discovered that the Pentecostal-Charismatic movement was the fastest-growing expression of religion in the world. And he foretold—and was absolutely right—that at the rate it was going, there would be at least one billion Charismatics in the world. That is exactly what is happening; the movement is sweeping the whole world. Vinson was like a prophet, able to tell the whole world what was happening.

He was a great man, a wonderful friend, and a magnificent dean for our school. He went on to Oral Roberts [University] and was dean out there also, with so many things he did subsequently. But he came from a family of the Synans, here in Virginia, where leaders for the Pentecostal movement were in the early, early days. They made Vinson their chronicler. And so his name will live forever in the annals of Christianity.

We miss him. We celebrate him. We celebrate his life and we celebrate his passing. My dear friend, God bless you as you are there with the angels. I'm sure you are going to teach them "The Wreck of Old 97" and what it was like on the line from Washington to Danville when that train got to roll. I'm sure the angels love singing with you in the heavenly places. God bless you.

Craig Walker

I want to thank Carol and the family for the privilege and honor of being able to speak to you today about my friend, my fishing partner, and my next-door neighbor, Vinson Synan. I'm going to refer to him now as "Vinson" because that's how I knew him, with no disrespect meant. We moved next door to Vinson and Carol not knowing who we were moving next door to. In the Tidewater area, with a million and a half people, we "coincidentally"—by God's divine plan—moved next door to Vinson and Carol.

I remember the first time I met Vinson, he walked around the corner to meet his new neighbor. When he found out that I was an IPHC minister, it was game on! He was so delighted, and I was too. I couldn't believe that the Lord had done this! Later, as we would reminisce, I came to find out that when I was just a little boy, Vinson came and preached a revival for my father in Ohio. As he was telling the story, I remembered sitting on the floor as a little boy—a big deal for a preacher's kid because, back then, after a revival, you got to stay up late past bedtime and sit and listen to the evangelist tell his stories. And I remember being a little boy, sitting there, listening to Vinson tell about the great revivals he had preached and the bridges he had built. What a divine set-up.

Getting to know Vinson and Carol was such a joy for us. Like I said, we had no idea about the giant of the faith that we lived next door to. Our last visit with Vinson and Carol was in Oklahoma. On that last visit, he gave me a copy of his autobiography. Upon reading it, there's no way not to conclude that Vinson was a peacemaker. That's just who Vinson Synan was. Vinson was a bridge-builder. And last week, as I was reflecting on Vinson's life after reading his autobiography, I'm embarrassed to tell scholars, theologians, and my presiding Bishop that as I thought about Jesus saying, "Blessed are the peacemakers…" for the life of me, I couldn't remember what the reward was. I happened to be in my pool at the time, and I was saying, "What is Vinson's reward? What is Vinson's reward?" And I couldn't remember, so I jumped out of the pool, went and got my Bible app, and looked it up. I openly wept when I read Vinson's reward: "for they shall be called the sons of God."

Can it get any better than that? Isn't that the greatest reward you could hope for? If you have a younger friend, and you say to them one day, "You're like a son to me," how endearing is that? That's what Vinson heard when he arrived in heaven. "Blessed are the peacemakers, for they shall be called the sons of God." A peacemaker is who Vinson was. He brought unity. He built bridges not walls. He served many denominations and faithfully served his own. We've found that to be tricky, but not for Vinson. Vinson naturally did it because of the kindness already spoken of. In 1973, in a meeting of national Catholic Charismatic leadership, Vinson stood and declared, "God has called us to build charismatic bridges, not charismatic walls!" And then he went on to do just that. "…For they shall be called the sons of God."

At the general conference of the Pentecostal Holiness Church in Oklahoma City, August 1977, one delegate stood and offered an emotional resolution which darkly warned about the dangers of the Charismatic movement to the life of the church. Once again, Vinson, the peacemaker, the bridge-builder, rose to his feet and confidently offered a substitute. His resolution passed, which placed the Pentecostal Holiness Church squarely in favor of the Charismatic Renewal. Another bridge had been erected. Vinson would later write, "I shudder to think of what might have happened if the church had officially opposed the charismatic renewal. We would've been fighting ourselves and opposing the very reason we existed as a church." … For they shall be called the sons of God."

Sadly, I never had the privilege of sitting in one of Dr. Vinson Synan's classes. I regrettably never heard him preach one sermon. I never experienced him as a denominational executive of the IPHC. Nor did I have the privilege of traveling with him to a faraway place like Rome or Chile. I only knew him as my neighbor before I became aware of all of his great accomplishments. Herein lies the outstanding testimony of all great men: that even as just a neighbor, my life and the life of my family has been profoundly impacted by Vinson and the wife he loved, Carol Lee. I came to know a man who had built bridges for tens of thousands of followers of Christ, but he also took time to build a bridge with just a neighbor next door. "…For they shall be called the sons of God."

I was always amazed at his recollections of his travels. I can only imagine the look on my face when he casually mentioned to me one day, "I remember the second time I talked to the Pope…" I remember thinking, "Is he joking? Is he serious?" Only to conclude that this was his life! Vinson was such a humble man. He could tell you these things and never skip a beat.

My family grew to love Vinson and Carol. We traveled back and forth between our homes: in the living rooms, on the deck together, and fishing together. One day I was in their living room and Vinson looked

Figure 11: Vinson Synan meeting Pope John Paul II. He also met Pope Francis in Rome in 2017. Used by permission. Copyright Holy Spirit Resource Center, Oral Roberts University.

at me and said, "Give me your hands." Then he said, "Craig, if you don't write books, you'll only be able to reach people for Jesus while you are here on earth. Your work will end when you go to heaven, except for the people you reach through people they have reached. But if you write books, even after you are in heaven, you can win more people to Christ." You see, this bridge-builder was not just concerned about building bridges while he was here. He was concerned about building bridges after he was gone.

I later learned that he said this to all his students. But then Vinson prayed for me. He left his mark. It took me seven years to write my first book. But then I went home and I wrote the next book in three days; Carol edited it for me. Seven books later, in many different languages around the world, I've seen nearly 800,000 people come to Christ since that prayer. It worked for just a neighbor! I'm left to wonder how many people have been impacted by the life of Vinson Synan.

The greatest bridge that Vinson always wanted to build was between heaven and earth—His name is Jesus. He's the mediator. And beloved, today Dr. Vinson Synan is wearing the crown of righteousness in a new body, in unspeakable joy. No more aches or pains. He's rooting us all on from the grandstands of heaven. First Corinthians 15:51–55 says:

> Behold, I show you a mystery: We shall not all sleep, but we shall all be changed; In a moment, in the twinkling of an eye, at the last trumpet: for the trumpet shall sound, and the dead shall be raised incorruptible, and we shall be changed…then shall be brought to pass the saying that is written,

Death is swallowed up in victory. O Death, where is thy sting? O Grave, where is thy victory?

Revelation 14:13 says, "Blessed are the dead which die in the Lord from henceforth. 'Yes' says the Spirit, 'that they may rest from their labors and their works do follow them.'" So, Vinson would have me say to you today, "Whatever you do, don't miss heaven!" [. . .] He would say, "Make sure your sins are forgiven, but don't arrive there empty-handed."

Continue his legacy. Continue building bridges. I wish Vinson were here so I could ask him, "How do I build bridges, Vinson? During such troubling times, turbulent times, how do I build bridges? What would *you* do, Vinson?" Because he could build bridges between different backgrounds, religious affiliations, creed and color. Yet I know that Vinson would answer, "It's found in *the* Bridge. It's found in Jesus. Jesus is the ONLY way."

Vinson crossed the finish line, and our reunion with him is closer than we could ever comprehend. It's going to be like a vapor and then we will be with him. But until then, make this your goal . . . Let's arrive in heaven not empty-handed. Let's continue his legacy and build the bridges that he gave his life to.

MEMORIAL SERVICE
AT ORAL ROBERTS UNIVERSITY

May 30, 2020

William M. Wilson

On behalf of the Synan family and the entire ORU community, we want to thank you for being here today. We welcome you in attendance and also everyone who will watch this service online around the world today.[1] We've gathered here to honor one of the greatest leaders among Pentecostals and Charismatics, in my opinion. We hoped to have leaders around the world here today, but, of course, we are in an unusual season with the pandemic. People are not traveling, therefore, we are really glad we can stream this service and it will be archived for people to watch for years to come.

It is difficult to find a way to honor a legend, and Vinson Synan was a legend in his own time. But today, during this service, we're going to do our best. We're going to celebrate our dear friend indeed. So, during this gathering today, feel free to laugh, cry, worship out loud, say "amen," embrace the Lord's presence together and rejoice in the hope of eternity through Jesus Christ. If there was anyone ever deserving of special honor, it was Dr. H. Vinson Synan. We believe this service will honor him and his ministry. And we are glad you're here today.

Would everyone stand, please, as we welcome to the stage Reverend Rodney Fouts, pastor of North Church in Oklahoma City, who will lead us in prayer as we begin this service.

Rodney Fouts

It is truly an honor to be able to stand here right now and be able to speak on behalf of an incredible man of God. Carol, we are praying for you and for the whole family. Let me just say, your strength—I watched you by his bedside, week after week—and I was amazed. I was encouraged. And [to the

---

1. Video of this service can be viewed at: "Synan Memorial Service at Oral Roberts University," Synan Audio and Video 3, Oral Roberts University Digital Showcase, 15 March 2020, https://digitalshowcase.oru.edu/synan_audio/3. The Synan family's tribute video, played at the service, can be found here: "Dr. Vinson Synan Tribute Video," Synan Audio and Video 1, 15 March 2020, https://digitalshowcase.oru.edu/synan_audio/1.

kids and grandkids] your dad, your grandfather—what an incredible example. From the words of one of the grandsons who married Elizabeth, "When I walked into his closet to try on some his clothes, I felt the anointing of God flowing out of that closet." Now I know that we've been delayed in this moment, but in order to commemorate a Pentecostal historian, we are stopping right now. At the setting of the sun today, Pentecost Sunday starts and continues through the next twenty-four hours. What an appropriate day to be able to stop and remember such a man of God. Let us pray:

> Father, we thank You. We thank You for the unity that Dr. Synan exemplified—bringing people together. That's exactly what Your heart is for us in the Church. It represents exactly what Pentecost is. On that day, they were all in one mind and one accord when suddenly there came a sound from heaven. That unity for the body of believers still comes together under the umbrella of Jesus Christ to receive more of His power and His anointing for our lives.

> And God, I thank you for Vinson's example: his is a legacy. May we learn. May we look. May we ask for a double anointing of that presence and power upon our own lives. That his mantle would be placed upon our shoulders. That his writings, that his memory, will encourage us and challenge us to be men and women of faith, unshaken by the tests and trials of this world. Comforted only by the power of the Holy Spirit, the great Comforter who now lives inside of us.

> God, we ask that Your hand would be upon Carol and upon the family, and that You would guide and direct them. We know that the blessings of a man of God goes not just to one or two generations, but to 1,000 generations. And so, we look forward. May Your grace and mercy upon this family, and upon all who are listening right now. May we learn and go forth, continuing to live out the legacy that has been set before us. We pray this in the name above every name, the name of Jesus Christ. Amen.

Connie Dawson

Good afternoon. My name is Connie Dawson, and I represent one of hundreds, thousands, maybe hundreds of thousands of students that Dr. Synan has touched around the world. Carol Lee, thank you. Thank you, Dr. Synan's family, for allowing me the privilege of representing his students this morning.

Dr. Vinson Synan was born December 1, 1934 in Hopewell, Virginia. He is the son of Bishop Joseph Alexander Synan, Sr. and Minnis Purdue Synan. He is preceded in death by his parents; and his brothers Joe Jr., Maurice, Ronald; sister, Doris Jean; twin brother, Hubert Vernon; and granddaughter, Rebecca Marie Synan. He is survived by his beautiful wife of fifty-nine years, Carol Lee Fuqua Synan. Dr. Synan loved to tell the story about when he first met Carol Lee. He was a young evangelist preaching at a summer youth camp.

He loved to say, "When I walked into the cafeteria, there she was—my dark-haired beauty, with a smile that lit up the room." That smile still lights up the room, Carol Lee. He is also survived by: his daughters, Mary Clark and her husband Curt, of Falcon, NC; and Virginia Taylor and her husband Mark, of Edmond, OK; sons Vince Synan Jr. and wife Laura, of Edmond, OK; and Joey Synan and wife Ashley, of Piedmont, OK; his eldest sister, Maurine Gminder, and eight grandchildren; and seven great-grandchildren.

Dr. Synan was an author, pastor, educator, and historian with widespread global influence. As he was making preparations for his academic career, Oral Roberts, a friend of the family, offered him a full scholarship to earn his Ph.D. in theology at Harvard, Yale, or Princeton. He could take his pick, whichever one, if he would just return to Oral Roberts University and teach. However, Dr. Synan declined the offer because he had already received a full scholarship with stipend from the state of Georgia to prepare for his calling as a historian.

In 1965, he earned a B.A. in history from the University of Richmond. Then later, an M.A. in history and Ph.D. in American social and intellectual history from the University of Georgia. In 1950, he along with William Menzies and Horace Ward formed the Society for Pentecostal Studies. Synan was elected as the first General Secretary and served as the editor of their newsletter for several years. In 1972, Dr. Synan was invited by Kilian McDonnell to speak to the third annual Catholic Charismatic conference at Notre Dame University. This was a life-changing experience that marked the beginning of many years of leadership in the ecumenical movement.

He was the author of twenty-five published books, many of which are university textbooks. His sales, according to Eerdmans publishing, have equalled the sales of C. S. Lewis. He served as pastor of four churches in Virginia and Georgia, and taught at Emmanuel College in Franklin Springs, Georgia. In 1974, the family moved to Oklahoma City, where he served the Pentecostal Holiness Church as the General Secretary, Assistant General Superintendent, and Director of Evangelism. He was the interim president of Southwestern Christian University. He was also the director of the Holy Spirit Research Center and professor at Oral Roberts University. In 1994, he returned to Virginia as the Dean of the School of Divinity at Regent University, where he inaugurated the seminary's Doctor of Ministry program and founded their Ph.D. program in Renewal Studies. In 2017, he returned to Oklahoma as the interim Dean of Oral Roberts University School of Theology and developed the school's Ph.D. Program in Theology. Until his death, he was Scholar-in-Residence here at ORU.

Dr. Synan's life and ministry reached around the globe. He spoke many times in the two largest churches in the world: one in Seoul, Korea and the other in Santiago, Chile. He played a significant role in uniting the 350,000 member Jotabeche Methodist Pentecostal Church in Chile with the

International Pentecostal Holiness denomination. He was focused on a vision of unifying the church at large and helped gather as many as 50,000 Christians—including Catholics, Pentecostals, and Charismatics—from every major denomination for the Congress on the Holy Spirit in the Superdome, Kansas City stadium, Orlando, Indianapolis, and St Louis. He dialoged with Pope John Paul II and preached at the Vatican. He recently spoke to 30,000 Catholics at the Circus Maximus in Rome, sharing the stage with Pope Francis. He was a frequent guest on television programs such as the PTL Club, Trinity Broadcasting Network, and the 700 Club, to discuss the renewal occurring among Catholics and the exploding growth of Pentecostalism around the world. In 2018, as a son of the Commonwealth of Virginia, he was named to the Historical Hall of Fame of the Virginia History Series, a nonprofit devoted to the collection and preservation of Virginia's history.

Dr. Synan loved playing golf, tennis, soccer, ping pong, swimming, sailing, water skiing, and snow skiing. He played basketball at Emmanuel College with a faculty team. He loved music and oil painting, and two of his pictures hang in his home office. He learned Morse Code and had a shortwave radio license. He loved the mountains and the seashore. And above all, he loved people.

Students were a big part of his life. In 2006, I began my Ph.D. studies at Regent University. I knew of Dr. Synan and had read his books. He had been a major influence in my choosing Regent University. When the new, incoming cohort arrived, Dr. Synan invited all of us to his house for a cookout. When I walked in the house, he looked at me and said, "Where are you from?" I told him I was a missionary to the Philippines and I would be flying in for our cohort classes. He said, "That's going to cost you a lot of money. You'd better stay here with Carol and I." And so, for the next six years during my Ph.D. studies, I lived in a beautiful room with a bay window overlooking the lake. They called it "Connie's room," and they adopted me into their family.

Not only did Dr. Synan chair my dissertation, he became like a father to me. I had the privilege of hearing his stories as we shared meals around the dinner table, but I learned so much more than history from Dr. Synan. He taught me about loving and caring for people. He taught me how to love my students. Today, I'm a better person, better pastor, and better teacher because Dr. Synan was my role model. I am one of countless students through the years who have called Dr. Synan their teacher, friend, mentor, and spiritual father. Never have I met a man so gracious and so kind. I can say along with many that he not only taught us history, he taught us how to love—and for that we will be forever grateful.

William M. Wilson

Thank you, that was so lovely. I think we can all envision Vinson kneeling at the throne of God, singing today, and worshipping his Savior.

"Harold Vinson Synan." We've seen the "H." in front of his name, and it is for "Harold." Today, in my thoughts, I want to use his more formal name. Names are important. Scripture says a good name is to be chosen rather than riches and honor (Prov 22:1). And many times a person's name is a key, unlocking understanding to who they are. "Synan:" this name means "old." I'm sorry to the others named "Synan" in the room, but the name means "old." It reflects on history; it's a historical name. "Harold:" this name means "power" or "brightness." It's a name for royalty and statesmanship. Five kings of Norway, three kings of Denmark, and two kings of England all bore the name "Harold." And "Vinson:" this name means "victory" or "victorious." So, Dr. Harold Vinson Synan was a historian, statesman, and victorious spiritual leader.

As I thought about this time today, I reflected on different characters through the Bible, looking for who might portray and help us understand this great man, Harold Vinson Synan. I first thought of Luke, who documented the work of the Holy Spirit in his generation, traveling and doing great exploits. But ultimately, I landed on an Old Testament prophet—perhaps the greatest prophet of the Old Testament—Isaiah. Isaiah was a historian. He was also a statesman and spiritual leader. I want to say today, as I begin my remarks, that Dr. Harold Vinson Synan was one of the greatest men I've ever known. He felt at home in a room full of Ph.D.s, but also fully comfortable in a room full of country preachers. He could astound you with his research capacity and then warm your heart, singing old hymns with his guitar, many times at the same meeting. He could prophesy in one moment and present a research paper in the next.

Vinson was revered in the Spirit-empowered movement around the world. Dr. Synan was an accurate and eloquent historian. In many ways, he was considered by many, including myself, the premier historian of the Pentecostal/Charismatic movement of all time. He wrote about history, and he made history. My introduction to Vinson came, before I ever met him in person, through reading his book, *The Pentecostal Holiness Movement in the United States.* This book helped me as a young preacher synthesize the spiritual and spirit-filled roots of the Church of God movement in connection with the Azusa Street revival. It was Vinson, in his book, that introduced me to G. B. Cashwell, the apostle of Pentecost in the southeast, at the Azusa Street meeting—and, during those years, a formational leader in the Pentecostal Holiness Church. Cashwell is the person who was preaching when A. J. Tomlinson, the first general overseer of the Church of God (the movement I was part of) received the baptism of the Holy Spirit in Cleveland, Tennessee.

Cashwell himself received the baptism of the Spirit at Azusa Street. In some ways, Vinson helped me connect the dots.

I was then further introduced to Vinson's work, without meeting him again, through the North American Renewal Service Committee at a large conference in the Superdome in New Orleans in 1987. Vinson led the organization of this event with over 40,000 people in attendance. Lisa and I were both touched mightily by the Holy Spirit during that meeting, but we still had never met Vinson Synan personally. Years later, as we began preparations for the Azusa Street Centennial celebration in 2006, I was finally able to meet Vinson myself.

I found him to be a kindred spirit. He became a life cheerleader for me, and over time became a wonderful friend. Dr. Synan was a prolific writer of history, as you heard today, with over 25 books to his credit as either author or editor. I'm sure Vinson would have agreed with the statement by Oscar Wilde who said, "Anybody can make history; only a great man can write it." And if you have ever read Vinson's work—and most of us in this room have—I think he also agreed with Winston Churchill who said, "History will be kind to me, for I intend to write it."

Dr. Synan was an amazing historian. He had a nose for history and a gifted pen to capture it for all to read. "Synan"—old, historical, historian; "Harold"—the name of kings, royalty, statesmanship. Harold Vinson Synan was a prince of a man. Like the prophet Isaiah, Harold was welcome in the palace while also understood in the most common home. Harold Vinson was a statesman. He made people feel good. He had a unique ability to bring people together. He was revered among Charismatic Catholics as well as historic Pentecostals. He was loyal to his denomination while also broad in his Kingdom reach. Vinson could speak in front of 50,000 people or more in dynamic ways or share before a class of eight to ten people with no less eloquence or energy. He was a common man's theologian, yet also peer reviewed at the highest level.

Vinson started numerous organizations over the years, as you've heard, and led scholars groups as well as church leader groups. He was instrumental in some of the most successful ecumenical movements in Spirit-empowered Christianity in the twentieth century. He welcomed everyone while he never stopped being himself. This was what was so unique about Vinson. He could reach out to everybody, but he never stopped being Harold Vinson Synan. In fact, if you were around him long enough, he would always find a way to throw in something about theology—about sanctification or the initial evidence of the Holy Spirit. It didn't matter who he was with, he would always throw it in. Yet at the same time, he'd put his arms around people that disagreed with him vehemently.

When we began the Empowered21 journey in 2008 and 2009, we started holding conversation events with voices, leaders, and scholars around the world. The first person I sought to help me with this journey was Vinson. He traveled with me on several continents, meeting with leaders in the movement. Invariably, when he walked into the room, he was welcomed with open arms and revered by all. He was a delight to travel with, a prince of a man. We had great times together and made memories that will last for my lifetime. "Synan, Harold, Vinson."

I've said that "Vinson" means "victory" or "victorious." Yes, Vinson Synan was a great historian and scholar, and he was an amazing statesman. But most importantly, Vinson was a victorious Christian. He had the victory. He was like Isaiah. Yes, a historian. Yes, a statesman, but also a spiritual leader in this movement. Some of my favorite times with Vinson were in worship sessions and worship services. When the Holy Spirit began to flow, Vinson would begin to flow with the Holy Spirit. Vinson's head may have been full of knowledge, but his heart was all on fire for Jesus and the Holy Spirit. Whether preaching with all of his energy at that great church in Chile (I was with him one time. It was fantastic!) or just laying his hands on one sick person in a prayer meeting here on campus at ORU, Vinson was a man of God. He loved God. It was not a pretense. He always welcomed the Holy Spirit and His work in his life.

Vinson was a gentleman in every way. He was gentle and kind on the outside to everyone. However, this gentleman was tough on the inside. I made a trip to Hong Kong with Vinson during the Empowered21 conversations, and he joined me on that flight. I think we met somewhere along the way to Hong Kong. We were flying across the Pacific Ocean, and Vinson was sitting in a seat. It wasn't beside me because I was in another area of the airplane. We had just barely said hello when I had gotten on the airplane. About halfway across the Pacific Ocean, I got up out of my seat and walked back to where Vinson was. I began to talk to him, and I looked down, and Vinson had a catheter bag on. I said, "What are you doing? You're flying to Hong Kong but you should not be. Why are you on this plane?" He looked at me very kindly and simply said, "I couldn't miss it, Billy. I wanted to be with you and in this conversation." He had this kind of savvy, a deep commitment to the work of God that drove him beyond where others would go.

A few years ago, the Lord spoke to me about Vinson, that we were to provide a place for him at ORU. After a few months of talking to him and Carol, I convinced them to move back to Tulsa. And they did. I am honored that he was able to finish here at ORU and serve with us. His presence on our campus was such a blessing. He was a strength and comfort to everyone. We are honored that Vinson finished his Kingdom service as part of our team. Here on campus, over the last few years, Vinson did not always feel like going, but he kept going anyway. He would stagger and struggle, but he never quit. He had a deep drive to maximize every minute of life to the fullest for Christ's Kingdom. He never stopped fighting the good fight of faith. Even when I saw him last, in a hospital in Oklahoma City, he could not talk because there were things down his throat that would not allow him to communicate verbally. Yet, he communicated. He was still strong in faith, still believing, still trusting.

Vinson's trust in the Lord turned the frailty of his human condition into a triumphant life pronouncement. The pronouncement was that Jesus is the victor, and in Him we have victory, even over death. The apostle Paul said in 1 Corinthians 15:54–57, "So, when this corruptible shall have put on incorruption and this mortal shall have put on immortality then shall be brought to pass the saying that is written, 'death is swallowed up in victory.' O death, where is thy sting? O grave, where is thy victory? The sting of death is sin, and the strength of sin is the law. But thanks be to God which giveth us the victory through our Lord Jesus Christ."

So I say again: "Synan, Harold, Vinson," historian, statesman, victorious spiritual leader. The Synan name—I want to go back to that surname for just a moment. It was an ancient name rising most notably in Ireland where the Synan clan was wealthy and prominent in County Cork, at least according to Vinson's own research. On the Synan coat of arms is a motto. The translation of that motto, in English, is this: "I trust in the Lord and do not die." The declaration that death is swallowed up in victory finds roots in the inspiration of that person that I think most exemplifies Vinson in Scripture, the prophet Isaiah. In Isaiah 25:8, Isaiah pronounces, "He will swallow up death in victory; and the Lord God will wipe away tears from off all faces; and the rebuke of his people shall he take away from off all the earth: for the Lord hath spoken it." Verse 9: "In that day they will say, 'Surely this is our God; we trusted in him, and he saved us. This is the Lord, we trusted in him; let us rejoice and be glad in his salvation.'"

This amazing and victorious life would not have been possible without his sweet, faithful, praying, godly wife, Carol. You have been such an example to us over the years here at ORU. Always there, always kind, always supportive, and always smiling. You amaze us. I became pretty well-convinced that somewhere in heaven there is a dictionary, and in that dictionary is the word "saint," and right beside it is the definition of saint that simply says: "Carol Synan." Thank you for loving Vinson so well and giving him to the world, Carol. You sacrificed a lot for Vinson to do what he did.

Almost two years ago, as I close here, Vinson and I first discussed writing a book together. I'm honored that this new book that we were finally able to complete is being released in e-book form tonight, as we enter Pentecost Sunday. The book is called *As the Waters Cover the Sea: The Story of Empowered21 and the Movement it Serves*. Carol, I want to let you know that this book is dedicated to Vinson. Here is the dedication:

This book is dedicated to my co-author, Dr. Harold Vinson Synan, who is without equal in the Spirit-empowered movement. He had a brilliant mind, insatiable desire to learn, exceptional personality, supernatural anointing, and far-reaching vision. He was respected in both the academy and the Church, and received by both Pentecostals and Charismatics. He was a bridge-builder, excellent preacher, teacher extraordinaire, exceptional writer, historian for a movement, faithful administrator, loving husband, great father, and my good friend. This volume contains what may be the final published work of Dr. Synan. He pushed me to do this project so he could help tell the story of Empowered21. He was ahead of me in getting Part I completed and cheered me on as I finished Part II. During the editorial process, Vinson left the shores of earth and landed in the presence of our King. The loss to the Spirit-empowered movement represented by his passing is inestimable. Thank you, Vinson, for your amazingly fruitful life. You will be missed and always loved within the Spirit-empowered movement.

May God bless the memory of Harold Vinson Synan, and may his family be blessed for generations to come.

Kathaleen Reid-Martinez

Vinson Synan—A life well-lived, filled with deep faith! On behalf of Oral Roberts University, the Provost's office, and the academic deans and faculty, I want to say thank you to Carol Synan and to the whole Synan family for sharing Dr. Synan with us. We are so honored to be with you here today, just as we were honored to have had him in our midst. And to give thanks to Jesus Christ on behalf of our beloved brother, colleague, and friend, "Dean" Vinson Synan.

I'll always know him as "Dean," because he and I walked arm-in-arm at Regent University. I was a brand-new, unseasoned dean, yet he was there beside me—praying, seeking the Holy Spirit, and guiding me through those wonderful days of learning how to lead. I had the blessing of working with Dr. Synan at two universities, and as a result, I have been twice-blessed.

Like so many who knew Dr. Synan, our friendship was a gentle camaraderie that allowed conversations to ebb and flow seamlessly across the miles and the decades. We would talk about what it meant to grow up Southern. He was born in Virginia, and I in the deep South. We discussed how geography had impacted our lives, and the lifelong blessing that came with a Southern sense of family and community. Naturally, as educators, we talked about our love for knowledge, academic research, scholarship. And yes, we talked about those academic administrative concerns as well, and how to manage them. The planning: I'll never forget my greatest joy of having him at my table for lunch with the other deans as we planned for the University. What would we do in the next year in academics and how the presence of the

Lord fell, and we worshipped God in the midst of the planning. It was beautiful!

As I reflect on these personal memories, I am reminded that Dr. Synan's influence extended far beyond our individual conversations—his legacy continues to shape our university and the broader faith community.

Dr. Dawson has expressed so beautifully our sentiments regarding Dr. Synan as an educator, and our experience of how he encouraged all of us, whether it was me as a new dean learning to do the job, or whether it was a student, or fellow faculty member. He brought people into what they never dreamed they could do or be. He loved—and we loved that he loved us, and we learned how to love others. In that process, we learned to shape young men and women for ministry and all the other professions. At the core of nearly every conversation I had with Dr. Synan, we found our way back to discussing our strongest shared commitments: our love for Jesus Christ, the growth and equipping of the church, our Pentecostal traditions and upbringing, and our belief in the infinite supernatural power of the Holy Spirit to transform human hearts and lives.

When I reflect upon Dr. Synan's life, I am reminded of a line in Madeleine L'Engle's memoir, *A Circle of Quiet*: "One cannot be humble and aware of oneself at the same time." I never knew Dr. Synan to be aware of himself or to feel the need to stand on his accomplishments, which were numerous. Rather, he was a man who demonstrated excellence with the greatest humility. Those of us who worked alongside him in academia counted on his steadfast intellect and professional experience. He continuously brought his expertise, gentleness, wisdom, and excellence to the work at hand—to both great and small tasks.

There are some people whom you encounter in life who teach you to appreciate and value life more deeply because of the way they lived. Dr. Synan was such a person. Spending time with him was to know Jesus, and to know Jesus a little better—because his life, his actions, and his words pointed the way to Christ and celebrated the uniqueness of the Spirit-empowered life. What a privilege: to feel the presence of Jesus and the power of the Holy Spirit in every conversation with him, whether the conversation was short and trivial or about important decision we had to make. We could call on him for wisdom, and he would always respond with grace and insight.

Indeed, his life and witness are reflected in 2 Timothy 1:12 (NASB), which says, "For I know whom I have believed, and I am convinced that He is able to guard what I have entrusted to Him until that day." As a charge to us, I know Dr. Synan would want us to remember the next verses: 2 Timothy 1:13–14 (NASB), "Retain the standard of sound words which you have heard from me, in the faith and love which are in Christ Jesus. Guard, through the Holy Spirit who dwells in us, the treasure which has been entrusted to you."

God, I thank You for Vinson's example—truly, he is a legacy. May we learn from his life. May we seek and receive a double portion of the Holy Spirit's presence and power upon our own lives. May his mantle rest upon our shoulders. May his writings and his memory continue to encourage and challenge us to be men and women of faith—unshaken by the tests and trials of this world, and comforted always by the power of the Holy Spirit, the great Comforter who now lives within us.

God, we ask right now that Your hand rest upon Carol and her family, guiding and directing them in every step. We know that the blessings of a man of God extend not just to one or two generations, but to a thousand generations. So, I look forward in faith, trusting Your grace and mercy for this family and for all who are listening—that we may learn, go forth, and continue to live out the legacy set before us.

We pray this in the name above every other name, the name of Jesus Christ. Amen.

Wonsuk Ma

My name is Wonsuk Ma, and I am Dean of the College of Theology and Ministry at Oral Roberts University. It is so nice to be with your family, Carol. Julie and I tried so hard to convert you and Vinson to Korean-ness as much as possible. Our friends in Asia say what a powerful and gentle statesman Vinson always was, a global statesman. I believe there are many unknown contributions he made throughout the world, one of them being in Asia.

It was 1998 when the Pentecostal World Conference met in South Korea, in Seoul. They met in Yoido Full Gospel Church. A group of Asian Pentecostal young scholars, including myself, gathered together to take full advantage of the presence of Dr. Vinson Synan along with William Menzies—two of the three founding fathers of the Society for Pentecostal Studies. They were there, so we asked them, and Dr. Synan in particular, if they could help birth the Asian Pentecostal Society. It was born there—with great blessing and wisdom coming from these two founding fathers of the Society for Pentecostal Studies.

I believe that there are many more stories like this that will surface in the coming decades. Now there is a thriving movement of Asian Pentecostal studies and a rise of Asian Pentecostal scholars. Dr. Synan didn't care about the seven or eight hour-long drive from Manila to Baguio City in the Philippines to meet with young Asian Pentecostal leaders and encourage them. It was a great experience. He was an encourager. He knew how to sit down and encourage people, challenge them.

Second—as we already heard—Dr. Synan came here to ORU once in 1990 as professor of Pentecostal-Charismatic Studies and also as the Director of the Holy Spirit Research Center. He told me quite a number of times that part of his assignment was to develop the Ph.D. program in theology. But only one meeting was initially held to discuss this. Fast forward: he came back—and this time, it was the right time. There was new leadership, global vision, and new energy. And when Julie and I joined Oral Roberts University in 2016, who was there? A half-Korean Dr. Synan and Carol, here welcoming us! We talked about how the new Ph.D. program could be shaped. Until his passing, Vinson was the Director of the Ph.D. program here. He gave birth to the program that was the dream and desire of the University from the very beginning. So we praise the Lord for his leadership, inspiration, and great contribution.

We had the first cohort of ten incredibly diverse Ph.D. scholars. They were perhaps the luckiest Ph.D. students at ORU because they had the tutelage of Dr. Synan; they were the only cohort that was privileged to have this. He knew the value of scholarship to be disseminated. He encouraged us to relaunch Oral Roberts' journal of theology, called *Spiritus*. We are now planning a special issue on Spirit-empowered leadership, dedicated to the life, work, and influence of Dr. Synan. Dr. Wilson mentioned how their new, co-authored book is coming out tomorrow. So, ORU Press, as a new venture, has received great influence and encouragement from Vinson. I think he was here by God's appointment to start something crucial in the coming days of the Spirit-empowered movement.

Lastly, I simply reflect as a person, as an individual. When Dr. Synan was retiring from his dean's post at Regent in 2006, he urged me to succeed him. Although our paths didn't come together then, and Julie and I spent ten years in England, we came to ORU only to find Dr. Synan. He was now my Dean! Finally, then, I became part of the team. As I said, Julie and I tried to be diligent in converting him and Carol into complete Korean-ness. We prayed, and all of sudden…nearby came a Korean restaurant opening! So, guess what? You ate more kimchi and bulgogi. Seriously, I'm so grateful. So grateful that he called me "Mr. Dean," while I said, "You are *my* dean forever." Every time we saw him, he would say *yesunim gamsahamnida* – in Korean, "Jesus, thank you."

So, I'm grateful. I'm truly grateful for his life, influence, and friendship. God bless you.

Harold Hunter

I'm Dr. Harold Hunter, Director of the IPHC Archives and Research Center. But my name does not matter because I am simply one of many who would stand here today and rejoice in the fact that they are counted among those who look to Dr. Synan as a mentor, colleague, and close personal friend.

It was one of his gifts to those of us who knew him. If I were speaking theologically, I would refer to Vinson as a "charism"—not only to his home church, the IPHC, but to Pentecostals around the world and many other Christian traditions. He was clearly the dean of Pentecostal historians in the United States for his generation.

But, of course, some stories get a little exaggerated over the years. Somebody said the other day that they thought that Vinson Synan knew more about the Azusa Street Revival than Jesus does. Vinson was like that too, always good about coming up with quips, quite clever ones, whenever he talked to an audience. I remember one time when he was in Cleveland, Tennessee. For those of us who have centered parts of our lives around that city, it is known for being the headquarters of Church of God and the Church of God of Prophecy. There are all kinds of universities, schools, headquarters, buildings, and printing presses. Churches are filled all over the city. But I remember one time that Vinson spoke there, in Cleveland, to a Pentecostal group that included all these folks and he quipped, "You know, since I've been in Cleveland, I've heard that there are more Baptists in here than there are people."

Well, you have heard Dr. Billy Wilson talk about his full name, Dr. Harold Vinson Synan. If you look at his 1971 book, *The Holiness Pentecostal Movement*, you'll see in the preface that he uses his full name. I met him in 1975, and later, after I got to know him, I accused him. I said "Vinson, I believe that since we met, you want to make sure that nobody confuses *us* Harold's, so you just go with H. Vinson Synan." That was a very smart move on his part.

Now the truth of the matter is, I have been in ninety countries around the world, and I have lost count of the times that I've been treated better than I should have—because I could say that Vinson Synan was a close personal friend. There was one time when, for example, in the 1990s when we were trying to do something with the World Council of Churches, we wanted Pentecostal engagement. I wanted the endorsement of a leading Pentecostal voice from around the world. I wanted Dr. Yonggi Cho, Pastor and Founder of Yoido Full Gospel Church. I wanted to talk to him. It was Vinson that made it possible for me to have a private meeting with Dr. Cho in his office in Seoul. And as a result of that conversation, Cho endorsed the meeting I discussed and sent a young Korean scholar to a subsequent meeting that we had later that year. It was Vinson, in one of the SPS meetings, who introduced me to that young man back then, Dr. Younghoon Lee. Now Dr. Younghoon Lee is a good friend, and he is the current senior pastor of Yoido Full Gospel Church.

On a much smaller scale, back in the 1980s when I was teaching at the Church of God Seminary, I was trying to broaden the horizons of the Church of God of Prophecy. When I went to visit, there was a PFNA meeting and the head of the Assemblies of God, Zimmerman, was in town. I said, "Vinson, is there some way that we can get something together?" I added, "Tomlinson won't move. I can't get him to come over. Is there any chance that Zimmerman would go to Brother Tomlinson?" Vinson made it happen. We even had a picture made, and it was published…but they cut me out of the picture, so you have to take me at my word!

Vinson was part of the group that led the transformation of PFNA to PCCNA. He does not get a lot of credit for that, but he was the key player. Yesterday in the IPHC Archives, I was going through some photos and there was a photo of Vinson, Ithiel Clemmons, and B. E. Underwood—the main players of that effort. Why were they together? Because they were all part of NARSC, the group that put on multiple conferences with 40,000–50,000 people. I was on the steering committee. I knew Ithiel Clemmons through SPS and his writings. But I saw personally, up close, the mentoring role that Vinson played in making that happen. This is another of his major contributions.

Vinson was also on the executive committee of an international group called ICCOWE. When I put together the first global conference for Pentecostal scholars around the world, with the help of Dr. Peter Hocken, and with Jürgen Moltmann as our keynote speaker, Vinson was the one who helped make sure that they allowed me to do what I wanted to do.

I remember when we were together at another conference related to the group in Malta. It was such a special meeting for me in a lot of different ways. In his typical way, he came up to me, put his arm around me, and started encouraging me. He could not stop taking time to come and encourage me and tell me to keep doing the work of ecumenism that I felt God had called me to. It was one of the reasons that I admired the fact that he sat on the boundary of the church and the academy. He was not only an IPHC executive, he was the primary founder of SPS.

I followed his footsteps to Rome, Geneva, and many other cities around the world. His global impact was remarkable. I have seen it myself. I am a first-hand witness of a lot of his work with these groups. I can confirm that, regardless of who he was surrounded by, he never compromised his Pentecostal identity. He never forsook his identity. On the other hand, when he was in an academic situation, he would be the first one to pick up a guitar and sing a song. He would invite everybody to get singing, standing, and praising the Lord, in order to lay hands on people and start praying in tongues for them.

I personally believe that we would not be honoring Vinson the same way we are today had he not married Carol. I believe her contribution is far much more than a lot of people know in public. God blessed this union and made them partners in ministry that has reached around the world. I am praying for the Synan family in this time.

When I first met Vinson, it was 1975. SPS was hosted by the Ann Arbor Catholic Charismatic Community, and I met him in a hallway. I remember I said, "I'm trying to learn about G. B. Cashwell." I had been in California, driving around on my motorcycle, going to Azusa Street on Bonnie Brae. I wanted to learn more about those links. So I went over to Vinson and said, "I want to know more than what you published. I want to know more about this story." And, you know, just a few days ago another thing came up about G. B. Cashwell. But I can't call Vinson anymore. I can't talk to him anymore. So I pray that somebody puts on the mantle to continue his work. Vinson had a remarkable memory. And so I say, with my friends, may the memory of Dr. Harold Vinson Synan be eternal. God bless you.

Daniel Isgrigg

My name is Daniel Isgrigg. I am the current Director of the Holy Spirit Research Center here at Oral Roberts University, standing on the broad shoulders of Dr. Synan, who of course came here in 1990 to serve as the Director of the HSRC and as a professor.

Dr. Synan first came to ORU in 1966 in the summer while he was working on his Ph.D. research. He came to what was, at that time, called the Pentecostal Research Center, which was the beginning of ORU's library. This was the first year the school was open. Vinson stayed in the library for two weeks, day and night. He said it was like heaven on earth, being surrounded by all the materials that were here. At that time, it was the best collection of materials on the Pentecostal and Charismatic movement, and it was a great place for him that forged his understanding and helped produced his material. So his roots go deep. I am just so thankful today to be standing on those shoulders.

I want to share two quick stories that encapsulate his influence on me as part of the next generation of Pentecostal scholars. I was, of course, a fan of Dr. Synan. I had read his books, but when I got to meet him in person, I though, "Oh my goodness, this is Vinson Synan—I can't believe it." The first time I met him I was trepidatious. I was so surprised at how kind he was, and how interested he was in me. I was nobody and he was somebody, but he made everybody feel that way. That really spoke to me.

I want to tell you one of the famous stories that he loved to tell. I won't do it as well as he did, but I told him that I had done some work on Howard Ervin, who is a founding faculty member here. He commented, "Howard Ervin is very important to me. One of my favorites." Then he said that many years ago, he went to his first Full Gospel Businessman Fellowship's meeting. At that meeting was a Presbyterian friend, and Ervin was the main speaker for the session. After the meeting, Ervin came off the stage and grabbed Dr. Synan. He said, "I want you to come with me to this room to help me pray with somebody to receive the baptism in the Holy Spirit." Now at this time, as a Pentecostal, Dr. Synan was still not sure about the Charismatic movement that was taking place in mainline denominations. But he agreed and walked with Dr. Ervin into a quiet little room. Immediately, Dr. Synan thought to himself, "This is not going to work." He had been told the man was a Lutheran pastor, and he said, "This is not going to work." Moreover, Dr. Ervin had the pastor sit down in a chair to be prayed over, and Synan said to himself again, "Well, this isn't going to work." Because he recalled, in Pentecostal tradition, "You have to hold their hands up and it is too quiet in here. It is not loud enough. We are not shouting enough. We are not patting him on the back enough." So that's why he had said, "There's no way that this is going to work."

But after they began to quietly pray over the Lutheran pastor, all of a sudden, the gentleman just burst forth in praise, praying in the Spirit and speaking in tongues! Dr. Synan said, "Wow, I didn't even think Lutherans could be Christians, let alone be filled with the Holy Spirit!" He later admitted that this was the moment that his identity began to shift from being a classic Pentecostal, born and raised, to seeing what the Holy Spirit can do all over the world in people of every tradition. Of course, fast forward: he becomes the leader of the Charismatic movement through his NARSC organization and all the Charismatic conferences that took place.

The second story I want to tell is that as a Scholar-in-Residence, his main job was to write and to do research. From time to time, he would come over to the Holy Spirit Research Center. I loved it when he came because I wanted to glean all that I could. He would come in and say, "I'm looking for this" or "I'm looking for that," and we would pull out materials. One time I pulled out some materials that we had, and it was the Eastern Conference News of the Pentecostal Holiness Church. We were looking at it and he said, "Do you see this?" I said, "See what?" And there was Oral Roberts' picture on the front of the paper. It had been 1943 and Oral served as the editor—and Dr. Synan had not known that. It was like a light bulb went on and he was an eight-year-old kid opening a Christmas present. Even in this period of his life, he never lost his curiosity. He never lost his ability to want to research and find out more. It was so fun to sit with him and to do research with him, looking at all these things. It was such a delight! And the fact that he wrote two books in his last two years of life is pretty amazing. Who else could do that but him? If you have already written 25 books, you would probably just hang it up—but not Vinson Synan. He was always curious, always still going, always producing, always investing.

I had the opportunity last March [2019] to go with Carol and Dr. Synan to SPS. They called me out of the blue and said, "Hey, we are going, but we are renting a car and wondered if you needed a ride from the airport to the place." That year, SPS was in Washington D.C. so I said, "Sure, I would be glad to." I got to spend that entire week being around Vinson and Carol. He was struggling a little bit with his health, but he still wanted to go. And I am glad he did because he was at what would be his last SPS. As he walked around and attended the various meetings, everybody stopped to talk. Everybody stopped to take a picture. It was like a farewell tour for this man who means so much to us as a community. We all got to fellowship with him. We all got to spend one more moment. I think that was really special.

And so, as a younger scholar, I just want to say that I am so thankful for Vinson Synan. He was a mentor. He was a friend. I am going to miss him dearly, and I will model my life after him.

Mary Carol Synan Clark

I'm Vinson's daughter Mary, and I'm here to bring him down to the human level. He had a family, and he didn't always talk about church and scholarly things. But before I present what I wrote, I was asked to read the following letter that we received [from the Holy See] on [May] 26. It says:

Dear Ms. Synan and Daughter, Mary;

Deacon Darrell Wentworth told me about the Memorial Service that will take place at the Oral Roberts University Chapel next Saturday, in memory of your husband and father Vinson. Allow me to join you in prayer and thanksgiving for the life of the faithful servant of the Lord that Vinson has been.

I had the privilege of knowing him and spend time with him when we were together in the Pentecostal-Catholic dialogue and keep the memory of Vinson as a deep spiritual and gentle person. I remember once, during a weeklong dialogue we were having in Venice, one evening we went together, Vinson and I, for a long walk and got lost in the intricate streets of the city, eventually arriving home after a long and very fraternal sharing. I have in addition a personal debt to Vinson. He was one of the organizers of the historic Kansas City ecumenical Rally back in 1977 which was the starting point of my Charismatic experience and a turning point in my life.

While mourning for his departure, you should rejoice at the thought that, being with the Lord Jesus in heaven, he is more alive than ever and closer than ever to his dear ones on earth.

I wish you a blessed Pentecost.

Sincerely and fraternally in Christ and in His Holy Spirit,

Fr. Raniero Cantalamessa

Preacher to the Papal Household

And what I want to read now is just some thoughts that I had about my dad. This was written back in March, when he passed: As I sit on the plane flying back to Oklahoma, my thoughts don't know where to go, what to say or to do. Words will never be enough to express the loss of my dad. At the age of 85, I thought I could justify his passing—after all, we're going to cross that bridge one day. Death can't be justified and it can't be cheated. But Dad did beat death on March 15 when he left his earthly body and his spirit rose to heaven to be with the Lord. The grave has no hold on him. He is in heaven and that I can accept.

I'm blessed to have been born into a family that has served the Lord for generations. With godly parents, I can say that accountability was always there, right behind what was my stubborn rebellion towards my parents and God. My life was filled with regret from the past, but my parents and my God are filled with forgiveness so I can have a future in Christ. Dad taught me a lot over the decades. Looking back at six years of age, I remember telling Dad that if he and Mom hadn't had my sister Virginia and my brother Vince, we could have had a Cadillac. To that he immediately replied, "Well, if I didn't have you, we could have had a Rolls-Royce." That perspective put me quickly in my place, and I never forgot it. (And we still don't have a Rolls-Royce.)

The life of a pastor's daughter was going to the Hartwell Pentecostal Holiness Church in Hartwell, GA. And it was not optional. We went to church on Sunday morning, Sunday night, Wednesday night, and every night during revival, like it or not. Most of the time, I didn't think twice about it. It was like attending school–it was not optional. But I will never forget one Sunday night, when I was around 7 years of age, going down to the altar and asking Jesus to come live in my heart and be my Savior. I remember Dad was there praying with me and it was the first time I remembered crying because I discovered that I love Jesus. And I've never stopped loving and crying for Jesus since that night.

I'm sure there were times that we made Mom and Dad cry out to Jesus, too. They needed His help because raising four kids was a job in itself, along with pastoring a church, teaching at Emmanuel College, and Mom working for the Pentecostal Holiness Church headquarters. Of course, I can't go any further without telling about my brother Vince, who was an avid fan of sleeping on a church pew through Dad's sermons. One Sunday night, my parents assumed he had gone home with some friends after service. That assumption when we got home was suddenly replaced with the stark reality that he must still be at church sleeping on the pew. Vince never woke up between the time the doors of the church were locked and when we finally picked him up. Mom and Dad were so thankful! I'm not sure if Vince still sleeps like that in church. Probably not.

For the first thirteen years of my life, I lived in Franklin Springs, GA. And life with Dad and his twin brother Vernon was always interesting. There were always silly songs like "My Bonnie Lies Over the Ocean," "I Went to a River and Couldn't Get Across," or "Found a Peanut." Laughter and music were always a part of our family when we were all together. I will never forget Dad playing his guitar, which by the way, he learned to play on his own. It was one of his passions. Just this past Christmas, I videoed him as he sat with Chad Synan, one of his grandsons, and played effortlessly and just as passionately as he did when I was a child.

About ten years ago, I went with him to hear a group of thirty classical guitarists all playing together on stage, and I understood that night why he loved classical guitar. As many of you know, in church, he took every opportunity to play and sing praise and worship music. Always carrying that guitar case all over the United States, from church to church, honoring the Lord with his talent he was blessed with. My sister Virginia loved to dance endlessly to the music as Dad played. No doubt they will have a father-daughter dance when she gets to heaven. Maybe they will dance before the Lord. How beautiful would that be? Maybe Dad will meet us in heaven with the guitar and a song. I look forward to that day.

I will fast forward to Mom and Dad's life in Virginia Beach. I spent as much time with them as possible. I loved being with them and really enjoyed the Virginia Beach area. I was constantly traveling up and down the interstate with my husband Curt and my children, Lauren and Justin. And eventually with my grandchildren—Jayden, Cazlyn, and Eli—to go see them. They loved seeing their Grammie and Granddaddy and hanging out at their house. And who wouldn't? They lived on a lake. The beach was twenty minutes away. The mall was also five minutes away (that was my favorite). Dad thrived in Virginia and loved teaching and being around the students at Regent University. Dad was a native Virginian, as well as Mom and I. And many of their brothers, sisters, nieces and nephews were fairly nearby to visit frequently. They loved entertaining friends and family. Mom and Dad also loved eating at restaurants on the ocean and traveling in their Winnebago camper to the Eastern Shores.

One year, Dad served as the Virginia State Chaplain of the Winnebago Club. He would get up and mix his history and gospel into his devotions presented to the campers. Mom said they always enjoyed hearing him speak. Life with Dad was busy, as he was always flying or driving to a meeting or preaching a conference. It was a way of life. And for all of the work he did for the Lord, we didn't always see it or recognize all of his accomplishments. There were always the accolades from others, but for us he was Dad. He would always greet me at the door and say, "You turned me into a daddy…" "…and then into a granddaddy; and now I'm a great granddaddy." I could quote it in my sleep. Every time I'd walk in that front door, he would say that to me, and I would respond, "I know, Dad. You always remind me." But what I wouldn't give to hear it one more time.

Two Novembers ago, my brother Joey and I went to Duck, NC to spend time at the beach with our parents, uncles, and aunts. One sunny afternoon, I remember sitting outside on a bench with Dad waiting for the others to come downstairs. As we sat there, he couldn't say it enough how glad he was that Joey and I came to be with them for the week. For Joey, that was one of the most special trips he had ever taken. We spent so much time fishing on the beach, talking, and eating together. I had driven my little Miata car up to Duck that week, and I suggested that we take the top down so Joey could drive Dad to the restaurant one evening. I asked Dad if he would be able to get into the car, to which he quickly replied, "Of course I can. I just don't know if I can get out." I have a picture of the two of them cruising down the road in my little car with the top down. Those are special moments that will never be forgotten. That trip was so special and something deep inside felt that it would be the last time he would spend at the beach. I was so happy to be there with him. Mom and Joey and I will forever cherish that in our hearts. They love the beach and all the amenities that come with living near the ocean. And I share that same passion.

Lastly, my Mom. This is a woman who stood by his side through thick and thin. She stayed by his side at the hospital and would rarely leave. She was with him through it all. Our mother is the essence of a Christian wife, mother, grandmother, and servant of the Lord. Dad loved and cherished her in all ways. They were the example of how God-ordained marriage should be. How do you leave the love of your life? How do you pick up the pieces, and where do you go to find peace? You run to the Savior who is always a part of your life. He brings joy in the morning. We love you, Mom.

I'm almost through. Dad loved the color yellow, and I don't know why, but I surmise that it is due to the beautiful sunshine, and he was our sunshine. The Synans originated from Ireland, and he was proud of his Irish heritage. He and Uncle Vernon loved digging into their ancestry and even made a couple of trips to Ireland. There they found distant cousins, the Synan Family Chalice from County Cork, and the ruins of what was once the Synan castle. What a life he led. As one of Dad's good friends, Dan Woods, reminded me just this past week, he lives on through us. He still lives on through his family. I could go on and on, but some memories are left in my heart and my mind. We will never be able to fill his shoes, but we will be able to follow in his footsteps. I can't say goodbye and I won't say goodbye. I would just say, "I will see you again someday. And I love you with all my heart."

Thank you, Lord, for letting me be Harold Vinson Synan's daughter. It was an amazing journey. I have a verse that makes me think about Dad when I read it, from Matthew 5:14–16: "You are the light of the world. A city that is set on a hill cannot be hidden. Nor do they light a lamp and put it under a basket, but on a lampstand, and it gives light to all who are in the house. Let your light so shine before men, that they may see your good works and glorify your Father in heaven." May his legacy live on for generations.

A. D. Beacham, Jr.

My name is Doug Beacham, and I'm the General Superintendent for the International Pentecostal Holiness Church.[2] H. Vinson Synan was a son of the Pentecostal Holiness Church. Earlier reference was made to Winston Churchill. That brought to my remembrance that in Churchill's preface to *The Gathering Storm*, he wrote this: "I followed Daniel Defoe's memoirs of a cavalier in which the author hangs the chronicle and discussion, a great military, and political events, upon the thread of the personal experience of an individual."[3] And Vinson Synan, like me and some of you, we are Cavaliers—we're Virginians. Well, it's not very difficult to hang the chronicle and discussion of great spiritual events upon the thread of Vinson Synan's personal experience.

In light of events transpiring in our nation at this time, and as a Virginian, I found myself wondering when the IPHC in its official magazine began to talk about racism. The most important resource for this is the *Pentecostal Holiness Advocate*, which began in 1917 and continued until the mid 1990s. For most of its history it was a weekly chronicle of what was occurring in our own denomination. I decided to do an online search through the entire magazine for the word "racism." The first instance of that word in the *Advocate* was on January 18, 1969. The writer used his article to describe the founding of Emmanuel College in Franklin Springs, Georgia in 1919. The year 1969 was the fiftieth anniversary of this IPHC flagship institution. The writer referenced that G. F. Taylor started the school during a global pandemic, the Spanish flu. He also mentioned the racism that was occurring during a time of rising white nationalism as the Ku Klux Klan spread. That writer was Vinson Synan.

As you know, Vinson Synan was a son of the South, a Virginian, as are many of us gathered here today. But instead of living his life conformed to the spirit of the dominant cultural mandate of his generation, he grasped the larger meaning of Scripture and the Pentecostal experience at Azusa Street. There, in 1906, William Seymour with blacks, whites, Asians, and Hispanics, came to understand that the Holy Spirit was at work bringing forth a new humanity and community. It's important to recognize that this was but ten years after *Plessy v Ferguson* in 1896, which institutionalized the civil and social

---

2. This eulogy combines content from Bishop Dr. Beacham's memorial message at Rock Church, Virginia and his message at Oral Roberts University, Oklahoma.

3. Winston Churchill, *The Gathering Storm* (Boston: Houghton Mifflin Company, 1948), iii. The reference is to Daniel Defoe's 1720 historical fiction account of a warrior during the Thirty Years' War (1618-1648) and English Civil War (1642–1651).

doctrine of "separate but equal."[4] Not only did Vinson Synan recognize that the Holy Spirit's work went beyond speaking in tongues and towards the greater view of the Spirit's work among all God's people, but he came to recognize the importance of the Spirit's work in bringing racial healing and hope.

He was just one of those who could sense what God was doing. In 1948 white Pentecostals formed the Pentecostal Fellowship of North America, and no black Pentecostal denominations were included. By 1994 many white Pentecostal leaders recognized the error of those earlier decades. Led by black leaders in the Church of God in Christ, and by Pentecostal leaders from the IPHC, Assemblies of God, Church of God, and others, these leaders met in Memphis, Tennessee and formed a new organization with a commitment to racial healing, the Pentecostal and Charismatic Churches of North America (PCCNA). If you go to IPHC Archives on Facebook, you will see a 15-minute video clip of the 1994 Memphis Miracle. In that clip you will hear Church of God in Christ leaders, you will hear IPHC General Superintendent B. E. Underwood, and you will hear Vinson Synan pointing us to the promise of Pentecost and the Azusa Street revival. You will hear Vinson Synan "yet speaking" to us of the promise of the Father. He "yet speaketh," calling us to what the Holy Spirit seeks to do among His people in this broken world.

It's been said and noted earlier, there are a lot of people who make history and there are a lot of people who write history. But fewer are the ones who do both—make it and write it. But you know the calling on our lives does not occur in isolation. There are many factors. Earlier, in one of the family video presentations, I was deeply moved to see those beautiful pictures of Vinson's daddy and your granddaddy, Bishop Joseph A. Synan. It's out of a home life that, for most of us, much of the great influences of our lives have been made. Bishop Synan was head of the 1961 General Conference to the Pentecostal Church, a conference held in Richmond, Virginia. A conference that ended up making a profound influence in my own life. Because that conference asked Bishop Synan to write an amplification of our denominational articles of faith. He referenced the theological connections of our articles of faith to John Wesley's articles of religion that were written for the Methodist Church. He then referenced the antecedent of that, the 39 articles for the Church of England. And then an antecedent of that, the Augsburg Confession. And then an antecedent that goes even further back, to the end of the first century AD and beginning of the second, the Apostles' Creed. I'm convinced that Bishop Synan's recognition of the historic depth and breadth of Pentecostalism had something to do with laying the

---

4. I am not aware of any writers of the Azusa Street era observing the sharp difference and the timeline between Plessy and Azusa Street. The closest may be Frank Bartleman's observation that at the Azusa Street the color line has been broken. This is a point that needs greater attention given that we continue to deal with racial division all these years afterwards.

foundation for Vinson Synan to move forward and take that giant leap into the Holy Spirit's presence in the historic churches of Luther, Calvin, and even the Vatican.

In light of that fatherly history/theology influence, it seems more than appropriate that we're remembering Dr. Synan on this campus, where on April 2, 1967 his father, Bishop Synan, read the Scriptures at the dedication of Oral Roberts University. And he was on the stage with Oral Roberts, and he was on the stage with Billy Graham, as was referenced earlier, in 1966. Vinson had come to ORU to do research, and not only did he revel in that historical research, but connections were made that led him to Santiago, Chile that put him immediately in connection with a relationship with a Pentecostal movement in Chile and the International Pentecostal Holiness Church that remains to this day. On a personal connection with the Chileans, who were then young men and women, who to this day still call him "Daddy."

It's also been noted how appropriate it is that this memorial service is being held for him on the weekend that commemorates the feast of weeks, or as we know from the New Testament, the day of Pentecost. I thought about Acts 2:1-4 as it inspired his witness to the present reality of the fullness of the Holy Spirit, from his personal devotional life to planting and pastoring churches, as a teacher to thousands of students, as the denominational executive, as an apostolic ambassador to the larger body of Christ, Vinson Synan walked in the power of the Spirit.

Now I need to admit to you today that I'm struggling referring to Dr. Synan in the past tense. Because I know, as all of you do, that Vinson Synan *is* fully alive in the presence of Jesus. He is in his place, in the communion of saints who are more than just past—they are present and future. He is in what the writer of Hebrews calls "so great a cloud of witnesses" (12:1). No doubt he's enjoying the presence of his parents and siblings. I have this mental picture of Vinson meeting his Irish Catholic ancestors, laughing together as they tell him they are delighted he figured it out. I'm also sure that by this time he's found heaven's archives. I'm convinced, Carol, that he has reserved a library. And no doubt he's already signed up for next semester's historical theology course that is, of course, taught by the Holy Spirit.

But most importantly, Vinson Synan is alive with Christ. It is that reality, as reflected in the hymn sung when at a Pentecostal Holiness Youth camp just outside of Memphis, TN, as a young man, he made his way to a Pentecostal altar and surrendered the paths of his life to Jesus. Hearing the refrains of that song we will sing in a few minutes, "*Where He Leads Me, I Will Follow,*" Dr. Synan followed Jesus to the ends of the earth. He's followed Jesus into the presence of the Lord. And when the Lord returns, he will still be following.

Where He Leads Me

I can hear my Savior calling,
I can hear my Savior calling,
I can hear my Savior calling,
"Take thy cross and follow, follow Me."

Where He leads me, I will follow
Where He leads me, I will follow
Where He leads me, I will follow
I'll go with Him, with Him all the way

He will give me grace and glory,
He will give me grace and glory,
He will give me grace and glory,
And go with me, with me all the way.

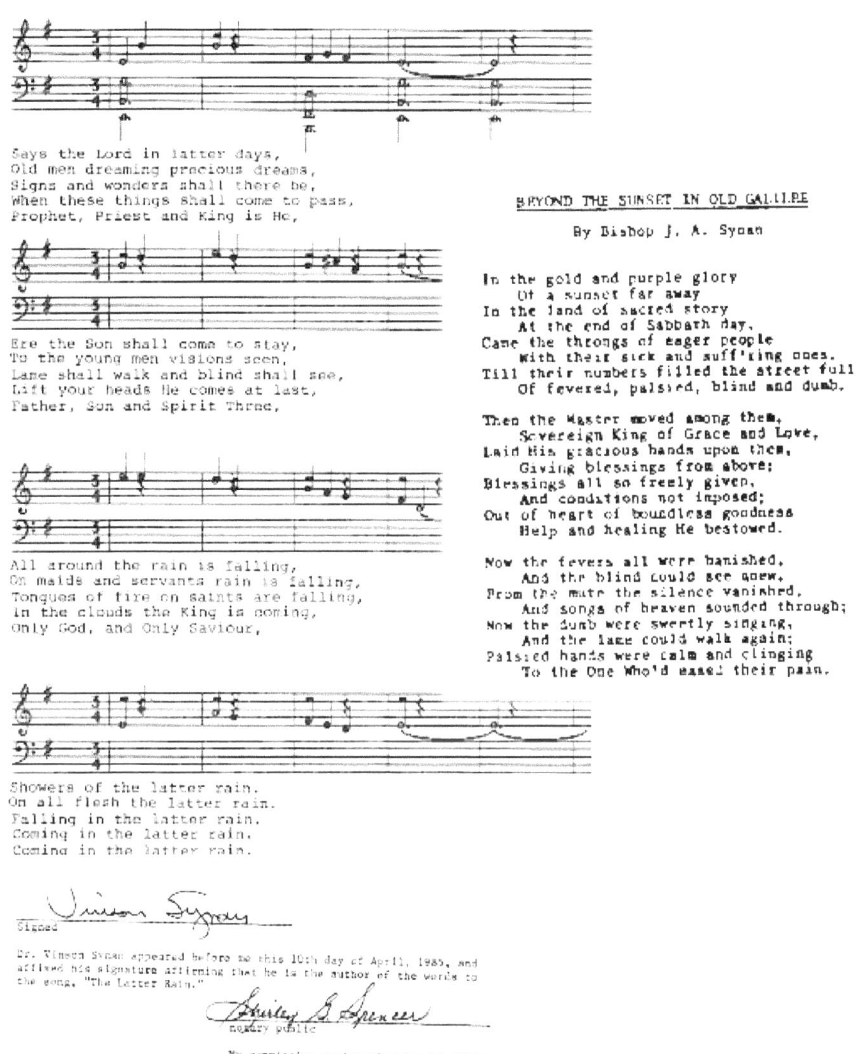

Figure 12: (Top left) A song, "Latter Rain," that Vinson wrote and had notarized in 1985, with Acts 2 in view. Recovered in his personal files, next to a song written by his father (right), Bishop J. A. Synan. Copyright Holy Spirit Resource Center, Oral Roberts University. Used with permission.

Figure 13: (Top left) A 2010 program celebrating the fiftieth wedding anniversary of twin brothers, Hubert Vernon and Harold Vinson Synan, with wives Phyllis Marie Sparks and Carol Lee Fuqua, respectively. (Top right & below): Vinson with Carol. Used with permission from the Synan-Taylor family.

In Memoriam
Carol Lee Fuqua Synan

July 31, 1942–March 18, 2021

CAROL LEE SYNAN

July 31, 1942 – March 18, 2021

Obituary

Carol Lee Fuqua Synan was born in Richmond, VA on July 31, 1942 to Gordon Lee and Hilda Jukes Fuqua, and passed to her heavenly home on March 18, 2021. She was the oldest of six children—herself, Shirley, Harold, Gordon, Janice, and Gary. She was born and raised in the Highland Park area of Richmond and graduated from John Marshall High School.

Carol married Harold Vinson Synan on August 13, 1960. He preceded her in death on March 15, 2020. She is survived by their four children—Mary Clark (Curt), Virginia Taylor (J. Mark), Vince Synan (Laura), and Joey Synan (Ashley); eight grandchildren—Lauren Smith (Brien), Elizabeth Ward (Jordan), Justin Clark (Mary Catherine), Lilly Synan, Preston Synan (Maddie), Priscilla Synan, Chad Synan, and Amelia Synan; and eight great-grandchildren- Joshua and Jeffrey Smith, Jayden, Cazlyn, and Elijah Brown, Noah and Harvest Ward, and Miles Synan.

Carol passionately loved her family and gathered them together for dinner and games every Friday night. She and Vinson loved opening their hearts and their home to friends, students, and other guests throughout their lives. They also loved sharing their vacation home in Duck, NC.

They say that behind every great man is a greater woman, and this was never more true than with Vinson and Carol. He was known for writing over 25 published books, but she meticulously edited every one of them. She kept the house and the family together, allowing him to travel the world in his ministry.

Carol exemplified grace and genuine kindness. She and Vinson lived as extraordinary examples of Christian love and dedication to the gospel. Above all, their children and extended family cherish this priceless legacy. In the midst of our grief, we remember Carol with joy and gratitude for her life. She is the epitome of a Proverbs 31 woman.

After a visitation service on Sunday, March 21, and a memorial service on Monday, March 22, Carol will be laid to rest beside her husband in Sunset Memorial Park in Chester, VA where Rev. Bert Synan will officiate.

Carol Lee Synan Memorial Service

Monday, March 21, 2021

North Church, Oklahoma City

William M. Wilson

I'm honored to be here today to honor and celebrate with you the life of Carol Lee Synan. It seems like just a few days ago that we said goodbye to Vinson. This was so unexpected for me. When I got the call about Carol passing, Lisa and I were blown away. Carol was an amazing lady! Sweet-spirited, gracious, faithful, wise, strong—so many adjectives could be used to describe her. I think one that really described Carol was simply "good." Scripture tells us that part of the fruit of the Spirit is goodness. When I was around Carol Synan, it was an experience with goodness. The goodness of God just flowed out of her life, her smile, her gentle ways. You would leave Carol saying, "That is a *good* woman."

I saw Carol in a number of different situations all over the world. We were at Jerusalem together for a week at a big conference; we were in Europe together at one point; in Virginia Beach; here in Oklahoma City; and, of course, in Tulsa at the university because Carol attended functions with Vinson when he was finishing his career there. I noticed that Carol was always a stabilizing factor. She was the anchor and a consistent force for good in Vinson's life, as well as in the lives of all of us that knew her. We just loved being around Carol. She was the kind of person that made everyone feel better.

It has been said today that she was the epitome of the Proverbs 31 woman, which is a wife of noble character—Scripture says, "worth more than rubies," very valuable, inestimable in worth. There are a couple of Scriptures in the description of the Proverbs 31 woman that I want to mention today because I think they speak so well of Carol and her journey and life's work. Proverbs 31:23 says, "Her husband is respected at the city gate, where he takes his seat among the elders of the land." A great woman is behind every good man. So great, in fact, that she helps make her husband known at the gate. In ancient times, the city gate was the place where business transpired—it was the public market of the day, the place where status was noticed. It is said of the Proverbs 31 woman that because of what she does and how she lives, her husband is respected at the city gate.

I think we see this with Vinson's life. Vinson was respected literally around the world—in many ways, considered to be the premier scholar of the Spirit-empowered movement for the last several decades. And behind him was always Carol. I didn't know until today, by the way, that she edited everything he ever wrote. I just thought he was a great writer! I thought his style was amazing. Now I know it is Carol's style that was amazing! Very easy to read and a great, great writer. And Vinson was respected at the city gate.

Another verse, Proverbs 31:28, says, "Her children arise and call her blessed. Her husband also praises her." These children sitting here today will tell you they were blessed by an amazing mom. Vinson was traveling all over the world, meeting everyone from the Pope on down—I mean *every* leader in the Christian world—and Carol was by his side over and over again. In the midst of all of that, her greatest calling was to be a mom. She did that with high excellence! And so today, her children call her blessed.

Proverbs 31:31 continues, "Honor her for all that her hands have done, and let her works praise her at the city gate." Yes, her husband is at the city gate, but someday—and I think even today as we reflect on Carol's life—we realize that *her* works were worthy of honor by those in authority. We honor Carol for her great work that she did for God, His Kingdom, and her family. She was an amazing lady, a true saint indeed. As Pastor Rodney mentioned earlier, "precious in the sight of the Lord is the death of His faithful servants," or "of His saints" (Ps 116:15). This past week, when Carol breathed her last breath and went into the presence of the Lord, the perspective from heaven was very different than what we felt here in this world. God saw that Carol's work was done. It was a precious moment when she crossed over into His presence to rest until He returns. It was a celebration time. It was a homecoming. It was a time when Carol's entire life was fulfilled. Her work was finished and her reward awaited her. In heaven, it was a blessed and beautiful moment. Heaven will be enriched by this amazing lady from now until Jesus returns, and even beyond.

However, on the earthly side last week, it might not have felt so precious to this family. First Corinthians 15:26 says, "The last enemy to be destroyed is death." I've reflected on this verse many times over the years. Death is an enemy. I hate death. It cuts us away from our loved ones. It's a stark and difficult goodbye—a sudden goodbye that none of us want. But Scripture says it is the *last* enemy that will be destroyed by Jesus Christ. Jesus came to defeat the enemy in every way, including to defeat death. This He did by His resurrection, giving us hope that we also will be victorious over death.

A story is told of an older dad traveling with his young daughter in a cab of a truck, out on a farm. She's 5 to 7 years old, sitting beside her dad, proud to be on a farm—but in the midst of their journey, with the windows rolled up, a bee had gotten into the cab of the truck. The bee is ominous to the child. As the bee circles around the truck, she's afraid that the bee is going to sting her, and she's worried about what the results will be. All of a sudden, her dad reaches into the air, catches the bee, and squeezes it tightly, being stung all the while. Then he releases the bee and says to his daughter, "You have nothing to fear. The stinger is gone." Now Scripture says in 1 Corinthians 15:55–57, "Where, O death, is your victory? Where, O death, is your sting?" The sting of death is sin; the power of sin is the law, but thanks be to God! He gives us the victory through our Lord Jesus Christ. On the cross, Jesus spread His hands out and took the sting of death. He became sin for us so that you and I don't have to be afraid of death any longer. The stinger is gone! Jesus accepted it into His own body.

The resurrection of Jesus also gives us amazing hope. Death is an enemy. Death is difficult for us. It's difficult for you and I to cope on this earth with our mortality. And for a world in a pandemic that has coped with death over and over again, and for this family that has coped with the deaths of their closest loved ones in the same year, it is difficult. And yet we have hope in Jesus Christ. He took the power of sin that was the sting of death—He took the stinger away. And He gave us hope by resurrecting from the dead, proving that someday we also will be resurrected.

Jesus came not just to save our soul and to redeem our spirit, but He also came to redeem our body. We forget this sometimes. He was in a mode of complete restoration when He came to earth. The redemption of the human body, because of Adam's sin, meant that we would need to be resurrected from the dead. So we have the promise today of Scripture that this body that we dwell in, when we pass away, will be sown into the ground as perishable. But, someday it will be raised. And when it is, it will be imperishable. It is sown in dishonor but will be raised in glory. It is sown in weakness but will be raised in power. It is sown a natural body, but one day will be raised a spiritual body that will never die, never cry, and never suffer disease or sickness again. Because of Jesus, we have the hope of resurrection so that today we do not sorrow like others sorrow.

Of course we do sorrow. Carol will be missed by so many, especially by this dear family. But we do not sorrow like everyone else because we have hope. The sting of death is gone, and the resurrection of Jesus has happened as a first fruits, that we too someday will be resurrected. God will change this body so that it will become imperishable, and we will have a new body in the presence of the Lord.

So let me finish by saying to the family that our prayers are with you today. From the Oral Roberts University community, my personal family, and the great Spirit-empowered community around the world, our prayers are with you. The legacy of Carol and Vinson Synan is amazing and will go on for decades and centuries to come. All the books they worked on remain.

The newest volume that Vinson and I worked on together is now a textbook in a class at ORU. Students will be reading and reflecting on Carol's and Vinson's work for years to come. So today, our prayers are that your memories will be sweet. That as you reflect on Carol, her journey, her beautiful smile, and her gentle spirit, a smile will cross your face. That you will remember her tender care and the love of an amazing mother, grandmother, great-grandmother, and on and on.

Also, we pray that you will have a sense of Vinson and Carol's prayers coming to fruition. Just because people go home to be with Jesus doesn't mean their prayers go unanswered. In fact, God's Word teaches that when people pray, it is laid up before God as a memorial. Many times, people's prayers are answered years after they have gone home to be with Jesus. Carol's prayers—some of the prayers she was praying last week—probably were for some of you. Those prayers are held in God's presence and will be answered someday. Those prayers are going to chase you the rest of your life. In fact, if you're here right now and don't know Jesus, those prayers are already chasing you—Carol's and Vinson's prayers. I heard them pray for their family many times when I was with them. They loved you, and those prayers will continue to chase generations to come, beyond the great-grandchildren. The prayers of Vinson and Carol Synan will go on.

Lastly, we pray for supernatural strength today. Grief comes in waves. Sometimes the waves are big. They feel like they're going to capsize our life. But we have an anchor so that, in those times when the grief comes, God will stabilize you and get you through it. We pray for the strength and comfort of the Holy Spirit. Vinson and Carol Synan were people of the Spirit. And I am convinced that in the days ahead, the Spirit of God will surround you, the Holy One will overshadow you, and He will bring comfort. He will be beside you. He will hold you. He is with you today. We are also, and our prayers will continue beyond this day. God bless you.

AFTERWORD:
HIS LEGACY LIVES ON

Jaime L. Riddle

What more could be said to appreciate the legacy of Dr. Harold Vinson Synan? Surely the contributors here represent untold numbers of those whose lives were changed by his teaching, leadership, and character. Testimony after testimony reinforces that those who knew Dr. Synan will forever treasure his contributions to the church and to academics—but even more, how he embodied them. Indeed, no list of achievements or timeline of events can fully capture a person's presence or the grace they carried. But presence and grace were Dr. Synan's strengths. They adorned his scholarship so that he could minister through the Spirit to people, including to those who were unfriendly to the idea. He led like a pastor and also a prophet. People felt better just because of his kind example that believed God for the way forward.

Now as it regards Dr. Synan's legacy, those who did not know him have the challenge of continuing his mission without personally experiencing what has been shared here. I myself am in this category. Being new to Tulsa and to Oral Roberts University, I am among those benefitting from a leader I never met: a professor whose time I just missed, a scholar who changed an entire conversation in church history, and a spokesperson whose vision persists to the very desk where I work. I sit in the renovated Holy Spirit Resource Center, next to a library that Dr. Synan once directed—even studied in, as a young doctoral student. Down the hall is a room endowed in his name, with part of his personal collections. A set of books from the scholars consultations that he helped found are now a big part of my life.

But it wasn't until I read *As the Waters Cover the Sea* that I began to understand the legacy I'd stepped into. I started reading Dr. Synan's published works—then his unpublished works and ministry magazines. I scoured *The Advocate* to fill in gaps, and I learned his voice and perspective. But in gathering the eulogies for this volume, I realized that I had still only scratched the surface of this amazing man and family. I understood the history but knew there was more that I'd missed.

In the end, it was tenderly going through the files that he had entrusted to ORU that made me feel like I was finally getting to know him: one manila folder at a time, one article at a time; some professionally completed, some brainstormed on assorted pieces of paper; some in his distinctively scrawled handwriting, others from an old typewriter. Tucked in were also conference bulletins in foreign languages, black and white photos from all over the world, drafts of articles, redrafts, outlines of books, and courses and degrees not formed yet. I could almost hear his voice in my head. And just when I thought that was as close to understanding that I would come, the Lord arranged a divine appointment with a dear friend of his. She showed me a fifteen-minute video of Dr. Synan at a kitchen table, in 2018, sharing his now-famous Notre Dame story. Tears came. His voice sounded exactly like the one I had been constructing in my mind. As his friend teared up beside me also, I became joined to those aspiring to carry on his legacy.

So for those wanting to connect to this living history but have no video yet, I offer a final story. There are many anecdotes that represent Dr. Synan well, including that pivotal moment at Notre Dame and also the Lutheran gentleman who surprised him by being filled with the Holy Spirit in the back room. His speeches at SPS are demonstrative, as are his two visits to the Vatican, and to Moscow after Communism fell. His "Please Sit Down in the Name of Jesus" story is incomparably great and may make you laugh out loud literally.[1] But the following story—understated, so easy to miss—brings together many elements of his character and imprinted my heart with what his gently reforming and humble leadership must have looked like in action.

In 1990, an ecumenical conference in Indianapolis that Dr. Synan chaired planned an Olympian-type torch run to kick off the event. Five thousand Christian runners ran a huge flaming torch through Mexico City, Los Angeles, Ottawa, and Washington DC to encourage prayer, unity, and evangelism across the four corners of North America. Very few knew, however, that the finances for the conference were depleted. The executive committee was praying unceasingly during the event about it. They had taken up multiple offerings but grew convicted about asking for more. As the final night drew to a close, Vernon Stoop, Jr. shares the following involving Dr. Synan and an unnamed Catholic lady at "the eleventh hour":

> We prayed and decided to leave it in the Lord's hands. With disappointment in our hearts, we began to leave the Hoosier Dome. It was then, while leaving the Dome with the last crowds, that a diminutive 75-year-old lady… approached Vinson Synan and asked if we were still short of funds. He told her that we still needed $150,000. She pleaded that he not ask for any more money. Instead, she said, she would write out a check for $150,000! Stunned, Synan asked if she had that kind of money. "Oh yes," she said.

> Her companions confirmed that this sweet Catholic lady indeed had the means. Awestruck, Vinson Synan thrust the [Olympian] torch just given to

---

1. "Please Sit Down in the Name of Jesus," *IPHC Advocate* (April 25, 1976): 16–17.

him by Jim Ryun [an Olympic silver medalist] into the lady's hands. Immediately, Catholic Bishop Sam Jacobs, who was standing nearby, blessed the torch.[2]

Now it was the charitable donor's turn to be overwhelmed as tears rolled down her cheeks....She told me that her reason for the gift was her gratitude for what she had witnessed at the Catholic youth Mass that afternoon, when Bishop Jacobs gave an altar call to young people. It was, she said, the first time in her 75 years as a Catholic that she had ever seen a priest or a bishop give an altar call. The experience so overwhelmed her that she felt led to give an expression of thanksgiving.

Many elements of this testimony could be highlighted, including faith for the finances, the depth of the conference, or the overall context of ecumenical and charismatic bridge-building that Dr. Synan and others labored for decades to cultivate, especially with Catholic believers. But what touched me most, as this memorial work closes, was the pure joy Dr. Synan was able to give this elderly lady as he responded, in the moment, to the Holy Spirit honoring her. The torch they had run across the country was very large. It had been passed among professional athletes and staff before being given to Dr. Synan to close the conference. But rather than guard it, or simply thank the lady verbally, he brought her into the Lord's circle of honor and grace surrounding the meeting. He gave her the experience of her lifetime—of being blessed by the Bishop (who was reciprocating her blessing!)—and recognizing her as a true torch-bearer, as much as him or any of the leaders.

These kinds of moments can only arise as a result of a lifetime of humility, love for God and others, and attentiveness to the Holy Spirit. They are the moments that don't go down in history but are the cups of cold water that speak volumes, even to Jesus eternally. And so Dr. Synan modeled, not just those acts, but a life that gives rise to those acts, as we pursue making a difference for God in the church, academy, or wherever God has placed us.

So I, like many to come, am a beneficiary of this book's record of Vinson Synan's Spirit-empowered legacy. I believe this concept will grow richer with time as we walk the path Dr. Synan prophetically walked. As we do, we will find his fingerprints on initiatives, conferences, and the historiography of the Spirit-empowered movement. We will also find his faith and optimism about what is still to come. In a sense, he has passed the torch to us. Let us guard it carefully and give thanks for the movement he helped shape. May the works of Vinson, Carol, and those they've touched live on for generations.

---

2. "Deficit Covered in Amazing Manner: 11th-Hour Miracle," *AD 2000 Together* 4, no. 4 (Fall 1990): 13.

THE PENTECOSTAL MOVEMENT
IN THE UNITED STATES

Harold Vinson Synan, Ph. D.
University of Georgia, 1967

Reprinted from DISSERTATION ABSTRACT!

Volume XXVIII, Number 11, 1968

Rev. H. Vinson Synan, a member of the faculty of Emmanuel College, was awarded the Ph.D. degree in history on August 18, 1967 at the University of Georgia. Dr. Synan made an intensive study in the field of Social and Intellectual history and wrote his dissertation on *The Pentecostal Movement in the United States*. Dr. Synan received his B.A. degree from the University of Richmond in 1958, and the M.A. degree from the University of Georgia in 1964.

In the preparation of his doctoral dissertation, Mr. Synan traveled widely in the southern United States and made two trips to Chile.

During his visits to Chile, Dr. Synan and Dr. R. O. Corvin succeeded in bringing about an agreement of affiliation between the Pentecostal Holiness Church and two pentecostal bodies in Chile (The Pentecostal Methodist Church and the Pentecostal Church of Chile). Membership of these affiliated churches is now more than 800,000.

While working on his doctorate, Vinson Synan organized and pastored a new Pentecostal Holiness Church in Hartwell, Georgia. This congregation built and moved into a new sanctuary within one year after its organization. (See P. H. *Advocate* for June 24, 1967.)

In addition to his duties as an instructor at Emmanuel College and as pastor of the Hartwell P. H. Church, Dr. Synan plans to devote some of his time to writing. He has already been commissioned to write a History of the Pentecostal Holiness Church, a task for which he is eminently qualified by virtue of the research he did for his doctoral dissertation.

Figure 14: The dissertation that started it all. Note the article's prescient comment that, upon finishing, Dr. Synan planned "to devote <u>some of his time</u> to writing…"

We are so thankful that he did.

SELECT BIBLIOGRAPHY

"If you don't write books, you'll only be able to reach people for Jesus while you are here on earth. Your work will end when you go to heaven, except for the people you reach through people they have reached. But if you write books, even after you are in heaven, you can win more people to Christ."

- H. V. Synan

Books[1]

Emmanuel College: The First Fifty Years. Washington, DC: North Washington Press, 1968.

The Holiness-Pentecostal Movement in the United States. Grand Rapids, MI: Eerdmans, 1971.

Old Time Power: A History of the Pentecostal Holiness Church. Franklin Springs, GA: Advocate Press, 1973. [Revised centennial edition, Life Springs Resources, 1998].

Charismatic Bridges. New York: Word of Life, 1974.

[Ed.]. *Aspects of Pentecostal/Charismatic Origins.* Plainfield, NJ: Logos, 1975.

In the Latter Days: The Outpouring of the Holy Spirit in the Twentieth Century. Ann Arbor, MI: Servant Publications, 1984. [Revised edition, Xulon, 2001].

The Twentieth-Century Pentecostal Explosion: The Exciting Growth of Pentecostal Churches and Charismatic Renewal Movements. Lake Mary, FL: Creation House, 1987.

[with Ralph Rath]. *Launching the Decade of Evangelism.* South Bend, IN: North American Renewal Service Committee, 1990.

Under His Banner: A History of the Full Gospel Businessmen's Fellowship International. Costa Mesa, CA: Gift Publications, 1992.

The Spirit Said "Grow": The Astounding Worldwide Expansion of Pentecostal and Charismatic Churches. Monrovia, CA: World Vision/MARC, 1992.

The Holiness-Pentecostal Tradition: Charismatic Movements in the Twentieth Century. Grand Rapids, MI: Eerdmans, 1997.

The Wesleyan Origins of Pentecostalism. Seoul: Korean Evangelical Holiness Church, 1998.

The Century of the Holy Spirit: 100 Years of Pentecostal and Charismatic Renewal, 1901–2001. Nashville, TN: Thomas Nelson, 2001.

Voices of Pentecost: Testimonies of Lives Touched by the Holy Spirit. Ann Arbor, MI: Servant Publications/Vine Books, 2003.

---

1. Works are listed in chronological order in each section. Author Vinson Synan is understood for each. Additional co-authors or editors are noted.

213

The Synans of Virginia: The Story of an Irish Family in America. Maitland, FL: Xulon, 2003.

An Eyewitness Remembers the Century of the Holy Spirit. Grand Rapids, MI: Chosen Books, 2010.

Spirit-Empowered Christianity in the Twenty-First Century. Lake Mary, FL: Charisma House, 2011.

[With Charles R. Fox, Jr.]. *William J. Seymour: Pioneer of the Azusa Street Revival.* Plainfield, NJ: Bridge-Logos, 2012.

[Ed. with Amos Yong]. *Global Renewal Christianity: Spirit-Empowered Movements Past, Present, and Future.* 4 vols. Lake Mary, FL: Charisma House, 2016.
> Vol. 1: *Asia and Oceania*
> Vol. 2: *Latin America*, with Miguel Alvarez, ed.
> Vol. 3: *Africa*, with J. Kwabena Asamoah-Gyadu, ed.
> Vol. 4: *Europe and North America*

Synan, and Daniel Woods. *Fire Baptized: The Many Lives and Works of Benjamin Hardin Irwin.* Lexington, KY: Emeth Press, 2017.

[Ed.]. *The Truth About Grace: Spirit-Empowered Perspectives.* Lake Mary, FL: Charisma House, 2018.

Where He Leads Me: The Vinson Synan Story. Franklin Springs, GA: Life Springs Resources, 2019.

Chapters in Books

"Theological Boundaries: The Arminian Tradition." In *The Evangelicals*, edited by David Wells and John Woodbridge. 38–57. Grand Rapids, MI: Baker, 1975.

"Introduction." In *Azusa Street: The Roots of Modern-Day Pentecost—An Eyewitness Account,* by Frank Bartleman. xi–xxv. Plainfield, NJ: Bridge-Logos, 1980. [Revised centennial edition, *Azusa Street: An Eyewitness Account, 1906–2006,* Bridge-Logos, 2006.]

"Speaking with Tongues." In *Roman Catholic-Pentecostal Dialogue (1977–1982).* 4–19. Frankfurt am Main/Verlag Peter Lang, 1987.

"An Equal Opportunity Movement." In *Pentecostals from the Inside Out,* edited by Harold B. Smith. 43–52. Wheaton, IL: Victor Books, 1990.

"The Role of Tongues as Initial Evidence." In *Spirit and Renewal: Essays in Honor of J. Rodman Williams,* edited by Mark W. Wilson. Journal of Pentecostal Theology Supplement Series 5. 67–82. Sheffield, UK: Sheffield Academic Press, 1994.

"Which Churches Are Growing and Why?" In *John Paul II and the New Evangelization,* edited by William Hauck, Ralph Martin, Peter Williamson. 111–121. Fort Collins, CO: Ignatius Press, 1995.

"The International Ministry of David Yonggi Cho." In *The Holy Spirit and Church: A Collection of Scholarly Papers in Celebration of the 40th Anniversary of Dr. Yonggi Cho's Ministry.* Vol. 1. 227–238. Seoul: Yoido Full Gospel Church, 1996.

"George Floyd Taylor: Conflicts and Crowns." In *Portraits of a Generation*, edited by James R. Goff and Grant Wacker. 325–346. Fayetteville, AR. University of Arkansas Press, 2002.

"Apostolic Practice." In *He Gave Apostles*, edited by Edgar Lee. 12–25. Springfield, MO: Gospel Publishing House, 2005.

"What You See, Write in a Book." In *Pentecostals in the Academy*, edited by Steven M. Fettke and Robert Waddell. 18–40. Cleveland, TN: CPT Press, 2012.

"The Many Lives of Benjamin Hardin Irwin." *In The Pastor & The Kingdom: Essays Honoring Jack W. Hayford*, edited by Hon Huntzinger and S. David Moore. 117–132. Southfield, TX: Gateway Academic and TKU Press, 2017.

Journal Articles

"Christian Initiation in the Pentecostal Holiness Church." *Studia Liturgica* 10, no. 1 (November 1974): 56–64.

"Theological Boundaries: The Arminian Tradition." *Pneuma* 3, no. 2 (Fall 1981): 38–53.

"Minutes and Financial Statement of the Society, 1981." *Pneuma* 4, no. 1 (Spring 1982): 57–60.

"Constitution and By-laws of the Society for Pentecostal Studies." *Pneuma* 4, no. 2 (Fall 1982): 46–52.

"In the Latter Days." *Church History: Studies in Christianity and Culture* 54 (September 1985): 446–447.

"Pentecostalism: Varieties and Contributions." *Pneuma* 9, no. 1 (Spring 1987): 31–49.

"The Holiness-Pentecostals." *Paraclete* 23 (Fall 1989): 1–6.

"The Yoido Full Gospel Church." *Cyberjournal for Pentecostal-Charismatic Research* 2 (1997). http://www.pctii.org/cyberj/cyberj2/synan.html.

"Responses to Perspectives on Koinonia." *Pneuma* 12, no. 2 (Fall 1990): 175–178.

"The Church of God in Christ." *Die Religion in Geschichte und Gegenwart* (December 1998).

"The Second Comers." *Christian History: Studies in Christianity and Culture* 61 (1999): 38–39.

"William J. Seymour." *Christian History: Studies in Christianity and Culture* 65 (2000): 17–19.

"A Healer in the House: A Historical Perspective on Healing in the Pentecostal/Charismatic Tradition," *Asian Journal of Pentecostal Studies* 3, no. 2 (July 2000): 189–201.

"The Pentecostal Movement in North America and Beyond." *Journal of Beliefs and Practices* 25, no. 2 (August 2004): 153–165.

"The Future: Strategies for Reconciliation." *Cyberjournal for Pentecostal-Charismatic Research* 14 (May 2005). http://www.pctii.org/cyberj/cyberj14/synan.html.

"The Beginnings of the Society For Pentecostal Studies." *2005 SPS Annual Conference Papers: That Which We Have Received We Now Pass On: Spirit, Word, and Tradition in Pentecostalism.* January 2005.

"Christ's Sanctified Holy Church: A Study in Black And White Holiness." *2013 SPS Annual Conference Papers: Holiness (Joint meeting with the Wesleyan Theological Society.* March 2013.

"Oral Roberts: Son of Pentecostalism, Father of the Charismatic Movement." *Spiritus: ORU Journal of Theology* 2, no. 2 (Fall 2017): 5–21.

[With Daniel D. Isgrigg]. "An Early Account of Oral Roberts' Healing Testimony." *Spiritus: ORU Journal of Theology* 3, no. 2 (Fall 2018): 169–177.

"The Pentecostal Roots of Oral Roberts' Healing Ministry." *Spiritus: ORU Journal of Theology* 3, no. 2 (Fall 2018): 287–302.

"Charles Stanley's Pentecostal Roots." *Spiritus: ORU Journal of Theology* 5, no. 2 (Fall 2020): 275–286.

Periodicals for Wider Readership

"Our Mother." *IPHC Advocate*[2] (May 9, 1959): 6.

"A Century of Holiness and Pentecost." *IPHC Advocate* (February 1967): 4–5.

"The Pentecostals of Chile." *IPHC Advocate* (March 18, 1967): 21.

[With A. M. Long]. "A New Church in Hartwell, Georgia." *IPHC Advocate* (June 24, 1967): 14–15.

"The Background of Chilean Affiliation." *IPHC Advocate* (October 28, 1967): 4–5.

"Emmanuel College: Its Founding and Development." *IPHC Advocate* (January 18, 1969): 3–6.

"The Pentecostal Methodists of Chile." *IPHC Advocate* (November 7, 1970): 12–13.

"Pulpit Power." *IPHC Advocate* (July 3, 1971): 4–5.

"Pentecostal Catholics at Notre Dame." *IPHC Advocate* (July 15, 1972): 12–13.

"Charismatic Walls." *New Covenant* (April 1973): 1–2.

"The Classical Pentecostals." *New Covenant* (May 1973): 7–27.

"Can a Child of God Be Demon-Possessed?" *IPHC Advocate* (October 20, 1973): 10–11.

"The World Pentecostal Conference." *IPHC Advocate* (November 3, 1973): 20–21.

"The Sunday School Supports the Family." *IPHC Advocate* (April 6, 1974): 27.

"World's Largest Congregation: A Cathedral in Chile." *Christianity Today* (January 17, 1975): 33–34.

---

2. *The Advocate* changes names several times between 1917–1996. To preserve continuity, *IPHC Advocate* is used here. To preserve space, all URLs to articles from *The Advocate* and *Assemblies of God Heritage* are available online at the Consortium of Pentecostal Archives here: https://pentecostalarchives.org/?a=cl&cl=CL1&sp=IPHCA&ai=1&e=------ -en-20--1--img-txIN------------.

"Pentecost in St. Peter's." *Christianity Today* (June 6, 1975): 45–46.

"American Tradition: Giving Thanks." *IPHC Advocate* (November 23, 1975): 8–9.

"Reconciling the Charismatics." *Christianity Today* (April 9, 1976): 46.

"Please Sit Down in the Name of Jesus." *IPHC Advocate* (April 25, 1976): 16–17.

"Pentecostal Tide Is Coming in." *Christianity Today* (November 5, 1976): 78–80.

"Will Renewal Come Out of Kansas City?" *Christian Life* (July 1977): 56.

"A Challenge to the Churches." *New Covenant* (October 1977): 11–12.

"The New Canterbury Tales." *Evangelical Press News Service Press Reports and Correspondence* (1978): 12.

"The Gifts of the Spirit in Church History." *IPHC Advocate* (October 22, 1978): 4–5.

"What is Family Night at Home?" *IPHC Advocate* (November 26, 1978): 16–17.

"God's Ideal for the Family." *IPHC Advocate* (April 13, 1980): 8.

"When Pentecost Came to Los Angeles: 75th Anniversary of the Azusa Street Revival, 1906–1981." *Assemblies of God Heritage* 1, no. 2 (Winter 1981-1982): 2–3.

"Azusa Street: The Roots of Revival." *Charisma* (March 1981): 10–13.

"100 New Pentecostal Holiness Churches in Four Years." *IPHC Advocate* (April 11, 1982): 4–5.

"Discerning the Charismatic Renewal: Reviewing Kilian McDonnell's 'Presence, Power, Praise.'" *Theology Today* 39, no. 2 (July 1, 1982): 187–193.

"World Pentecostal Conference Meets in Nairobi." *Christianity Today* (November 26, 1982): 66–67.

"Speaking in Tongues." *One in Christ* 19, no. 4 (November 4, 1983): 321–323.

"The Third Force in Christendom." *Charisma* (November 1984): 92–96.

"The Latter Rain Falls in America." *Charisma* (December 1984): 71–72.

"Pentecost Scorned, Pentecost Reconsidered." *Charisma* (January 1985): 54–56.

"The Renewal Intensifies." *Charisma* (February 1985): 73–74.

"Are We the Latter Day People?" *Christian Life* (March 1985): 54–59.

"Holiness the Priority." *IPHC Advocate* (May 1985): 10–12.

"Trend Toward Worldwide Charismatic Revival." *Charisma* (August 1985): 40–46.

"The Charismatic Canterbury Tale." *Charisma* (March 1986): 63–68.

"The Presbyterian Pentecostal Pioneers." *Charisma* (April 1986): 37–39.

"Oral Roberts: Serving Fellow Ministers." *Charisma* (April 1986): 82–84.

"The Quite Rise of Black Pentecostals." *Charisma* (June 1986): 45–55.

"A Miracle at Strawberry Lake." *Charisma* (July 1986): 45–47.

"That Old-Time Pentecostal Religion." *Charisma* (August 1986): 53–57.

"Fire in the Lutheran Church." *Charisma* (September 1986): 78–80.

"A Long Road to Renewal." *Charisma* (October 1986): 61–65.

"Baptists Ride the Third Wave." *Charisma* (December 1986): 52–57.

"Pentecostalism: Varieties and Contributions." *One in Christ* 1, no. 2 (1987): 97–109.

"From the Hills of Tennessee." *Charisma* (January 1987): 58–62.

"Joint Witness Leads to World Evangelization." *AD 2000 Together* 1, no. 1 (February 1987): 1.

"Surprise of the Spirit." *Charisma* (March 1987): 26–29.

"A Tribute to Mr. Pentecost." *Charisma* (April 1987): 18–23.

"The Unexpected Transformation of the Pentecostal Holiness Church." *Charisma* (April 1987): 55–56.

"The Great Methodist Awakening." *Charisma* (May 1987): 55–61.

"Where Do We Go From Here?" *AD 2000 Together* 1, no. 6 (July 1987): 1, 5.

"God's Timing for New Orleans." *AD 2000 Together* 1, no. 6 (July 1987): 5.

"Fulfilling Sister Aimee's Dream." *Charisma* (July 1987): 53–54.

"We Must Stand Together." *New Covenant* (July/August 1987): 5.

"The Vision for the Year 2000." *Charisma* (August 1987): 42–44.

"Unity Felt." *AD 2000 Together* (Fall 1987): 6–7.

"Pentecostal Fires Lit in Germany." *AD 2000 Together* (Fall 1987): 13.

"West Germans Show Their Charisma." *Charisma* (November 1987): 84–90.

"Evangelicals and Charismatics." *AD 2000 Together* 2, no. 1 (January 1988): 1.

" A Son that Sleeps in Harvest Causes Shame." *AD 2000 Together* (January 1988): 4.

"Ecumenical Energy." *New Covenant* (February 1988): 15.

"Pentecostals Differ From Fundamentalists: Evangelical Ties." *AD 2000 Together* 2, no. 2 (March/April 1988): 14–18.

"The Wisdom of Reverend Wise." *Charisma* (June 1988): 56–61.

"Episcopal Charismatic Leader David Collins." *AD 2000 Together* (July/August 1988): 4–5, 10.

"Renewal Grows in Reformed Church in America," *AD 2000 Together* (July/August 1988): 5, 15.

"The Unexpected Renewal." *Charisma* (September 1988): 84–90.

"Restoration Movement: Renewal Spreads in Church of Christ." *AD 2000 Together* 2, no. 5 (Fall 1988): 4–7.

"Euro-Fire '88." *AD 2000 Together* 2, no. 5 (Fall 1988): 14–25.

"The Holiness Pentecostal Movement." *Assemblies of God Heritage* 8, no. 4 (December 1988): 4–6.

"A.D. 2000 the Target," *AD 2000 Together* (Spring 1989): 4–7, 10.

"Can the World Be Evangelized by AD 2000?" *Ministries Today* (March/April 1989): 52–53.

"Charismatic Pioneer Don Basham Dies at 62." *AD 2000 Together* 3, no. 2 (May/June 1989): 2.

"The Hope of Bangkok Church." *Witness Ministries* 1, no. 2 (July 1990): 2–3.

"108 Leaders Meet in Jerusalem: Pentecost Revisited." *AD 2000 Together* (July/August 1989): 4–7.

"The Faith of Kenneth Hagin." *Charisma* (June 1990): 62–70.

"Charismatics Make Their Presence Felt at Lausanne II." *AD 2000 Together* 3, no. 4 (August 15–19, 1990) ["Evangelize the World Now"!— Indianapolis 1990 Edition]: 28.

"Congress Participants Challenged: Keynote Address." *AD 2000 Together* (Fall 1990): 14–15.

"Nigeria's Super Church." *Charisma* (October 1990): 84–87.

"Pentecostals Meet in Singapore World Conference." *AD 2000 Together* 4, no. 1 (Winter 1990): 18–19.

"New Light on Pentecost," *New Covenant* (June 1991): 30–31.

"'AD 2000 Together' Becomes 'Timelines.'" *Timelines: A Quarterly Report of Pentecostal-Charismatic Trends* 1, no. 1 (Summer 1991): 1.

> Editor's note: *Timelines* quarterly newsletters were each four pages long, 10–12 headlines per issue, written by Vinson Synan. He began these circulars after *AD 2000 Together* magazine ended. For six years, from Summer 1991–Summer 1996, he produced *Timelines* vols. 1-6, nos. 1-4, pages 1-4. Notable entries include:
>
> "Pentecostal Renewal Among Seventh-Day Adventists," (April 1991): 4.
> "The Holy Spirit Invades Eastern Europe," (Fall 1991): 2.
> "Catholic Charismatics Celebrate 25 Years," (Winter 1992): 1.
> "Black Churches Experience Renewal," (Winter 1992): 1.
> "Chinese Intellectuals Turn to Christ," (Winter 1992): 4.
> "Muslims Converting to Christianity in Increasing Rates," (Fall 1992): 4.
> "One Million Catholic Charismatics in India," (Winter 1993): 4.
> "The Miracle in Memphis: Racial Reconciliation," (Fall 1994): 1–2.
> "The Toronto Vineyard: A Summary," (Summer 1996): 2–3.

"Who are the Modern Apostles?" *Ministries Today* (March/April 1992): 43–47.

"Women in Ministry: A History of Women's Roles in the Pentecostal and Charismatic Movement." *Ministries Today* (January/February 1993): 44–50.

"Graceless Law versus Lawless Grace." *IPHC Advocate* (February 1994): 4–5.

"The Calamity of Lawless Grace." *New Covenant* (March 1994): 23–25.

"Christianity's Astounding Growth." *New Covenant* (March 1995): 7–10.

"Overcoming Ancient Divisions." *Charisma* (July 1995): 30–31.

"Major Movers and Shakers." *IPHC Advocate* (December 1996): 4–7.

"The Apostle: A Film Review." *Journal of Southern Religion* 1, no. 1 (1998).

"The Memphis Miracle." PCCNA Reconciliation 1 (Summer 1998): 14–18.

"Pentecostal Trends of the 1990s." *Ministries Today* (Mary/June 1999): 60.

"Rediscovering the Holy Spirit." *Crosspoint* (Fall 1999): 2–7.

"The Pentecostal Twentieth Century." *Ministries Today* (November/ December 1999): 27–35.

"Regent University Celebrates 25 Years of Spirit-Filled Education." *Charisma* (May 2003): 84.

"Ambrose Jessup Tomlinson: His Place in History (1865–1943)." *The White Wing Messenger* (June 2003): 19–21.

"2000 Years of Prophecy." *Ministries Today* (September/October 2004): 24–28.

"The Azusa Street Revival: Celebrating 100 Years." *Assemblies of God Heritage* 25, no. 4 (Winter 2005–2006): 6–11.

"Rome Stadium Message" [transcription]. *Hugh's News* [blog]. June 16, 2006. https://www.hughsnews.com/newsletter-posts/rome-stadium-talk-by-vinson-synan-ph-d.

"What's so Attractive about the Prosperity Gospel?" Originally published online at Religious Freedom in America. April 28, 2008. https:/religiousfreedom.org/. Currently unavailable.

"Oral Roberts [1918–2009]: A Son of the Pentecostal Holiness Church." *IPHC Experience* (March 2010): 8–9.

"Reviving the Classics." *Charisma* [blog]. January 12, 2012. https://mycharisma.com/culture/reviving-the-classics/.

"Notable History: The Quiet Rise of Black Pentecostals." *Charisma* [blog]. February 26, 2016. https://mycharisma.com/culture/notable-history-the-quiet-rise-of-black-pentecostals/.

Other

"The Pentecostal Movement in the United States." Ph.D diss., University of Georgia, 1967. ProQuest. 685087.

"Pentecostal Churches." In *Britannica Book of the Year 1973*, 23.

"Pentecostalism." In *Evangelical Dictionary of Theology*, edited by Walter A. Elwell. 834. Grand Rapids, MI: Baker Books, 1984.

22 Articles in Stanley Burgess, Gary McGee, and Patrick Alexander, eds. *Dictionary of Pentecostal and Charismatic Movements*. Grand Rapids, MI: Zondervan, 1988.

> "Reinhard Bonnke," "Willard Cantelon," "Gaston Cashwell," "Laurence Christenson," "Classical Pentecostalism," "Normal Correll," "Ambrose Crumpler," "Evangelicalism," "Fire-Baptized Holiness Church," "Fire-Baptized Holiness Church of God of the Americas," "William Fuller," "Fundamentalism," "Nickels Holmes," "International Pentecostal Holiness Church," "Kansas City Conference," "Benjamin Hardin Irwin," "Joseph Hillery King," "Pastor (role of)," "Pentecostal Holiness Church of Canada," "Presbyterian and Reformed Charismatics," "William Seymour," "Joseph Alexander Synan."

21 Articles in Stanley Burgess and Eduard M. van der Maas, eds. *The New International Dictionary of Pentecostal and Charismatic Movements*. Grand Rapids, MI: Zondervan, 2002.

> "Reinhard Bonnke," "Charles Emmitt Capps," "Gaston Barnabas Cashwell," "Laurence Donald Christenson," "Classical Pentecostalism," "Raymond Othel Corvin," "Ambrose Blackman Crumpler," "Evangelicalism," "Fire-Baptized Holiness Church," "William E. Fuller," "Fundamentalism," "Nickels John Holmes," "International Pentecostal Holiness Church," "Benjamin Hardin Irwin," "Kansas

City Conference (1977)," "Joseph Hillery King," "Pentecostal Holiness Church of Canada," "Presbyterian and Reformed Charismatics," "Mary Rumsey," "Joseph Alexander Synan," "George Floyd Taylor."

"The Beginnings of the Society for Pentecost Studies," 34th Annual Meeting, 2004. https://sps-us.org/download/history/synan_sps_beginnings.pdf.

3 Articles in Stanley M. Burgess, ed. *Encyclopedia of Pentecostal and Charismatic Christianity*. London/New York: Routledge Publishers, 2006.

"North America," "Sanctification," "Second Work of Grace."

"Pentecostal Revivals." In *Encyclopedia of Religious Revivals in America*. 2 vols. Edited by Michael McClymond. Greenwood, 2006.

A Seminary to Change the World: Regent University School of Divinity at 25 Years. Virginia Beach, VA: Regent University, 2007.

Audio-Visual

"The Age of the Holy Spirit." (1974). 3 cassette tapes. Witness Ministries/Advocate Press: Franklin Springs, GA.

"The Charismatic Restoration." (1974). 4 cassette tapes. Witness Ministries/ Advocate Press: Franklin Springs, GA.

"Vinson Synan Testimony." (1975). *Charismatic Renewal Audio Collection* 30. ORU Holy Spirit Resource Center. https://digitalshowcase.oru.edu/renewal/30.

"The Wesleyan Origins of Pentecostal Worship - Vinson Synan - SPS 1977." (1977). *Synan Audio and Video 4*. ORU Holy Spirit Resource Center. https://digitalshowcase.oru.edu/synan_audio/4.

"Fifteen Years of the Society For Pentecostal Studies (11-14-1985) - Vinson Synan." (1984). Synan Audio and Video 5. ORU Holy Spirit Resource Center. https://digitalshowcase.oru.edu/synan_audio/5.

"United Methodist Session - Vinson Synan - 1987 Congress on the Holy Spirit." (1987). *1987 Congress on the Holy Spirit and World Evangelism 7*. ORU Holy Spirit Resource Center. https://digitalshowcase.oru.edu/narsc1987/7.

"Pentecostals and Charismatics: Barriers and Bridges - Vinson Synan - 1987 Congress on the Holy Spirit." (1987). *1987 Congress on the Holy Spirit and World Evangelism* 8. ORU Holy Spirit Resource Center. https://digitalshowcase.oru.edu/narsc1987/8.

"Renewal History and Theology Symposium: A Tribute to Vinson Synan." (2006). *Renewal History and Theology: A Symposium in Honor of Vinson Synan* 3. https://digitalshowcase.oru.edu/rht/3.

"International Pentecostal Holiness Church History." (2017). *International Pentecostal Holiness Church History* 1. ORU Holy Spirit Resource Center. https://digitalshowcase.oru.edu/iphch/1.

[With Daniel D. Isgrigg]. "Where the Spirit Leads Me: An Oral History of the Life and Ministry of Vinson Synan, Ph.D." (2019). 19 recordings. ORU Holy Spirit Resource Center. https://digitalshowcase.oru.edu/synan.

[With Daniel D. Isgrigg]. "A Short History of the Society for Pentecostal Studies - Dr. Vinson Synan." (2019). *Synan Audio and Video 2*. ORU Holy Spirit Resource Center. https://digitalshowcase.oru.edu/synan_audio/2.

[Posthumous]. "Dr. Vinson Synan Tribute Video." (2020). *Synan Audio and Video* 1. ORU Holy Spirit Resource Center. https://digitalshowcase.oru.edu/synan_audio/1. [Played at Dr. Synan's Memorial Service at Oral Roberts University.]

[Posthumous]. "Synan Memorial Service at Oral Roberts University." (2020). *Synan Audio and Video* 3. ORU Holy Spirit Resource Center. https://digitalshowcase.oru.edu/synan_audio/3. [Recording of Dr. Synan's Memorial Service at Oral Roberts University.]

CONTRIBUTORS

Authors

Daniel D. Isgrigg is Associate Professor of History of Spirit-Empowered Christianity at Oral Roberts University, Tulsa, OK, USA.

Younghoon Lee is Senior Pastor of Yoido Full Gospel Church in Seoul, South Korea. He previously served as President of Bethesda Christian University in Anaheim, California; professor of theology at Hansei University, Korea; Senior Pastor of Tokyo Full Gospel Church and Los Angeles Full Gospel Church; and Chairman of the Theological Committee for the National Council of Churches of Korea.

Kunle Ogunkolati is Vice President of Churches at FullStature Missions International and served as pastor and church planter for over thirty years at Deeper Life Bible Church in Abuja, Ibadan, and Lagos, Nigeria.

Jaime L. Riddle serves as Research Coordinator for the Holy Spirit Resource Center in the Center for Spirit-Empowered Research at Oral Roberts University, Tulsa, Oklahoma, USA.

Sally Jo Shelton is retired after serving 24 years as Theological Librarian and Associate Professor of Learning Resources at Oral Roberts University, Tulsa, Oklahoma, USA.

William M. Wilson serves as President of Oral Roberts University, Tulsa, Oklahoma, USA, while leading Empowered21 and Pentecostal World Fellowship as Chair.

Tributes & Memorials

A. Douglas Beacham, Jr. is General Superintendent of the International Pentecostal Holiness Church and member of the Executive Council of Bishops.

Matteo Calisi is the founder and President of United in Christ International. He also is former President of the Catholic Fraternity of Charismatic Covenant Communities.

Mary Carol Synan Clark is the oldest child of Vinson and Carol Synan. She has been married to Curtis Clark for 45 years, is the mother of two, Lauren Smith and Justin Clark, and grandmother to seven.

Connie Dawson is an international speaker, pastor, and missionary who trains future leaders and serves as Professor of Church History at Global Awakening Theological Seminary.

Rodney Fouts is Senior and Founding Pastor of North Church in Oklahoma City, Oklahoma.

Harold Hunter is the creator and Director of the International Pentecostal Holiness Church Archives & Research Center in Oklahoma City, Oklahoma. He helped launch the Consortium of Pentecostal Archives.

Wonsuk Ma is Distinguished Professor of Global Christianity and Executive Director of the Center for Spirit-Empowered Research at Oral Roberts University in Tulsa, Oklahoma, USA.

Kevin Ranaghan is the principal leader of the Catholic Charismatic Renewal since its inception. He served as Executive Director of the National Service Committee for the Catholic Charismatic Renewal, as well as the Holy See's international renewal office, which, since 2018, has been known as the Catholic Charismatic Renewal International Service (CHARIS).

Kathaleen Reid-Martinez is Provost and Chief Academic Officer of Oral Roberts University in Tulsa, Oklahoma, USA.

Pat Robertson[†] served as Founder and Chairman of the Christian Broadcasting Network, and also as co-founder, Chancellor, and Chief Executive Officer of Regent University until his passing in 2023.

Craig Walker is Founding Lead Pastor of Upward Church, a multi-site church in Norfolk, Virginia; Williamsburg, Virginia; and Pensacola, Florida.

INDEX

Brown, Michael L., 63
Brownsville, 7, 38
Bryant, Garry, 106
Buckingham, Jamie, 54
Buena Vista Church, 100
Bullard, Rayford, 78
Buskirk, James, 74, 85, 134
Butler, James, 130

C
Calisi, Matteo, 161
Canada, 35–36, 47, 59, 86, 88
Canadian Pentecostal Research
	Network, 47
Cantalamessa, Raniero, 191
Canterbury, 166
Carey, George, 166
Carnegie, Dale, 91
Carter, Kelso, 20, 87
Cashwell, Gaston B., 33, 67
Catholic Charismatic movement,
	4–5, 7, 18, 35–37, 53, 71, 107–
	109, 113, 118, 160, 166, 171,
	177, 211
Catholic-Pentecostal dialogue, 123,
	133, 159, 166
Chapel Hour, The, 104
Chappell, Paul, 71, 75
Charismatic Catholics, 110, 123, 133–
	134, 180
Charismatic Christianity, 1, 3–8, 10–
	11, 27, 32, 36–37, 48, 53–54, 58,
	61, 75–76, 93
Charismatic Concerns Committee, 6,
	53–54
Charismatic Leaders Conference, 54
Charismatic Renewal International
	Service (CHARIS), 48, 159–60,
	163
Charismatic renewal movements,
	1–4, 6–11, 34, 36–37, 47, 51,
	53–55, 58, 62–63, 65, 70–72,
	74–76, 84–85, 114, 117, 119,
	124, 131, 139, 141–42, 162–64,
	167, 185–86
Chile, 8, 33, 59, 115, 171, 178, 181,
	197

China, 10, 33
Cho, David Yonggi, 40, 55, 140, 143,
	145, 183
Christenson, Larry, 2, 6, 36, 52, 54
Christian Broadcasting Network
	(CBN), 142
Churchill, Winston, 176, 191
Church of God in Christ (COGIC),
	18, 51, 55
Clark, Gary, 2
Clark, Mary C. Synan, x, 177, 191, 203
Clark, Steve, 109
classical Pentecostalism, 3, 8–9, 18,
	32, 37, 53, 71, 93, 186
Clemmons, Ithiel, 55, 162, 188
Coe, Jack, 52
Colombia, 63
Commonwealth of Virginia, 164, 166,
	174
Communism, 10, 34, 41, 123, 127,
	145, 206
Conatser, Howard, 2, 36
Congregational Holiness Church, 25,
	83, 90–91
Consortium of Pentecostal Archives,
	132, 208
contextual theology, 40–45, 81, 145,
	149, 152, 207
Corvin, Raymond O., 70, 72–73, 92
Corvin, R. O., 73
Cox, Harvey G., 10–11
Cremeens, Timothy B., 53
Crouch, Paul, 5
Crumpler, Abner B., 88
Crutchfield, Finis, 73, 93
Culbreth, J. A., 69
Cullis, Charles, 19–20, 27, 87

D
Dail, F. A., 98
Deeper Life Bible Church, 147–51
Derstine, Gerald, 2, 36
DeWeese, Bob, 69
Discipleship Ministries, 106
dispensationalism, 41, 48–49
divine healing, 17–20, 23–26, 69, 86–
	91, 93, 98